MY
MIDNIGHT
YEARS

MY MIDNIGHT YEARS

SURVIVING JON BURGE'S
POLICE TORTURE RING AND DEATH ROW

RONALD KITCHEN
WITH THAI JONES AND LOGAN M. McBRIDE

Lawrence Hill Books
Chicago

Copyright © 2018 by Ronald Kitchen with Thai Jones and Logan M. McBride
All rights reserved
Published by Lawrence Hill Books
An imprint of Chicago Review Press Incorporated
814 North Franklin Street
Chicago, Illinois 60610
ISBN 978-1-61373-766-8

Library of Congress Cataloging-in-Publication Data

Names: Kitchen, Ronald, 1966– author. | Jones, Thai, 1977– author. |
    McBride, Logan M., author.
Title: My midnight years : surviving Jon Burge's police torture ring and
    death row / Ronald Kitchen ; with Thai Jones and Logan M. McBride.
Description: Chicago, Illinois : Lawrence Hill Books, [2018]
Identifiers: LCCN 2017058175 (print) | LCCN 2017055722 (ebook) | ISBN
    9781613737675 (adobe pdf) | ISBN 9781613737682 (kindle) | ISBN
    9781613737699 (epub) | ISBN 9781613737668 (cloth)
Subjects: LCSH: Kitchen, Ronald, 1966- | Burge, Jon. | Death row
    inmates—United States—Biography. | Police brutality—United States. |
    Torture—United States. | Judicial error—United States.
Classification: LCC HV8701.K57 (print) | LCC HV8701.K57 A3 2018
    (ebook) | DDC 364.66092 [B] —dc23
LC record available at https://lccn.loc.gov/2017058175

Typesetting: Nord Compo

Printed in the United States of America
5 4 3 2 1

CONTENTS

———

PROLOGUE

THE MIDNIGHT CREW

———

SHOUTS, CURSES, CHAOS everywhere as the sergeant marched me upstairs to the third floor of the precinct building. In my twenty-two years I had experienced a lifetime of nasty encounters with the Chicago police. But I had never been here before. This was the Homicide Division. My hands strained in cuffs behind my back. We walked in silence through a corridor of noise. I could hear cries from all directions. Somebody yelled, "The fat one's throwing up!" and I smelled the sick scent of vomit coming from one of the side rooms. Confused, I turned my head right and left, trying to figure out why they had brought me here. A detective snapped me back to the present, sneaking up from behind and smashing the side of my face with a hollow clank into the cold steel of a locker on the wall.

"Look straight ahead!" he screamed.

They led me into a grim room with a scuffed-up desk, chairs, and a bank of telephones. Long fluorescent tubes cast a harsh yellow-green light. They chucked me down roughly into a chair and bolted my cuffed hands through a steel hoop in the wall. As soon as I was secured, the detective—a wiry man with a hard face—started screaming at me.

"Who have you been talking to?" His mouth was just inches from me. "Who have you been talking to?"

"I talk to a whole lot of people," I replied, trying to keep cool and make sense of the question. Wrong answer. The detective punched me in the chest. He kicked my stomach and legs. He smacked my face with his open palms. The thuds from the blows echoed from floor to ceiling. He asked again and again: "Who have you been talking to? Who have you been talking to?"

I had done my share of bad things—criminal things—but there was no reason I should be in this part of the precinct. I did not know what offense he was investigating, or how I could be involved. *Damn*, I thought, *what am I doing in homicide?* Maybe they suspected I was a gang member or something. I had no idea. No idea.

"Who are you talking to?"

"I told you," I said. "I talk to a lot of people." Wrong again. The blows thrashed down all over me.

Those first strikes that fell on my body were the start of a long, long night. For me, it was a night that has never ended. I have told the story so many times: to judges and juries, to friends and family, to students and teachers. Every time I describe it, I relive these experiences. Not a day goes by when I do not think about what happened to me back then—during that dark night of August 25, 1988.

And yet the morning had showed such promise. Dawn came hazy and humid to the South Side of Chicago. I opened my eyes. Birds tweeted in the oak trees outside my apartment. It was a Thursday, a special day. I remember it like yesterday. I woke up filled with the kind of hope I hadn't felt in years.

It was my day off, and I'd been looking forward to it all week. I tiptoed down the hall to my son's room and coaxed him out of bed. In the kitchen, I set Ronnie Jr. in his high chair while I fixed our favorite breakfast: oatmeal with raisins and Cap'n Crunch. Then I sat up on the tabletop while he ate and chattered to me about his birthday. He'd be turning three in a couple weeks and the party was the only thing he had any interest in discussing. My girlfriend, Tiffany, joined us in the kitchen. Our relationship was coming to an end—at least in my opinion—but she was pregnant again and hoping that a second baby would draw us back together as a couple.

Apart from my feeling of hopefulness, it was an otherwise normal morning. I felt the typical cares that I experienced at the beginning of every day: fatherhood worries, relationship stress, and the uncertainty of surviving. But still I had a sense from the start that it was somehow different.

After eating I got set to go out on my regular hustle. I took my time getting ready, laying out a pair of parachute pants and a baggy linen shirt while brushing my hair. I peered through the front door. South Aberdeen Street looked as it always did. Although the streets all around us were filled with litter and decay, our block was pretty tidy, thanks mostly to my grandmother's insistence that everyone in the family did their bit. When I was a kid she had made sure I cleaned the gutters and mowed the lawns. Now that I was older I'd give younger family members a couple bucks to do these chores for me. I checked both directions for trouble. Nothing seemed out of place. No suspicious cars idling, no strangers loitering on the corner. I knew that later in the day neighborhood life would pour from these homes out into the open, but for now all was quiet.

When I stepped outside, the temperature was in the mid-seventies, with a slight breeze. Sunlight gleamed like money off the chrome grille of my Cadillac Eldorado. I climbed in and cranked up the new Keith Sweat album so high that people could hear me coming from two blocks away. So far the summer had been fun. A lot of fun. Pool parties, women, clubs. It had been a nonstop bash. And I stood atop my game. All day and all night, the streets of the South Side—trash piles, broken glass, boarded-up windows, and all—were my domain.

When I say my "regular hustle," what that meant was seeing girls and selling cocaine. Dealing drugs was the path I took to support my family. I was not a kingpin or anything. Most of my business was local. But I had graduated from selling on the streets to the next level in the industry. Customers would come up to a couple dope houses I rented and buy $10 and $20 bags from my employees there. I was rarely even present when these transactions happened. This lessened the risk. It made what I was doing seem almost like a real business. Maybe that was why so many people I knew had gone into narcotics and made a lifestyle out of it. They joined one of Chicago's prominent gangs—the Stones, Vice Lords, Latin Kings, or Disciples—and turned cocaine into a career. That wasn't going to be me. I never affiliated with a gang. For me it was get in and get out. I had friends and family on both sides of the gang wars, though, and since I had cousins belonging to all of the rival crews, everyone tended to leave me alone.

When you're a teenager, and you're getting this money, you feel untouchable. You feel like, *they can't fuck with me.* In fact, I used to always say just that. I had never been locked up. I had never even seen the inside of a police station. Then I turned twenty-one and shit got hectic real quick. It got really real. In the 1980s everybody was coming up dead somewhere. If it wasn't in a garbage can, it was in the river. If it wasn't in the river, it was in a car. And every one of them that you heard about coming up dead was a dope dealer. I was getting antsy. Police had busted into my house in June and discovered seven hundred grams of cocaine. That was troubling, and I knew I was probably looking at several years behind bars.

But it wasn't the cops who scared me most. Dudes in the neighborhood knew I had money on me—and that played heck on my mind. My nerves were gone. I was taking all sorts of precautions. I never let Ronnie Jr. or his mom ride in the car with me, just in case someone tried to shoot me down. I had been robbed at gunpoint in a darkened hallway and that made me paranoid. I didn't feel safe in my own house. Now, if I got home and saw that the rooms were dark, I would call from my car phone and have someone turn on the lights before I ventured inside.

I was telling myself constantly that it was time to call it quits and get out of the dope game. I had one son, and a second on the way. I had bought Ronnie Jr. a bike with training wheels. I wanted to be there to teach him how to ride it around the block. I knew I'd probably be away for a little while on that cocaine bust, but because of that I was trying to get things in order. I was trying to get it so my family would be all right while I was away. I was trying to live. And on August 25 I was finally ready to make the change.

That afternoon, my mom and I had a serious sitdown. I told her "I'm through with this drug stuff." I had a little more product to sell—about half a kilo's worth. I was going to get rid of my stash and be done with it. This was the plan that I had been thinking about all morning; this is why I thought this one particular day was going to be a milestone in my life.

The building where my mom lived, just a block away from us, had a ground floor storefront, which we had turned into a video-game arcade called the Game Room. We had six or seven machines, Pac-Man, Ms. Pac-Man, Galaxy, and a few more of the latest hits. And business was booming. Because we owned the machines, all the quarters that went into those slots belonged to us. And, since we were around the corner from a grammar school and a karate studio, we were making more than $1,200 a week. That afternoon my mom and I sat on her front porch and discussed a proposal to expand. If we closed the Game Room for about a month for renovations, we knew that we could earn significantly more money for the family. Soon we would be selling popcorn, snowballs, ice cream, and candy. Our income was going to skyrocket. I imagined myself owning twenty Game Rooms in a couple years' time. This was my plan to change my life. This was the vision that was filling me with hope that day. And, at the very least, even if I did a few years in the penitentiary, I was getting my ducks in a row so that Ronnie Jr. and the coming baby would be all right while I was away. Just thinking about it calmed my nerves.

As my mom and I were talking, a blue-and-white police car pulled up. Officer Dowling, the local beat cop with whom I was all too familiar, rolled down his window and called me over. "Ronnie," he said, "where you been?"

"I've been in the house."

"You staying out of trouble?"

"I'm always out of trouble," I replied.

"Good," he said, and drove off.

I didn't think nothing of it at the time. Police harassment was an everyday occurrence for people in my neighborhood. Because I had a high profile, I probably dealt with them more than most of my friends did, but I wasn't particularly concerned. The police didn't scare me. I said good night to my mom and called Tiffany to tell her to turn the light on—I was coming home. She asked me to stop in at the corner store to pick up a gallon of milk and a package of cookie dough.

Evening had come as I walked to the shop. The air was cooler. I felt more at ease than I had in weeks. This was the time of day when the whole hood came out to socialize. Aromas of fish fry and fried chicken hung in the air. Every night that summer the street had just come alive around sundown. The adults would have a gossip about who was doing what with whose husband. My uncles would come over to drink beers and the neighbors would stop by to sit on the porch. The little kids might be playing "one, two, three, red light," or "catch a girl, kiss a girl," or else zipping around on their go-karts. I would open the trunk of my car, turn up the speakers of the radio, and tie on my roller skates. The street was paved flat enough to serve as a perfect rink, and I could skate my ass off. Big wheel, crazy legs, the shuffle, the nutcracker—I had all the fancy moves. This was the summer. And it was beautiful.

Before I got to the store, though, Officer Dowling rolled up on me a second time. He asked some meaningless questions, and I figured he was just giving me trouble. Then, while I stood by the side of his cruiser, another vehicle—a burgundy Oldsmobile Cutlass—skidded to a stop next to us—an unmarked police car. The driver told me to come over, and I walked from one officer to the other. "Somebody just pointed you out for auto theft," said the man in the Oldsmobile.

"That's impossible," I answered. "If I had done something wrong, would I be standing here talking to a uniform in a squad car?" The whole idea was laughable. "And anyway," I continued, "I don't need to steal no car."

But the driver wasn't laughing. Instead, he slowly and deliberately took out his gun and rested it on the windowsill. The barrel was aimed directly at me. Then he stepped out of the car and started to clip handcuffs on my wrists. By this time, Tiffany, my mother, my grandmother, and my aunties, had all come down the street to see what was going on. They were worried, but I was calm. I knew that I hadn't stolen any cars. This was a misunderstanding that we could easily clear up. As the sergeant conducted me into the back seat of his vehicle, I turned to reassure my family.

"I'll be back in forty-five minutes," I hollered to them.

I had lost track of the hours. But a whole lot more than forty-five minutes had gone by—and yet here I was, still chained to the wall in the Area 3 precinct house. I had plenty of time to think back on my interactions with the police. I had known them my whole life. Or at least I thought I had. They always fucked with us. They would say some shit. I would say shit back. Harassment was a constant fact of life.

But here in this room—this was something else. The interrogators did everything they could to baffle and disorient me. They left me waiting for hours. Sometimes I squinted into bright lights; at other points I sat by myself in absolute darkness. Then the officers would crash into the stillness with a terrifying outburst of violence. The physical pain was excruciating. But the uncertainty and confusion—that was torture.

The hard-faced detective—his name was Michael Kill—stormed in and out of my room repeatedly over the course of several hours. Each visit resulted in blows and kicks. The third time, he returned with another man. They were a mismatched team. Whereas Kill was lean, thin-faced, and blond, the second man was fat and ruddy with a full head of red hair. I knew by the white uniform shirt he wore that he was a high-ranking officer in the Chicago Police Department, maybe a sergeant. That was all I could tell of his identity, however, because the first thing he did upon entering the room was remove the nametag from his chest.

No questions this time. Kill came at me again. He punched me in the left side of my face and I went down. With my hands still cuffed to the wall behind my back, I was completely helpless when I fell. Contorted half-on and half-off the chair, my shoulders were in agony. As I lay twisting there Kill kicked me in the chest, the midsection, the testicles, the ribs. The fat commander clambered up on top of the desk and began stomping me in the back. His heavy shoes thumped into my ribs and spine. It went on for a matter of minutes. Then—just as suddenly as they had entered—the two men disappeared, leaving me alone again, bewildered and gasping painfully to breathe.

———————

Only later—years later—would I finally discover the name of that fat man who was so determined to keep his identity a secret. Today, anyone who has read a newspaper in the past decade is likely to have heard of him. But back in 1988, as far as the general public knew, Jon Burge was just another Chicago cop.

Born—like me—on the South Side, Burge had served with distinction in Vietnam before returning home to be promoted through the ranks of the police department. By the time I encountered him, he had already been a detective for sixteen years. From 1981 until 1986, he led the Violent Crimes Unit in Area 2—a vast jurisdiction covering many of the city's African American neighborhoods. In January 1988—only seven months before I was brought to his precinct—he was promoted again, to command the entire detective branch in Area 3.

Wherever Burge went, his units amassed impressive records for speedy arrests and high conviction rates. But other patterns also emerged, if only anyone cared to search for them: accusations of violence, racism, torture, and coerced confessions. In 1988, these were just whispers. Soon, though, they would emerge into open court. Revelations about Burge and his men would help spark a popular movement against mass incarceration and the death penalty. In Chicago, a town with a high tolerance for—and a rich history of—scandal, this would become the most notorious outrage in a generation. Lives have been ruined. The total costs to the city can only be estimated, but the victims have already been awarded over $100 million. And even these costs do not include the funds wasted prosecuting and incarcerating innocent people, litigating abuse cases, and defending Burge, his accomplices, and his protégés. The psychological and emotional expenditures go far beyond currency, and they can never be tallied—let alone compensated.

At the latest count—and the number keeps rising—120 victims have come forward. The earliest incidents dated from 1972, the very start of Burge's career as a detective, and they continued until 1993, when he was dismissed from the force. Each case differed in its details. Some victims were identified by witnesses. Others, like me, had a reputation in the neighborhood. A few found themselves targeted in retribution for protesting police activities. Many just chanced to be in the wrong place at a very bad time. But a crucial similarity endured. In every case—without a single exception—the victim was black.

Detectives routinely employed fists and boots against their prisoners. Racial epithets and verbal assaults just rolled off their tongues. Burge and his men used whatever lay at hand to perpetrate their enhanced interrogations: people in custody were suffocated with plastic bags, burned against radiators, pistol whipped, had gun barrels placed in their mouths, took beatings with baseball bats and flashlights, had their fingers vised in bolt cutters, and felt nooses tightened around their necks. Burge's favorite implement was an electrocution device he had used against enemy prisoners in Vietnam. A rewired telephone unit called the Black Box, it was employed on dozens of victims who received electric shocks all over their bodies: ears, chest, armpits, testicles, and penis.

Within the police department some referred to the Area 2 and Area 3 detectives as the "asskickers." But Burge and his team had a different name for one another. They called themselves the Midnight Crew.

"This is what you did," Detective Kill sneered at me, as he shuffled the photographs around on the desk. "Nigger, we know you did this."

Hours more had slipped away. The ordeal had destroyed any sense of time. I had no idea how long I had been here, or whether it was day or night. Despite all that I had been through, I still had only the most general notion about what crime the homicide squad was even investigating.

Now that changed.

I glanced for an instant at the pictures on the tabletop and turned away in horror: they were too gruesome to look at for long. The officer clutched my head and forced it down, making me stare at the photos. I saw crime scene snapshots of dead, disfigured bodies—the charred and burned remains of two young women and three little babies. "Nigger," Kill sneered, "we got you on record saying you did this."

With a sinking feeling, I suddenly understood the depths of my trouble. The mystery of my ordeal—the secrecy and torture—finally snapped into focus. They wanted me for a mass murder.

Even for Chicago, the crime had been brutal and tragic. A month earlier, firefighters had discovered these five corpses inside a burning bungalow on a quiet street in the Mexican area of Gage Park. One of the women had been beaten, and the children were smothered with pillows. The fire had been set by the assailant in hopes of destroying the evidence of violence. It was a sensational case, and Burge was under strong pressure to find the perpetrators. The women were mothers, hardworking teacher's aides, popular and friendly with neighbors and coworkers. There was another factor, too. One of the victims was the daughter of a Chicago cop.

The story had drawn some media attention, but in those days I was not exactly up on current events. I had never heard of these murders until the moment when I found myself confronted with the pictures. I never spent time in the neighborhood where the crime had occurred. In the drug business, I'd had no contact with any Mexicans. But now I understood what the police were claiming I had done. The realization that I was being charged with five murders should have been terrifying. Or, if I was thinking clearly, it might have even felt like a relief—since I knew I was innocent of the charges. But it was not like a normal encounter when someone comes straight up into your face and accuses you of something you didn't do. In that situation you would say, "I don't know what you're talking about." My thought processes were so jumbled by the beatings that this knowledge just added to my bewilderment. Confused isn't even the word. Mentally and emotionally I was not even in the room anymore. I was totally someplace else. I was in the land of *What the fuck is going on?* I sure knew it was not a joke though. Hell no, it was not a joke. And though I now knew my supposed crime, I still had no idea why the detectives thought I was the perpetrator.

Later on, I got my first hint of their case against me. Detective Thomas Byron, the big officer who had brought me into custody, entered the interrogation room. Playing the role of "good cop," he asked if I was OK and offered me something to eat. I told him I wanted to know what evidence they had on me. He brought out the case file. My hands were still cuffed, so he set the papers on the desk and turned the pages. My one idea was to scan the document in order to see the name of the person who had fingered me to the detectives. When I did see the name—Willie Williams—I almost laughed. Willie was an acquaintance, at best—a neighborhood guy whose sister was dating my cousin. In the statement, he claimed that we had talked over the telephone, and that during several of these conversations I had bragged to him about committing the murders.

"I don't know why this dude told you this," I said. "I don't socialize with him and he don't come to my house." I asked Byron if I could use the phone to call my lawyer. With a smile he walked over and lifted the receiver. Then the smile vanished. He unplugged the handset from its cord and smashed me with it on the side of my head. "Do you hear ringing now?" he asked, and thundered out, switching off the lights as he left.

Hell yeah, I heard ringing. Sitting there in the dark I heard a lot of ringing. Over the course of hours the police had gradually moved forward with their plan to break me down. They had starved me and refused to let me use the toilet. I was injured and disoriented. I knew they wanted me for murder, and now I had learned who their informant was. Only one step remained: confession.

Now it was just a matter of time. I was moved into a holding area and then to a second room. During these transfers I saw that other people were involved. My cousin Eric Wilson was there. He was "the fat one" who had been vomiting the previous night when I had arrived in the police station. I was allowed to catch a momentary glance of Marvin Reeves, my grandmother's godson, who was in a different interrogation room and had a massive black eye. It was morning. I could see the sunlight through the window. It had been maybe twelve hours and I hadn't had a scrap of food or a sip of water.

"We have ways of making niggers talk," boasted Detective John Smith, the next officer to enter. "I'm going to introduce you to the telephone book and the blackjack." He then placed the phone directory on my skull and wailed on it with his nightstick. Oh my God, it hurt. It felt like he was trying to knock my brains into my neck. He jabbed me in the gut with the baton until I rose to my feet, and then he shoved it between my legs and ground it into my testicles, lifting me onto my tippy toes and almost into the air with the force. "Admit you spoke to Willie Williams," he commanded. "I never said this shit to him," I repeated. "I don't know why he's lying to y'all. He's a damn liar."

The detectives appeared and departed. If their tactics differed slightly they all showed the same rage. Each one made the same threat, in so many words, *You will say what we tell you to say.* After an entire night in the police station, I hurt everywhere. My testicles were swollen and my ribs ached with every breath. When the police finally did let me use the bathroom later that morning my urine was red with blood. But the officers at Area 3 were experienced in the art of torture. They knew how to mess up someone real bad without leaving any incriminating wounds. Too-obvious bruises and broken bones could jeopardize a case. That's why Kill had used open-palm slaps when he hit my face, why Burge had kicked me in the back, why Byron had smashed the phone on the top of my head, and why Smith had employed the telephone book to reduce the visible damage from his nightstick. The beatings would worsen. Only two paths existed:

they were going to torture me to death, or I would have to confess to this terrible crime. *You will say what we tell you to say.*

———————

When the assistant state's attorney first entered the room I hoped he might be a lifeline to the outside. That was naive. The prosecutor—his name was Mark Lukanich—asked if anyone had read me my rights. I told him they had not, and he began with the formalities—fifteen hours after my arrest.

"You have the right to remain silent," Lukanich informed me. *Is that a fact?* I thought. *Someone should tell that to Detective Kill.* "Anything you say can and will be used against you in a court of law.

"You have the right to talk to a lawyer and have him present with you while you are being questioned. If you cannot afford to hire—" I wanted to interrupt him right there. I did have a lawyer—a longtime family friend, who had represented me before—and I was frantic to speak with him. I told Lukanich my attorney's name and telephone number and asked him to contact the man for me. He promised to look into it and left the room.

Detective Kill came roaring back in moments later, shouting, "Nigger, you just don't know how to do what we say to do." He smacked and slapped me around. He said he knew that we did it— Marvin and me. Everyone knew we did it. Over and over, he issued the same dark threat, "We have ways of making niggers talk." Whatever the laws of the state, inside Area 3—or any precinct worked by the Midnight Crew—different statutes were enforced. "You don't have but two rights when you come in here," Burge liked to tell his victims, "to confess or get your ass kicked."

I finally agreed to speak to the prosecutor again, but then when Lukanich came back, I told him, "I don't want to talk to you. I—I want to talk to my lawyer." He left. And here came Kill. "Everyone knows you did it," he shouted, punching me again and again. "We have ways of making niggers talk." It seemed like they could go on forever. But, I'd had enough.

"All right," I sighed, "I'll talk to him." This time, when Lukanich returned, Kill stayed with us. Exhausted, desperate, aching and throbbing, and no longer able to keep up the fight, I finally said, "I'll do whatever you want."

This was when I gave my so-called confession. Here's how it went. Detective Kill stood behind me and told the entire story directly to Lukanich. According to the narrative he created, Marvin and I had murdered the women because of a drug debt. The figure he concocted—$1,200—would be cited by newspapers as evidence of our cruelty. Doing the math, reporters would claim that we had valued our victims' lives at just over $200 apiece. Sitting across the desk, the prosecutor dutifully wrote it all down on a piece of paper. All I did was agree to it. Whatever Kill told me to say, I said it. The attorney never asked me about any particulars. All he asked was "Is this how it happened?" And I just said *yes, yes.* "Anything else?" No. The entire statement came from Kill. I did not add a single detail, and I did not object to anything. I never said, "I don't know." I never said, "I don't remember." During this whole time the only two words I ever said were "yes" and "no."

I had no choice but to confess. Once I realized that the prosecutor and the police were working together, I knew that there was no other way out. Even as I said "yes, yes" to all of Kill's outrageous lies, I was already thinking about the future. I couldn't imagine this statement ever holding up in court. Long before we even reached the trial, I thought, the arraignment judges would see my wounds and set me free. The intake doctors would examine me and testify on my behalf. The entire system—I truly believed this—was designed to protect me from the actions of the likes of Burge and Kill. It was designed to protect the innocent and punish the guilty. The moment I escaped the clutches of the Midnight Crew, my "confession" would be seen for what it obviously was—a bunch of lies.

When the prosecutor finished scribbling, he passed the document across the table for me to see. There were large block letters written across the top that said, "Statement of Ronald Kitchen." Beneath the heading a paragraph read, "I understand I have the right to remain silent. Anything I say can be used against me in a court of law." I signed my name beneath those words. And I signed again on the bottom left-hand of the page. I signed it on page two. I signed it on page three. I signed every page of the confession. I didn't even bother to read it. I knew what it said. Then the state's attorney signed it, and he and Kill left. Drained, bruised, starving, and exhausted I found myself alone.

The life I had led up to that moment was stolen from me by Jon Burge, Michael Kill, and the Chicago police. Precious God-given years were taken away due to a lie that strangers told about me. Responsibility for what happened—to me, and to scores of other survivors—does not rest with the Midnight Crew alone. Widely held assumptions about poor black men and upstanding police officers made this possible. Prosecutors and politicians, including at least three mayors, abetted a conspiracy of silence. Because of who I was, and the way I looked, others were eager to believe that I was a monster and a murderer. Few would show any interest—at first—in listening to my version of events. If the whole truth of what took place was told, it would implicate them all.

I bear witness to this history. When I speak, it is not only for myself, but for other survivors and victims of a society that incarcerates one-in-three black men and where black men and women can be gunned down by police, who get a pass by saying, "I feared for my life." All of our lives other people have tried to define us, whether it was the teachers, social workers, or sociologists on the South Side or the lawyers and journalists involved in my cases. It has taken time for me to find my own voice. We have lots of stereotypes on our back, and I have suffered for the assumptions others have made about me. I love to prove people wrong, but I get tired of having to prove myself over and over again. I know my self-worth, and I don't have to prove a thing.

The time has now come. I am Ronald Kitchen. This is my story.

1

BORN IN THE PROJECTS

I TOOK A LOT of chances on stuff when I was a kid. I did. Ever since I can remember, I took risks. But they were calculated risks.

In the late 1970s, for example, when we were living on the South Side of Chicago, my uncle Earl owned two Doberman pinschers named Bonnie and Clyde. He had kept attack dogs for as long as I could recall, and I knew he had the skills to train them to a T. Bonnie and Clyde were new, and he was going through the delicate process of transforming them into deadly weapons. "Don't touch my dogs," he told everyone. "Don't go 'round them."

I was twelve or thirteen years old at the time. What did I do? I snuck over there and started feeding them. I didn't exactly have a set purpose in mind. I just knew there wasn't any way in the world I was going to spend time in a house that had two attack dogs in it—and not try to get on good terms with them. Every night, after Earl left for work, I headed over to his place. Chicken bones, leftovers, I grabbed whatever was in the fridge. At first I just threw it to them from the window. Then I came down the stairs, right up to their cages, and let them sniff me. For a month or more I did this, until I felt I had a deal with these dogs. I was pretty sure they wouldn't bite the hand that fed them.

One day a bunch of us were hanging out on the sidewalk near Earl's yard. He was feeling good or cocky, or something, because he suddenly boasted, "I bet none of you will walk to the fence and try to rub my dogs." At first I was kind of leery. Maybe he had caught an inkling about what I had been up to. But I barely hesitated.

"Man," I said, "I'll do it."

He looked at me with disbelief. "You gonna try to rub them?"

"Yeah."

"If you rub both of them," he said, "I'll give you a hundred dollars apiece."

Now this was interesting.

"Show me the money," I replied.

"I got it."

"No, show me the money," I insisted, knowing better. "Give the money to Tommie. Give the money to him. I'm going to do it." I watched as Earl handed over the cash.

"Hold it out," I said to my other uncle. "I'm gonna get my money."

Now Earl was a little worried. Not over his money—he figured I had no chance of collecting—but he was probably thinking about what he'd tell his big sister, my mother, if his dogs tore me up. "You gonna do it for real?" he asked anxiously.

"Yeah," I replied. "But what are you gonna say? You're not going to tell them to attack me, right?"

"I'm just going to tell them to watch you."

I took a step toward the fence. Bonnie and Clyde stood up, their keen dark eyes staring daggers at me. Another step. They raised their front paws, suddenly on full alert. *Oh shit*, I thought.

"Watch him!" Earl commanded. Their canine focus sharpened even tighter.

I got a little closer and I could see that even though they were watching me, they were not growling. A tiny bit more relaxed now, I walked over to the deadly attack dogs. They sniffed and licked my hands playfully, like puppies, as I laughed and rubbed them all up and down their backs.

"What did you do to my dogs?" shouted Earl.

That memory says volumes about me as a youngster. I was always a little different, even from my brothers, cousins, and friends. I hadn't started out to win that cash, just with a general feeling that it would be a smart idea to be on good terms with those dogs. But when the moment came to earn a buck—or sneak a kiss—I was ready to act. I got a reputation for thinking ahead, for reading angles and sensing possibilities that others maybe didn't see. So when I took a chance, I was generally pretty sure it would pay off.

Things seemed to come my way—the good and the bad. Money. Girls. Trouble. I put it down to my smarts and to protecting what was mine. Others had a different interpretation: they said, "This boy's got issues." In either view, it related to my general attitude. Part of it was just who I was. Me. But it was also all about my upbringing, the people who raised me up: my grandmother, my mother, and my uncles.

————————

My people had always lived in the South. My grandmother, Geraldine Howard, was born in the town of Baxley, Georgia, about a hundred miles west of Savannah, in 1929. Her father—Roy Bell—had lived in the area all his life, earning a meager living as a pulp wooder, cutting timber for the local paper mills. For all that backbreaking work he was only able to afford a little old country house—a shack, really—to shelter his family. It had no lights and no plumbing. The kitchen featured a coal stove, but the family was too poor to buy fuel, so instead they used wood shavings for all the cooking and heating.

Geraldine was basically still a kid herself—she had only just celebrated her own sixteenth birthday—when she gave birth to her first child, my mother, Louva Grace Bell. They were still in Georgia then. The year was 1945. Nine other children followed after. There were so many of them that my mother sometimes lost count of who was who. To remember their ages she had to work her way down the whole list of names to figure out which one came when. Regardless, my mother was big sister to them all. She and my grandmother were so close in age that they basically raised up the entire family together as a team. They were remarkable women, fighters who had big dreams for their kin. And it didn't take long for them to outgrow the family shack. They had eight or nine people crammed into a couple rooms. It was time to move. First they went to Jacksonville, Florida. Then, in 1960, the whole clan up and moved to Chicago.

Geraldine brought her children north for a chance at wider opportunities and a better life. She wanted the same thing my mother wanted for us—the same thing I want for my kids, the same thing everybody wants for their children—to allow her children to grow up in a better environment and to be better than their parents ever were, to be a better provider and a better spouse. Upon arriving in the city, the family lived for a while in some of the South Side's dilapidated, falling-down tenements. Seventeen years old and eager for a place of her own, my mother became one of the first tenants to move into the city's newest and most famous housing development—the Robert Taylor Homes.

In later years the Taylor Homes, like many of Chicago's other huge projects, would come to have a notorious reputation. But when they first opened in the early 1960s their construction was greeted with joy. Carefully selected families—with good jobs and steady incomes—felt lucky to be chosen to move into their pristine apartments. To my family, who had only known grinding poverty, the Taylor Homes were like a dream: running water, elevators, massive apartments with bedrooms for all—or nearly all—the children. For us, these weren't the "projects"—they were the "high rises."

But the dream didn't last long. The Taylor Homes were too large and isolated to thrive. Stretching for two miles down South State Street, the complex consisted of more than two dozen dreary, identical towers. It was the largest public housing project in the country. Thirty thousand people lived there—nearly every last one of them black. The Dan Ryan Expressway ran alongside the development, serving as a barrier between the residents and the rest of the city. The apartment towers had been built on the cheap. Before long, the elevators and heating systems started breaking down. As working families increasingly moved out—replaced by the underemployed and single mothers on welfare—the project became known as a place of crime and delinquency. Within a year of its opening, tenants were staging protests demanding more police protection and better conditions. During Martin Luther King Jr.'s visit to the city in 1965, civil rights leaders dubbed the Taylor Homes Chicago's "high-rise ghetto."

And this is where I came into this world. I was literally born in these projects. My mother was twenty years old when she gave birth to me in unit number 1101 of 4444 S. State Street, right in the middle of the Robert Taylor Homes. It was January 13, 1966. My great-aunt served as midwife. My brother Pat had been born a few years earlier—in a more theatrical fashion—right on the dining room table, but for me the experience was not quite so dramatic. I first drew breath in the back bedroom of our apartment.

I had a child's eye view of the Homes. Big things like crime and politics escaped my notice, but I sure felt the little things. What I remember best was the day care center down on the first story of the building. In my bones I can feel the way the wind would blast in through the cheaply constructed walls. For a young baby down on hands and knees, the floors were always gusty and freezing. And I can almost still smell the hot dogs, nachos, hamburgers, and sweets that the older kids bought with extra pocket money from the "Candy Lady," who had turned her apartment into a makeshift food stand.

In those early years, the Homes retained some of their original shine. The walls were being painted semi-regularly by the Chicago Housing Authority. Pleasant patches of lawn had been planted between the buildings. Playground equipment, the Laundromat, and other services still functioned—at least part of the time. But on the whole, living conditions on the South Side were desperate enough to draw the attention of national civil rights leaders. Two weeks after I was born, Martin Luther King Jr. returned to Chicago to take a public and courageous stand against northern slum conditions. That summer, while I was still too young to sit up on my own, he and hundreds of his followers participated in a series of demonstrations in all-white neighborhoods to demand better jobs and integrated housing.

I recall listening to my grandmother's stories, years later, about these events. We were sitting on our front porch late at night—approaching midnight, if I am remembering this correctly—when one of my cousins asked her about King and the summer of 1966. These confrontations were still fresh in her memory. She had been there, on the front lines. Organizers had hoped these demonstrations would be nonviolent, but the rage and fear of local residents had ensured the shedding of blood. Mobs of angry white Chicagoans waved Confederate flags and chanted "Niggers, go home!" During one march in Marquette Park, they threw stones, eggs, bottles, whatever they could get their hands on. King was hit and knocked to the ground by a brick. He told reporters, "I've been in many demonstrations all across the South, but I can say that I have never seen—even in Mississippi and Alabama—mobs as hostile and as hate-filled as I've seen here in Chicago."

My grandma had other stories about the time two years later—in April 1968—when King was assassinated in Memphis, Tennessee. In Chicago, days of open rebellion and violence followed the tragic news.

As African Americans demonstrated their frustrations, thousands of soldiers were deployed to the city's South and West Sides to try to restore order. Mayor Richard Daley issued a "shoot to kill" order that was basically a declaration of war against black residents. Over the course of several hellish days, more than two hundred buildings were destroyed. The human cost was great, too. Hundreds were injured, and many were killed—all of them black. Although black folks' anger was focused on whites, the devastation of April 1968 was confined almost entirely to our own neighborhoods, mostly on the West Side. Some of Chicago's public housing high-rises had turned into furious battle-grounds during the uprising. Entire business districts were leveled.

For my grandmother, surveying the damage from the window of our eleventh floor apartment, the scenes of rebellion were heart-breaking and filled with frustration. Geraldine hated to see these self-destructive acts. Everything she did was to bring stuff back to the community, and she could not understand why people—even in the depths of frustration—would choose to tear it down. Rioting and looting and stuff, she wasn't for that. She knew that when black people tore things down like this, it would be hard to ever get these areas rebuilt. And she was right. Many of the damaged areas have never been mended.

Seeing that the projects were on a downward slide, and that black neighborhoods would take decades to recover, she and my mother made a difficult and courageous choice. It was time to leave the Tay-lor Homes. The family would work its way into a better area, a place with nice houses, good schools, and pleasant parks—in other words, a white neighborhood. They knew this would mean a long, hard fight. But they wanted the kinds of opportunities that any parent wants for their kids, and they refused to be intimidated.

I was about four years old, in 1970, when we left the Taylor Homes and moved into our own house on Emerald Avenue at Fifty-First Street, on the city's Southwest Side. My family had put away enough money to purchase an older home divided into twin units. We would live on one side, my grandmother on the other. The main thing I remember is how fun it was to live next door to Geraldine. Whenever she called me over—or if I wanted to visit—I could go into the bathroom, unhook the grate, and crawl through the heating vent across to her side. To me, the houses seemed huge, especially after the cinder-block walls and dark corridors of apartment living. We had upstairs, downstairs, a basement, and a porch. In our backyard there were apple trees, cherry trees, and even grapes growing. My older brothers, Pat and Darnell, shared one room; I shared another with my little brother, Charlie. My sister, Leslie, had one to herself. By other people's standards it might have been rather modest, but for us at the time it was a little bit of the American Dream.

My favorite memories from these years all take place in my grand-mother's kitchen. It was white and beige, with all new appliances and curtains decorated with flowers. The living room was off limits to us children; the furniture in there was covered in plastic sheeting. The formal dining room was also for adult guests. She didn't want anything broken or messed with in either of those areas. The kitchen, though, was the place for us. It was large enough for a full-size table, two chairs to a side, and we spent hours sitting there playing cards, doing homework, and just hanging out.

During the afternoons or on weekends we'd play out front, remembering always to keep within sight of the door. In the evening, when the streetlights switched on, we knew it was time to head inside. My mother would step onto the porch and call us all in. Anyone who was even a little bit late could expect to be greeted by anxious looks, or a quick smack. We were one of the first African American families in the area, and our parents understood the reality of our situation. Anyone who could remember those demonstrations that King had led knew how fiercely white Chicagoans were going to fight even the first hint at integration. Our elders shielded us from it all. We didn't think about it or question anything. It was just a simple fact of life: when the lights came on everybody who was black had to be in the house.

The area we had moved into was very much a working-class white enclave. Filled with Irish and Polish immigrants, or the children of immigrants, it was a flourishing area of small bungalows with lawns and yards, set back from the tree-lined streets. Our specific area of Chicago—east of Racine and north of Fifty-Fifth Street—was at the meeting point of several neighborhoods. It had character but not a lot of renown. Our part of town didn't even have an agreed-upon name. Depending on who you asked, this small pocket was Back of the Yards, Englewood, New City, or Moe Town. For generations, the nearby stockyards and packinghouses had served as the main local employers. Men went off to work at the factories, or to city jobs, while their children played with friends in the nearby parks after school and their wives kept house, running errands at the many local shops and stores. The row on row of neat single-family houses and two-story brick flats were clean and spacious, with all the modern conveniences. These thriving stores—these nice homes—they had all been built for the white working-class families, at a time when the city's bright future had seemed certain.

None of these nice things had been intended for us. And as we, and a few other black families—including the Loves, Gilberts, Carrs, and some others—started to move into the neighborhood, white homeowners saw us as a threat to everything they'd worked to build. They cared more about keeping us out than about working to provide good times for all—even if it meant the destruction of their own community. We were greeted with ruthless terror and violence.

To drive out any pioneering black family, and deter others considering the move, the area's white residents threw rocks and bricks at our cars and homes. They launched bottles, shot BB guns and arrows at black kids playing outside, and even tossed firebombs onto our front porch. The war was waged block by block, made more brutal as the tide of integration pressed further into formerly white spaces. Only a few blocks away, a number of black families were already in place. More and more were moving west of the Dan Ryan, as we had, with the dream of owning their own homes. But whites in our area were trying hard to stop the influx of new black families, holding the line first at Halstead, and then, when that fell in 1971, at Racine.

The authorities offered no help. They seemed to blame the victims, those black families with the uppitiness to move into the neighborhood in the first place. Police officials knew that racial tensions were growing in the district, but they downplayed the threat, saying that these were harmless acts of vandalism perpetrated by local kids. Whenever any violence occurred the police would always blame the black participants first.

They could deny it all they wanted to. I was there to see it. When I think back to my earliest memories what I recall most are fights. Lots of fights. I was just a preschooler but I remember listening to my uncles describe their daily struggles. Their fifteen-minute walk up Union Avenue to Tilden High School was like crossing through a minefield. They had to avoid any passing police cars, confront white gangs on Forty-Ninth and Fiftieth Streets, and then—just when they thought they would be safe—the firefighters would come bursting out of the station house and soak them with a water hose to slow them down. When I was still a kid, my uncle Earl got caught on Forty-Second Street at the wrong time, got into it with some white gang members and police, and was struck in the head with a hammer. The blow cost him his eye. Even if the confrontations didn't turn physical, there was name-calling, the persistent call of "Niggers, you ain't wanted here!"

On a good day we might face a rain of insults; most times we had to deal with punches, rocks, BBs, or worse. We weren't allowed to cross the street. We couldn't cross Halsted to go the store. The Laundromat was a no-no. If you went there at a certain time it was a death sentence. Lowe Park was a block away, but we couldn't go there. We had to devise our own recreations. There were no public pools available in the neighborhood. The nearest one was half a mile west in Sherman Park on Racine, and it was off limits to us. One summer day we spent a few hours cooling off in the water spraying out of an open fire hydrant. The next day we came back and found that the firefighters had encased the entire thing in concrete, making sure we would never be able to use it again. We were surrounded, surrounded by nothing but white. There was never a moment of being safe, no matter which direction you took.

We lived in a sea of racism.

Not every single white person in the neighborhood was bad—a handful of black and white teens would sometimes play basketball together, and some adults occasionally offered sympathies for what we were going through. But the racial hatred controlled everything. Good intentions were not enough. No one was willing to be too friendly. Established white families didn't want to risk ostracism. And it went further than that. There were other matters that reached beyond the neighborhood. Our white neighbors soon learned that banks deemed their properties to have lessened in value now that there were black families nearby, and auto insurance companies denied them coverage because black neighbors made the area too "dangerous." The whole system was designed to separate us, to keep Chicagoans from getting along. It worked. Chicago remains one of the most segregated cities in the country.

I remember looking out my bedroom window to the street. A police car drove up and some officers stepped out. They started arguing with my mother and grandmother. I could hear the cops shouting at them, "You niggers shouldn't be around here! Niggers should go back to the jungle!" My grandmother wasn't no punk. Nor my mother neither. They were not ones to back down from anyone, even policemen. While I watched, the taunts and curses turned into punches and scuffling. I was just a small kid, but I ran down the stairs and pushed one of the cops off my mother. Another one of them tossed me to the ground and put me in cuffs until I calmed down. This is one of my first memories. From an early age, therefore, I was learning that the police were really just another enemy for us.

In the years we lived in the neighborhood, we were the frequent targets of attacks. Bullets would smash into the walls of our house. All of the windows on our car would be shattered and the tires slashed. Explosives were even placed in my mother's vehicle. Some people might have said to call the police and find out who was behind this. But we knew they didn't care. Neighbors called the police all the time, but the cops took their time arriving and never did anything to help. As far as we were concerned, it was just as likely that it was the police themselves committing these acts of terror. Despite these assaults, our elders held their ground. They were fighters. That's where we got our fight from.

I had another kind of early experience with the law that also helped to shape my complicated feelings about men in uniforms. My father, Rudolph Lamont Kitchen, served in the sheriff's office, working at times as hospital security and later in the county jail. His brother was in the Chicago Police Department. Their family was from Tennessee, but I don't know many details about their story. He just wasn't around very often when we were kids. By the time I was five or six years old he had separated from my mom. A few times when I was in grammar school he would come and pick me up. He never came around on Christmas. At the time I took this all personally, but looking back I can tell that he was under pressures of his own. I was his first child, but at the time they hooked up my mother had two children already. He wanted to get married, but his family didn't approve. His father questioned whether I was even his son: in his mind it was a "mother's baby, daddy's maybe" situation. Here he was, an upstanding man of the law. But I didn't really see my father and uncle as men in uniform, they were just my relatives. They never invited me to go with them to any law-enforcement events. And if they had, I probably would have said no. I really didn't care for the police and these two men in my family didn't do much to alter that opinion.

My loyalties were to my mother. She was the one who was there for us. She wanted us to be better and to do better. She ensured we stayed in school for as long as she could keep us there. She packed us off to church on Sundays. Having already played a major role in raising her own brothers and sisters, she now worked to provide for us. My earliest memories of her all involve labor. When she was at home she would be in the kitchen cooking, making sure we did our homework and tidied up our rooms. Then she would work as an accountant at Tabernacle Hospital. She went to school and held a full-time job. She earned a bachelor's degree and then a master's in social work. And she did this all with five kids and no man. When I picture her in these years, I see a woman in an Afro who was always on the go. Changing from work clothes to school clothes, from scrubs to jeans, and back again. Yet, despite my mom's efforts, there were always times when it just wasn't enough.

When mother was away, our grandmother would watch us, but she too had lots to keep her busy. Geraldine Howard was not one for waiting around. Despite the care of ten children and all us grandkids, she fought on and on. Neighbors widely regarded her as a community pillar. In 1970, right around the time we moved to our new house, she got involved with the South Side chapter of an old philanthropic organization known as the Chicago Commons Association. She joined a neighborhood improvement group as its secretary and helped to organize several other organizations as well. She began to work on the issues that mattered most to us: providing children of the neighborhood—black and white—with day care, summer camps, afternoon activities. She took in battered women and served as a mediator in housing disputes. Her colleagues at the office saw her get worn down and tired—even sad—but she kept going.

Expecting no help from the authorities, my grandmother insisted that we follow the path of self-help. She made it her job to get in touch with newly arrived black families. She would warn them about what to expect, inform them of the support that awaited them, and—most important—get them organized. She went door-to-door, canvassing, setting up meetings, establishing block clubs, gathering information, and referring newcomers to local community services. She was a great organizer. Anything you needed, she would fix it, get it, or fight for it. Sometimes even the little stuff, like giving away donated clothes or extra food. And, knowing that most of the arriving families had moved up from the South like she had, she helped people get hold of their birth certificates from way back, and then aided them in filling out forms for services they were eligible for in Chicago. For her, the neighborhood wasn't streets and houses, it was people and community.

The area of the city we lived in was at the center of the population shift. It was going from white to black quickly. "White people moved out so fast you didn't even know they had been here," our neighbors would say. Between white flight and a lack of investment in the community, many of the things that had first attracted my family to the neighborhood disappeared. Within a few short years of our arrival, despite the efforts of women like my grandmother, a lot of those nice houses had been demolished and the busy stores—like the A&P on Fifty-Second and Halstead, and smaller shops—had closed down. Many blocks on the South Side were filling up with abandoned homes, sidewalks and yards were covered with trash.

When I went back to visit friends in the Taylor Homes, I could see that the same trend was happening in the projects. The elevators were always out of order, the hallways smelled like piss and shit. The buildings were filthy. Metal was corroded, windows had been broken. There were holes in the walls. I saw it and smelled it. With public housing going to ruin, white families fighting out newcomers, and integrated neighborhoods falling into disrepair, it seemed like there were no good options for black families looking to improve their lot in life. But our street was different. Every day my grandmother would put a broom and a shovel in my hand and scoot me out the door to clean things up. My job was to tidy up the street, from one end of the block to the other, on both sides. On my grandmother's street all the grass was cut and the gutters were clean. The alleys were empty of trash. We did that, not the city.

In these ways, we made that community our home. Over the next few decades, my uncles and aunties, my brothers, my mother, and even myself moved into different apartments and houses in the neighborhood—on Union Avenue, Carpenter Street, Aberdeen Street. We visited, stayed with, and hung out with family here and there, but the family homestead was on Emerald Avenue, and Sundays—every Sunday—centered around dinner at my grandmother's house. It was a big event. She would start preparing food the previous day. Then after getting home from church she would get the main course in the oven. The gospel records would start spinning as she set to making greens, cornbread, oxtails, red beans and rice, corn on the cob, ham, and cakes. My mom and aunties would be right there, too, cooking alongside her. As a child I was invariably up under her, tangling in her skirts, constantly underfoot. When she was done mixing up the cake I made sure to be the one who licked the bowl. I always had a taste for cake batter. When she baked banana pudding there would be a small pan just for me. Everybody said I was her favorite, but I'm not sure about that. I just loved being around her. By the afternoons the gospel LPs would give way to blues and country and our uncles and friends would start arriving for the feast. Grandma would sit at the chair closest to the sink, ready to keep things moving. The rest of us would find a seat where we could; uncles would eat standing up.

My grandmother was a born organizer. Even in the worst times in the neighborhood she worked to ensure that the children—black as well as white—had a chance to enjoy some simple pleasures. All she was trying to do was to bring decent services to Englewood. But she had to fight the entire way for everything she accomplished. And she was putting her life on the line to do it. One day she arrived in the office of her supervisor at work, a veteran civil rights activist named John Salter Jr., and pulled out two brand new .38 caliber Saturday Night Specials, which she had obtained for self-defense. Salter was an experienced gun user and spent a few hours with her going through the basics. He warned her to keep the weapons away from us children and to beware the legal ramifications of illegal possession of a handgun. If trouble came, he urged her to employ the pistol as a deterrent only, firing it into the air or down into the floor to scare off any threat. My grandmother was not the only one exploring this option. Many black neighbors were arming themselves for self-defense and to protect their homes. I remember her always carrying that little revolver in her pocket. I saw her pull it in numerous confrontations. When the police came by and threatened her, she would verbally fire back, saying, "You're not the only ones who got guns." She didn't back down. My grandmother did not back down.

The holiday season was her favorite time, and she never did it halfway. On an average year she would gather food and clothes for at least fifty families and distribute as many as two thousand toys. But never did she score a bigger success than for Christmas in 1973. All December she had been pushing for the US Marine Corps to donate presents to needy children in our neighborhood as part of its Toys for Tots program. When the local unit refused, my grandmother went further afield, contacting the post in an affluent North Shore suburb, and they agreed to step in and help. On the afternoon of Christmas

Eve a fleet of cars drove up from Englewood to Glenview to pick up the toys, which my grandmother then distributed from the back of a local nightclub. The channel two news came to film the celebration as my grandmother passed presents of toys, food, and clothes around to more than 150 children who lived on Emerald and the other nearby avenues. The entire city watched her that night, beamed to their televisions on the evening news, larger than life, head thrown back in joyous laughter. In that one news segment, at least, a little bit of our story reached the wider metropolis.

A black kid on the South Side in the 1970s did not have to go searching high and low for trouble. It would seek you out. But even so I seemed to turn up more than my share. Down the block there was one family with girls about my age. Their mother was as strict as could be and wouldn't let us even get close to her babies. Like us, they had apple and cherry trees in their yard, so we would go over and pretend to be interested in the fruit. One of the sisters dared me to climb up the cherry tree and into the window of her house. This was a dangerous proposition; the long branch did not look like it could support much weight, and I could only guess at the kind of trouble that might await me inside.

"What will I get if I do that?" I asked innocently.

"I'll give you a kiss," she answered. ". . . and you can rub it." Shit. You think I didn't get across that tree branch and into that house? I guess there had to be something at the end of that rainbow that I wanted in order to make me take that chance, but I took chances. Plus, knowing she'd get in at least as much trouble as I would, I figured she knew her mama wasn't home to catch us.

Other times I just did what had to be done. When I was in the third grade I was hanging out just a couple blocks from home in the asphalt play yard behind Dewey Elementary School one afternoon when the fourth-grade bully came up to me and said he was going to go slap my little sister, who was a first grader at the time. I didn't even hesitate. Looking down, I saw a brick sitting right there on the ground. I picked it up and smacked him in the side of his head, knocking him down instantly. My mother had a saying, "street fights, house rules," meaning in a confrontation there's nothing you shouldn't do. If it's there, use it. You don't give them a chance, especially if they're bigger than you. And I stuck to that. I did not care how big this kid was. Of course, now I had done hit the bully, and so from then on every time I looked around somebody was trying to fight me.

More African American families kept moving into our part of Englewood, and the whites were fleeing to the suburbs. Before a few years had gone by the area had gone from all white to nearly all black. In Chicago, urban activists have said, "Integration was that brief period of time between when the first black family moved in and the last white family moved out." In our community, then, "integration" lasted from the time I was four until I was ready for school. By the time I was a kindergartener the days of having to fight your way to class had ended. I walked out of the house every morning by myself without worrying about whether or not the ten-minute stroll would involve danger. But the black parents still kept up their guard. As the other children came out of their houses to join me, their families would get on their phones and call each other up. As we progressed from block to block the mothers and grandmothers would telephone ahead to let the next house know we were on the way. This network was always watching over us.

When I was still in grade school, after five years or so on Emerald Avenue, my mother had had enough of living next door to my grandmother. The arrangement may have worked for a lot of reasons, but the two of them had started arguing more and more. My grandmother was hard, and especially so on my mother, her oldest child.

She needled her about her choice in men, for not helping out, and for being too giving with the family savings. Eventually enough was enough. We moved back into the projects—not the Taylor Homes this time, but another housing development on Forty-Third Street and Lake Park. And though our new place was just a few minutes' walk from the waterfront that gave the complex—the Lake Michigan Homes—its name, the string of projects were anything but a beach-front paradise.

My mother had big plans; she would make an R&B group out of us. Pat was on the drums and also played the sax. My brother Darnell played lead guitar and bass. They were good. Meanwhile, I suffered through piano lessons every Saturday and struggled to keep up with the others. In the end we didn't have the talent to match our mother's vision. The musician gig had at least one positive effect, though; the girls in our apartment building certainly knew who we were. We made a big impression in the neighborhood. And not everyone was pleased by our arrival. My oldest brother got into a fistfight with a local gang member. That night, someone blasted a flurry of bullets through our front door. One stray slug struck a kitchen cabinet and lodged in a jar of peanut butter. If it hadn't, it would have hit my auntie who was standing at that moment by the stove.

This was around the same time that neighbors started to look at me with a bit of wariness. Word started spreading about me in the streets. I got into a fight in the projects with twins and beat them both up at the same time. In third grade I was kicked out of school for fighting. People who knew me best, my family, had a different take. They said I took no barter; I didn't bend. Even my older brother Pat came to rely on me when things got hectic for him in the streets. I was eleven years old when Mama sent the two of us on an errand to the One-Stop, a local convenience store. Just as we got there a full-grown adult came out from behind a clinic and demanded our money. He looked at me—I was a little bitty tiny brother—and then didn't give me a second notice. Without saying another word he reached his hand into Pat's pants and started rooting around for cash.

"You going to let this dude go in your pocket?" I asked, amazed. "You not going to do nothing about it?" Pat just stood there in some kind of shock.

"Do something," I said. "Don't let this man go in your pocket!"

"Shut up, shorty!" the thief ordered.

I glanced down at the ground and sure enough, there was an empty forty-ounce bottle lying right there. I picked it up and smashed it across the man's face. He collapsed to the ground, streaming blood. Looking at my brother disgustedly, I asked, "Pat, are you going to help now?"

While many areas on the South Side transformed, other Chicago enclaves clung stubbornly and steadfast to segregation. The West Side neighborhood of Bridgeport, in particular, symbolized white people's absolute refusal to welcome the changes transforming the city. It was the stretch of neat bungalows where Mayor Daley was born and raised, the seat of his power. It was also—though no one yet knew the name—the home of an ambitious young Vietnam vet named Jon Burge. This was Klan territory, where children grew up fearing and hating black people. They looked down on us like they were better. That was the mentality there, that the white race was better and that black people were less than human. If crossing the street back by home was the ticket to a beating, wandering into Bridgeport was considered a death sentence. We never went near there if we had the choice. But we didn't always have a choice.

The police would harass us constantly. It was a fact of life for black Chicagoans, even for kids. The same cruiser that would pass by paying no attention to twenty little white girls and boys listening to rock and roll music would screech to a halt at the sight of four black boys standing by the curb. We would be waiting at the bus stop and a cop car would stop in front of us.

"What do you think you're doing?" they'd ask.

"Waiting for the bus."

"The fuck you are."

These confrontations could be terrifying. You lost control of your life in the clutches of the law. I was only in seventh grade when police grabbed five or six of us from a corner, tossed us into the back seat of their car, and started driving. We watched the signs in mounting terror as the street numbers steadily descended. Around Thirty-Fourth Street and Halsted—right at the heart of Bridgeport, where the Richard J. Daley branch of the public library stands today—the officers pulled over and shoved us out onto the streets.

"Start running!" they commanded. "We better not see you try to hail a cab or get on a bus." As we started to move they shouted through their window, "We got some niggers out here!"

Then the chase began. Suddenly all these white folks were coming out with blood in their eyes. They piled into their cars, waving bats, throwing bricks and bottles. It was the middle of the night. This was a real racist neighborhood, probably the worst in the city. So we knew we had to get east, past the expressway, almost a mile and a half away. The Robert Taylor Homes may have been notorious—and they sure had their troubles—but if you were a young man running from a gang of racist whites, the Homes could seem like heaven. We raced toward the black people. And that night we were some running fucks.

2

PENITENTIARY OR DEATH

I SLIPPED INTO SOME boots and put on my Tilden High School letterman's jacket. Pocketing wallet and keys, I grabbed a roll of toilet paper and headed out the front door of my mom's house on South Union Street. The clock struck midnight on a summer evening in 1982. I was sixteen years old, and it was time to go to work.

A few minutes' walk brought me to the old Catholic church on Fiftieth Place, where the other guys were already assembling. After about ten of us had gathered, we piled into a blue van and steered north toward Chinatown. Conversation among the crew faltered as we neared our destination. By the time we finally pulled over and I got out, nervous tension was twisting my stomach. I was too on edge to speak in anything other than tight, clipped sentences.

We faced a fifteen-foot-tall concrete wall stretching block on block, to the north and south, farther than the eye could follow. Looming above this barrier we could see the ghostly outlines of shipping containers—hundreds, thousands of them—stacked three and four high. Glancing around to ensure there were no witnesses, we quickly scaled the wall and dropped silently down the other side, into the restricted zone of the freight yards.

After nearly a year pulling jobs in the yards, much of the process had become routine. We waited till shift change in the middle of the night, snuck into one of the many huge railroad and trucking depots scattered throughout the city, and disappeared back into the streets carrying boxes of stolen goods. But no matter how many trips you took, the fear did not go away. You never got used to it. As soon as we were inside the walls the guys would all fan out to find a concealed place to take a shit. The first time that I had ventured out with some older guys to the yards, I had nearly crapped in my pants. In desperation I had been forced to wipe my ass with my T-shirt. Ever since that embarrassing rookie mistake I'd known to include a roll of toilet paper as part of my kit. We called the feeling "bubble gut," and it happened to every person at every heist.

On this night in Chinatown, once we'd all handled that piece of our business, we got down to the real work. Someone produced a set of bolt cutters and snapped the lock off the back of a truck. Inside we found boxes and boxes of stereo equipment. Everything was going smoothly. We packed the van with one load and then returned for a second batch. By this time it was after 2:00 AM. The boxes were heavy and awkward to maneuver. Everyone was ready to head home for sleep. We moved more slowly and with less coordination. Then we froze. Cars were rapidly approaching. We instantly snapped back into motion. Experience had taught us the distinctive sound of the vehicles used by the freight dicks—detectives hired to guard the merchandise—and in a flash we had dropped the goods and were fleeing.

I tore through the crowded aisles of the yards. The dicks were shouting and speeding toward me. I wasn't a fast runner, but I was smart enough to know not to travel with the rest of the pack. The lanes were dark and littered with debris. I leapt over railroad tracks, dodging scattered crates and shipping pallets. Going at full stride, I tripped over something in the road and flew headfirst to the ground. Looking down I saw in disgust that it was a dead dog. For long minutes I lay next to that rotting body, waiting for the guards to pass on. I could hear shouting as several of the other guys were being arrested.

When the voices were gone, I raced to the edge of the yards and disappeared over the wall into a residential neighborhood. I knew my outfit was far too conspicuous. The blue and gold Tilden High School colors on my shiny windbreaker would be easy for the police to identify. I needed to get off the streets—fast. Without pausing to think I ran into a yard and kicked open someone's back door. Crouching and panting in this random basement, eyes gradually adjusting to the darkness, the thought dawned on me that this could be anyone's house. For all I knew, this could be a serial killer's house—and at that moment I felt pretty sure it was. I waited for someone to come downstairs, but nothing happened. After several minutes I cautiously started exploring. Seeing a laundry line, I swapped my clothes for a ridiculously oversized T-shirt. After a few more minutes, I headed out again.

I was miles from home, and at this time of night public transportation was shut down. White neighborhoods along Ashland Avenue and Halsted Street were off limits, so I walked south on State Street, painfully alone and conspicuous in my ill-fitting garments. I had gone about a mile before the van came pulling up alongside me. The dudes cracked up when they saw me, scared and exhausted. But I didn't care. I was too annoyed about losing my clothes: whoever owned that house sure got themselves a good jacket.

That windbreaker had been my last tie to high school and the life my family had taken such pains—and risks—to map out for me. My mother had brought me up the best way she knew how. She had sacrificed and fought to leave the South, move to Chicago, and then integrate the neighborhood. She raised me in the church. I had been a junior deacon as a boy, a lead singer in the choir, and a star in the pageants. She had wanted me to finish my education, go to college— everything. But none of it turned out how she had imagined. In fact, I had stopped going to classes long before that night in the yards. I had strayed far from the course that my family had hoped I would take. Before most other kids had even outgrown childhood things, I was moving out of the house to embrace the life of the streets.

In these years, I stole, got into fights, and sold drugs. I knew many of the city's underworld kingpins, and for a little while it looked like I might become one myself. I was accused, arrested, and targeted by police on numerous occasions. I also started a family and tried to dedicate myself to supporting my young son. They always say when you lead the life of crime, being on the streets, you got two things that's gonna come to you: penitentiary or death. In the 1980s I had seen both of them.

Watching my mother's struggles only motivated me more to succeed. Despite her best efforts, there were times when Mom's labors just weren't enough. There was only one of her, and five kids, not to mention all of her brothers and the influence of the neighborhood. In the mid-1980s we were experiencing the hardest times. "I never asked for help," Louva would say. "I'm one of those people who always tried to solve my own problems." But some problems went far beyond individual strength and resolve. She found herself feeling sick and missing work. There were constant battles with the power companies. When the gas in our house was cut off we were reduced to using a kerosene heater to keep a single room warm in the winter. Half her paycheck went to pay rent. The house was falling apart; our linoleum floors were cracked and peeling. Only a few secondhand pieces of furniture were scattered around the rooms. When the water was shut off, we would have to walk over to my grandmother's house to use the bathroom.

We weren't alone. The whole country was suffering. As was often the case in difficult times, black Americans suffered most. In Chicago this was especially true. Instead of waging a war on poverty, the Reagan administration decided to wage a war on poor people. They slashed food-stamp and school-lunch programs, unemployment benefits, housing assistance, and aid to single mothers. African American neighborhoods in Chicago were hit especially hard. My grandmother had a subscription to the *Defender*—Chicago's most famous black newspaper—and copies were always lying around her house. I remember seeing stories about the hard times around us. Headlines talked about joblessness, welfare, inflation, hopelessness, crime. Between 1970 and 1980, the unemployment rate tripled for the city's African American men. Around half of Chicago's black teenagers said they were unable to find jobs. In those same years, our neighborhood had completely flipped from being about 95 percent white in 1970 to being almost entirely black by 1980. It seemed like almost everyone around us was struggling.

Poverty in Chicago was painfully visible—to anyone paying any kind of attention. Lines at the city's employment centers stretched around the block, full of black guys, along with the occasional Latino or white person, hoping to find work. "I'll take anything," was the general attitude of the thousands of people who were desperately seeking jobs that might pay only $3.50 an hour. For those who came up short, turning to crime was often the only logical choice to put food on the table and make ends meet. Welfare checks didn't cover rent. To feed a family, a person might steal some food from the grocery store, only to find themselves arrested. The prisons grew while every avenue of help was cut off. I couldn't have rattled off a bunch of employment statistics at the time, but these larger trends were shaping my life.

In this country, education is often seen as a path out of poverty. But I didn't stand a chance in school. Because no teacher had ever inspired me to excel as a student, I never became much of a scholar. In grade school my attention would focus a little bit during Black History Month, when we studied Rosa Parks and Martin Luther King Jr., but for the most part the education offered to me was entirely irrelevant to my daily life. By middle school I was already getting into trouble more regularly than I was getting into my lessons. The only organized learning that I actually enjoyed were the sessions at my uncle's karate school. We started a club called the Black Dragon Slayers. Dressing up like ninjas, we'd have competitions and beat other dojos. Everybody I hung out with did karate. It was discipline but at the same time it was fun. Classroom learning didn't have the same appeal. Things did not improve when I arrived at Tilden High, which by the early 1980s was one of the lowest-performing schools in the city. Gangs operated openly in the halls, and only about a third of freshmen made it to their graduation four years later. About as soon as I got there, I entirely lost interest. I usually went to one class—that was first-period homeroom—and the rest of the day I was ditching. After sophomore year, I dropped out for good.

Typical teenage fun did not really appeal to me. When I graduated out of eighth grade, my uncle said I could use one of his cars if I would have a beer with him. That was the first time I ever drank, and I actually got sick. After that, I never drank again. When I turned fifteen, another uncle kept me out one night on the porch smoking reefer. When I came in the house, probably around four or five in the morning, my mama beat the shit out of me. That was the last time I smoked reefer. I never touched either substance ever again. On Friday nights, I didn't hang out in bars or clubs. No, on my weekends I used to go roller skating. Skating was the air that I breathed back then.

The hobby was in style in the early 1980s. There were popular skating establishments all across the city—Motion Explosion, The Oval,

Screamin' Wheels, Skate City, Loop Roller Disco—and everyone was doing good business. My uncle Earl owned a roller skating club on Eighty-Ninth and Ashland called The Rink. It was a little matchbox of a place. The floor was the size of a typical living room, but it was kept up and polished to perfection. We'd refinish the wood ourselves by hand each year. Earl often employed me to guard the door or handle the equipment rentals.

There was something for everyone at The Rink: Wednesdays were family night, we had adult skating for professional people, and special times set aside for kids. But for serious skaters, center stage was the weekly Midnight Ramble, which lasted from 11:00 PM on Friday to 3:00 AM on Saturday. The Midnight Ramble would be jam-packed and filled with excess. Out in the parking lots, dudes from the car and motorcycle clubs would be checking out each others' Cadillacs and Corvettes. Everyone was gussied up and eager to show off their boyfriends and girlfriends. Sometimes the entire place would gasp and stare as one of the big drug kingpins would arrive surrounded by an over-the-top entourage. Inside, the DJs would be spinning Donna Summer or Michael Jackson while the disco balls flashed red, blue, and green. A few times each night the colored lights would snap off, a Stevie Wonder slow jam would begin, and the patrons would clear the floor for a "couples only" skate.

And when the moment was right, I'd come strutting right into the center of this kaleidoscope, wearing Levi's jeans, a tight turtleneck sweater, and the most expensive necklace I could afford. Everyone knew I was a sharp dresser. I was famous for it. I'd have my precision skates in my hand, ready to strap up and hit the floor. I laced up my Gem 2 boots—this was pro stuff, the equipment you wore if you were good enough. Back then I could get down, and so could the rest of the karate club. All we wanted to do was skate, have a good time, and get close to some girls. But somehow it never seemed to work out that way.

The Rink was in a different neighborhood from where we lived, and we were seen as newcomers to the area. Our status as karate students was well known, too. So even though we didn't mess with anybody and just went about our business, people would still come and try to show us up. Other crews would be challenged to skate; we got challenged to fight. Every single Friday night—and I mean for years—dudes would come out to The Rink for that sole purpose. The thing is, in all those years, we never started nothing in that skating rink. The other guys always initiated the trouble. My uncle told us: "If it come to y'all, take care of it. But don't never go out there looking for it." And so every week we had to whoop somebody's ass.

Shit usually kicked off inside. We'd be passing out skates or just having a conversation with each other. Someone on the far side of the room would see us huddling up and think we were being confrontational. Next thing I knew some guy would strut up to us and get in our face.

"Y'all talking about us?" he'd say.

"Nah, you the last thing in our minds," I'd shoot back.

And it'd go from there. It would just escalate. I don't recall a single time when we fought an even match. We were always outnumbered. Sometimes the violence got so out of hand that there would be a full-scale riot in the parking lot, big brawls involving ten guys or more. I'd get hit in the eye or get knocked down but nothing could make me quit. In all these fights, the police never got called. No guns, no knives—just fisting it out. This was all part of a process where we were being tested. It took years, but finally we had our ups—we had proven ourselves. Word went out about us across Chicago: *Them dudes don't need to be played with.* And then, at last, the fighting stopped.

After dropping out of Tilden I bounced around between relatives. I couldn't just sit in the house all day, especially since my mother was almost always working or in school, and so for a couple years I stayed with one or another of my mother's brothers. This side of my family was pretty notorious in Chicago. Uncle Earl acted as bodyguard for Flukey Stokes, a legendary gambler and dope kingpin. Another uncle had been convicted of repeated robberies. The two halves of my family could not have been more different. On my father's side the law was respected to a fault. Whenever I got together with my dad or his brother, they would point out the flaws—as they saw them—of my mother's brothers. Finally, I said to them, "Don't tell me about it. Go tell them yourself how you really feel." Of course they did nothing of the sort.

My mother's kin were black gangsters, kind of like the South Side version of the Italian Mob. Let's just say this didn't always make us the most popular family on the block. While some lived in awe, others lived in fear. People always assumed that my uncles trained me in illegal activities, but it wasn't like that at all. At home we were just family. They would feed me and clothe me and give me a place to lay my head. Although my father wasn't around much, I always grew up surrounded by men who loved me. I looked up to them as male role models, not as criminal masterminds. They didn't have me out there doing crazy shit. When I got old enough, I went out and did crazy shit on my own. I didn't need persuasion.

The very first time I went up to the freight yards, I was no more than fifteen years old. Some guys invited me along because they needed a ride and knew I could borrow my uncle's car. We drove up to Chinatown, which was known for lax security. Parking in one of the lots at a nearby public housing project, we waited till shift change at one or two in the morning. That night we made two or three trips and came away with a bunch of Casio keyboards and some Apple computers, which were just hitting the market. Over the course of the next several months our techniques diversified. We disabled a streetlight near the yards, forcing truck drivers to sit idling at a red that would never change, while we scrambled into the back and offloaded as many boxes as we could. We rode the freight trains, tossing goods off the tracks and then returning in a rented U-Haul to gather things up again. If we came across big pieces of furniture, like sofas or pianos, we'd leave them. Otherwise, it was ours: TVs, clock-radios, lamps, tools. If it wasn't nailed to the floor, we'd take it.

I was suddenly making serious money. We'd get a hundred cases of Reeboks, with each case containing forty-eight pairs, and we'd get twenty dollars for each pair. We'd get a hundred windbreakers and sell them each for ten bucks. Guess Jeans went for fifteen dollars a pair. Needing to stash the goods somewhere, I chose my mom's basement and my grandmother's attic. It didn't take long for suspicions to arise. Every time I strutted past in a stylish coat or a new pair of sneakers, they would ask, "Where you get this at? Where you get that at?" Neighborhood people started knocking on the door inquiring after goods, even placing orders for specific items. Someone would tell my mom, "I need this size jacket," or ask, "Have you seen Ronnie? I need this size pair of jeans, or this size gym shoes."

My mother was furious. There I was, sixteen years old. I wasn't going to school, I wasn't coming home when I was supposed to. I was stealing. I was staying out all night. She tried talking to me, but it didn't do any good. She was worried to death, but there was nothing she could do. No matter how much she preached to me, no matter how much we argued and turned blue in the face, she soon realized that school had nothing to offer me. Life on the streets was my calling. "I can't tell you nothing," she admitted. "You're going to do it your way, but I'm going to be here for you." I was as honest with her as I could be. And she knew who I was—understood my true character and capabilities—and so she trusted me. Of course, that supportiveness went through ups and downs. When she discovered

I was stashing stolen goods in her basement, she was angry all over again and demanded I remove the merchandise immediately. On the other extreme, after one score where we came away with a truckload of furs, the complaints quieted down for a while. Every female in my family got a rabbit or fox coat as a gift, and we had the whole of Fifty-First Street walking around looking like millionaires.

After a couple years, though, the risks and rewards no longer balanced out. We robbed a UPS truck and made off with about $100,000 in cash. This seemed like the score of a lifetime until we spent a few bucks in local businesses. Suddenly, police and federal agents were everywhere in our neighborhood searching for the money—it turns out we had stolen marked bills that were intended for some government investigation. We burned every last dollar and were thankful not to have been caught. The night I lost my Tilden jacket in Chinatown was another reminder of the dangers of this type of theft.

It was another terrifying night, when I was eighteen or nineteen, that finally convinced me to give it up for good. We were in a predominantly white neighborhood with a car loaded to the rooftop with stolen goods. It was well past midnight when we realized with rising panic that our vehicle wouldn't start. I opened the hood and tapped on the cables with the jack handle, looking for a problem. In a terrible coincidence, the instant the metal in my hand touched the negative and positive terminals on the battery, my partner in the driver's seat happened to turn the ignition key. The battery exploded with a huge detonation right in my face. Acid burned the shirt off my body and scarred my chest and cheeks. Immediately blinded, I started screaming, "My eyes! Oh, my eyes! Not my eyes! Jesus, are you going to take my eyes away from me?"

Lights started switching on in the houses around us. White folks came rushing out of their front doors to find a black teenager clutching his face and hollering wildly about being blinded. Immediately assuming there had been a shooting, they fled back inside and called the police. When the ambulance arrived, the medics washed my face under a fire hydrant before taking me to an emergency room on the West Side. I was lying in the hospital bed a few hours later with bandages all over my head when my mom stormed into the room screaming about how she was going to beat my ass. "Are you crazy?" I said, "I can't even see!" After she calmed down, we settled into a grueling recovery period. I had to go to the doctor every day for six months. As bad as it was, it could have been worse. Somehow, by a miracle, the cops hadn't checked out the car—if they had even given a hasty glance in that direction they would have instantly found all the stolen goods inside.

This was a turning point for me. At the height of my panic, when the battery acid was searing into my face, I had shouted to heaven, "Oh Jesus, don't take my eyes away from me! I swear I'm not going to steal no more." After my vision recovered I decided that this was a promise worth keeping. I still needed to earn an income, however, and my part-time job as skating rink attendant didn't quite provide the cash flow to which I'd become accustomed. That left but one option: narcotics.

———————

I started out by selling reefer on the sidewalk. I'd stand out on South Aberdeen Street, or over on Emerald near my grandmother's house, and sell bags to people who came by. I'd sit on the corners or circulate through the local lounges and hotspots, letting people know what I had available. This was the lowest step of the ladder, with the shortest profits and the highest chance of getting caught. But it gave me a chance to build a clientele. By keeping at it for about a year I earned a large and loyal base of customers. When one of them asked casually if I happened to have any cocaine, too, it gave me the inspiration to expand into the dope business. I invested in an eight ball, mixed and bagged it up, and went back out to the corner. Ten minutes later I had sold out. Next, I bought a half ounce; that took thirty minutes to sell. And things just took off from there.

I went into partnership with my cousin Eric, who was also my best friend. We used to go to parties, the movies, we did a lot of things together. As kids we even slept in the same bed. Together, we planned it out and pooled our money. By watching the way other dealers maneuvered, we began to get our operation in shape. Between us we started renting a couple of dope houses; these were apartments where our personnel would handle the actual transactions with customers. This allowed us to move more product while minimizing our risk of arrest. Success required expertise in every aspect of the trade. Dope had a vocabulary to it: an eight ball was "two girls," a "teenager" was a sixteenth, and an ounce was an "onion." There was a body language, too, and I became sensitive to its details. One afternoon I was on Aberdeen talking to some friends, when a white dude approached us casually—too casually—and asked if we could sell him a dime bag of cocaine.

"We don't sell cocaine, *officer*," I responded.

"What are you talking about?" he replied, acting offended. "Do I look like a police officer to you?

"Yes, *officer*, you do."

Our instincts served us well. Fast forward a year or so, and business was flourishing. We had fat bankrolls, Cadillac cars, suede jackets, leather pants, big gold ropes, girls, and whatever else, to go with it. It was every young dude's fantasy. The big drug dealers were—to us—the heroes in the neighborhood. We saw them at the skating rinks and the clubs, driving customized Cadillacs, throwing hundred-thousand-dollar parties, surrounded by women, dripping with diamonds. And this was our chance to go for that lifestyle.

I was a player now, and with that came a reputation. The words, "Oh shit . . ." were in my ears constantly. I heard them over and over and over again. Every time I came around and pulled up on the block that was all people had to say. "Ronnie's here, oh shit . . ." If someone in my family had any trouble I'd get a call or a beep and I'd head over to intervene. Family and neighbors said I didn't barter. When people saw me, they knew I wasn't going to sit there arguing. There wasn't really anything to talk about. To me it was simple. I just wasn't going to let anyone take anything off me or hurt me. When I got involved there was nothing to say—nothing, that is, except "oh shit . . . "

No situation was more likely to end in an "oh shit" moment than the sight of a man committing violence against a woman. My hatred for this type of behavior went all the way back to childhood, when I had seen one of my mama's boyfriends put his hands on her. I was just twelve or thirteen years old. But I warned that man that if he ever touched her again, I would kill him. And I meant it. Over the years I did a lot of things to dudes. If somebody did something to me as a man, then he got what he had coming to him. But except for a couple childish fights in school, I never put a hand on a woman or a child. That was not in my character. Nor was I willing to sit by and watch it happen. There was one time when I was riding in the car and saw a dude beating up his girl at a bus stop. I screeched to a stop, jumped out, and beat the shit out of him. After an abusive husband moved his family to Aberdeen Street, I went right into his house and whooped him so bad he jumped headfirst out of his own window to get away. When he came back with the police to have us arrested, the officers instead saw evidence of his domestic abuse and locked him away rather than pressing charges against us. Sometimes this instinct of mine led me into trouble, but it didn't matter—those who knew me best understood that it was a deep part of who I was, and nothing was going to change it.

The other thing that made me different was my refusal to join one of Chicago's powerful gangs. These street organizations controlled most of the drug sales in the neighborhood, and were normally rapid and ruthless in stomping down competition. But I never had any problems with them. This was so unusual that even the police were confused. One day they'd see me with a group of Vice Lords and think they had me pegged; the next time they saw me in the streets, I'd be hanging out with some Stones, and they'd have to rework their theories. I knew people in gangs. I had family members in gangs. In fact, I had a high-ranking brother in the Disciples and a high-ranking cousin in the Stones. Maybe that's why I could go wherever I wanted to and didn't have problems.

My family connections gave me some degree of security. But the reason I avoided joining up was more personal. I wasn't one to give away my earnings for dues, and in my experience you can't make money gangbanging. Furthermore, I certainly have never been OK with other people telling me what to do. More than that, though, I never wanted to make a long-term career in a gang or in the dope business. You can't retire from a gang. You are in that for life. Even when you're old, you still pay homage to the organization. The only way you retire is in a box. No, that wasn't happening. Gangs weren't for me. I was just out there hustling. I wasn't a gangbanger, I was an entrepreneur. I had other interests.

For a few years in the 1980s my luck was always with me. Narcotics afforded me money and neighborhood recognition. As far as I was concerned the good times never had to end. I knew there were dangers out there: I watched as competitors got killed. I saw first one uncle and then another get locked up. Yet as a teenager I somehow felt certain that I personally would not suffer these same fates. On the streets of the South Side I was respected and feared. And for a while at least I dreaded nothing. But there was a bigger world beyond the blocks where I ran my hustle. All you had to do was go over to the lake to see the gleaming skyline of center city Chicago. I was no stranger to downtown. The Loop was a favorite spot to hang out during the summer, to bring a girl to a club, or to pick up some new gear. Yet,

I had only a general sense that the businessmen and politicians who occupied those buildings and nearby city hall were making decisions that deeply affected our daily lives.

The workings of power were both obvious and invisible. We could see the poverty and neglect in our neighborhoods, the lack of jobs, crowded schools, homes in disrepair. And we had constant, direct confrontations with the bitter racism of police and many white Chicagoans. But the network of institutions that were operating to keep us from our dreams of full equality were largely out of sight.

As a result, I didn't involve myself deeply in politics. Ronald Reagan, the cowboy actor, was president. Our TVs were always airing warnings to "Say No to Drugs." And yet, as we learned during the Iran–Contra scandal, his administration was involved with trafficking cocaine all across the world. They were selling more dope and more guns than anybody. As an aspiring drug dealer myself, how could I hate this man? How could I hate the biggest dope dealer in the world? He made a lot of people rich, and also revealed the hypocrisy of the "Say No to Drugs" message. That was politics for me—the big picture stuff. I wasn't registered to vote and paid little attention to city issues.

Many others felt the same way. Blacks didn't vote much in Chicago and as a result politicians from city government to the White House felt they didn't need to listen to our concerns. Rather than working through party politics, community activists like my grandmother focused on self-help and local assistance. As the decade continued, the neighborhoods continued to suffer. Boarded-up buildings, vacant lots, rising crime rates, and gang violence were everywhere. Things had gotten much worse than they'd been in April 1968, during the riots after Martin Luther King Jr. had been killed. Many wondered whether the city would soon burn again. But this was the world we knew.

My life was the South Side. I had never flown on an airplane. Except for summer camp and a few family vacations, I had rarely left the neighborhoods that I called home. Due to the city's strict racial boundaries, many white and Latino areas—even those just a few blocks from my home—were as foreign to me as if they had been in a distant country. I almost never went past Western Avenue, for instance, which was the agreed-upon border between the black and Latino parts of the South Side. And I would certainly not have ventured there alone. Just like Bridgeport, it would have been hell to pay for a black guy to get caught in the wrong place after hours. As far as my day-to-day was concerned, the primary connection to the metropolis came through brushes with the police department. I knew all the regular officers who patrolled Fifty-First Street—and they knew me. They'd constantly stop and harass me. They'd say some shit to me, and I'd say shit back to them.

But politics occasionally did offer some hope for change. In early 1983, Harold Washington ran an inspirational campaign to become the first African American mayor of Chicago. My mother and grandmother committed themselves heart and soul to this effort. In order to win, Washington had to defeat the incumbent, as well as Richard M. Daley, son of the mayor who had been so responsible for creating the segregated city we lived in. Racism, inevitably, was the key issue in the campaign. Catcalls and curses greeted Washington every time he took his message to Marquette Park and other white neighborhoods. But in African American districts, he was a hero. In the final days of his campaign, he led a caravan of fifty vehicles through the Robert Taylor Homes and other projects while residents cheered him on from the high-rise windows.

The enthusiasm and anger in that election were enormous. Everyone in my neighborhood voted for Washington. In Bridgeport, and the other white districts, he ran dead last. But the huge turnout in the South Side gave us hope. We watched the results at home, cheered with every new update from the polls. It was well past midnight when

Washington finally declared victory. "Yeah, yeah, praise God! We did it," shouted black people all over the city.

The celebrations in our neighborhood went on for days. And in the coming years much of that happiness would prove to be justified, as Washington's administration would have a real impact on me and the city. He brought in jobs, funded community groups, like the one my grandmother worked with, and constructed new housing for low-income families. But like so many moments in Chicago during these years, our optimism always had to contend with the realities of hatred. On the day after Harold Washington's election I was chatting with some friends on the sidewalk when we suddenly heard shouting about a "nigger getting elected." A car screeched up in front of us and a group of white guys leapt out to try to start something with us. That was their mistake. We beat their asses. But then an older black man drove by and gave us a warning: more whites were coming into the neighborhood looking to start trouble. Heeding his advice, we got off the streets for safety—driven indoors by the threat of violence at the very moment when we had achieved our greatest electoral victory.

————

With my expanding business interests demanding so much of my attention, it was often difficult to find time for family. My mother was working around the clock, it seemed, and when I did happen to visit her place and find her in, she was usually lying in bed trying to enjoy a few minutes of rest. We would sit there together on the bed to chat and catch up. My brother Pat still lived at home, as well as my sister, who by then already had two kids of her own. Most of the time, though, when I went back to Fifty-First Street it was to see my grandmother. We all still gathered together every single Sunday at her house for her traditional weekly dinner party. It was during a Sunday night feast in September 1985 when the phone rang with the news that my girlfriend, Tiffany, had gone into labor. Dropping everything, I raced over to the hospital to be by her side. When I arrived, Tiffany was surrounded by her mother and aunties. The whole family was in the delivery room with her. She was in real bad pain, screaming every few minutes. At one particularly violent contraction she let out a heart-stopping wail. Overcome at the sight and sound, her mother shrieked even louder and then collapsed in a faint. From the hospital bed, Tiffany shouted to the doctors and nurses, "Can somebody get this bitch out of here?"

My family had reservations about the relationship. And frankly, so did I. Geraldine feared that Tiffany was using the pregnancy to trap me into marriage—but, then again, my grandmother was the type to suspect everyone of scheming. My mother had her concerns, too, I'm sure. But she was mostly excited about the arrival of a grandchild. As I held Ronnie Jr. for the first time I knew one thing for certain: I wasn't going to be an absentee father. I would be there for him, even if things didn't work out with his mother. Fatherhood soon changed my attitude toward life. Spending time with Ronnie was too much fun to risk losing, and I was eager to figure out a plan that would make life safer for all of us. That's one thing that separated me from rival drug dealers in the neighborhood. Most of the others were in the game for the lifestyle. And—yes—I enjoyed the benefits of wealth and reputation, too, but for me the primary concern was always to make a living. I was doing it to live. I was doing it for my family. I had to take care of my son and his mama.

By the late 1980s, I could feel my luck changing. After three years in the narcotics business, dangers suddenly lurked everywhere. Formerly secure connections—friends, and even family—no longer provided any guarantee of safety. With stakes and desperation this high anyone could turn against you. I learned this the hard way. A guy I knew called for me to come by his house with some product. I arrived at night and made my way up to the second story landing of his building. The stairs were dark, but I hardly gave it a thought. Suddenly, I could sense that I was surrounded by multiple people. Then, instantly, I was struck down by the butt of a gun and I heard voices shouting at me: "Break yo'self! Break yo'self!" They grabbed the drugs, which was basically all I had on me.

"Just shoot his ass," someone shouted. "Just shoot that motherfucker. Just shoot him."

Thinking quickly, I started reasoning with the attackers. "What you gotta shoot me for?" I said. "I don't know who you are. I don't see no faces. Y'all took everything I got."

"Just shoot him. Shoot that motherfucker. Shoot him."

"Man, you don't have to shoot me," I said. "I done gave you everything. Matter of fact, you could have the car. I got money in the car. You can have that shit, too. I can get that shit back. I can't get me back." They took the shoes off my feet. They took the keys to the car, took money out of the car, left the keys in the trunk, and I got my head split wide open. But I survived.

After that I knew I had to arm myself. But I hated it. When people carry guns, it's because they're looking for trouble. When you have to go with bare fists you're looking for a way to calm stuff down. But when people got a gun, shit is gonna get real tricky, real fast. If people have a gun, they have it for a reason. I started carrying a gun, but my gun was not for show, my gun was to protect. And it was while trying to protect my family that I got arrested on a gun charge. The day after Christmas in 1987, right after I had just started carrying a gun, I happened upon a bunch of Vice Lords beating up my cousin's cousin. There were six of them and just little ol' me—I probably weighed about a buck ten. I chased after them until the police arrived, and I was given a year's court supervision for gun possession. I never carried a gun after that.

Now, every time I looked around, I was in jail for this, for that. Most of it never came to trial; charges were dropped, a lot of it was nonsense. That was the life I was leading. Times were changing. More and more people were sticking up and murdering, getting into all crazy types of shit. I was getting tired of that. I was sick of being paranoid. When you start feeling that way, there's no need to even try to be into that stuff anymore. Then, someone I knew—a drug dealer named Boo, who lived on the next block—had his son kidnapped to extort money from him. That was too close. I didn't want to live like that. The drug game was a business to me, and when it started getting to be more dangerous than I could handle, I knew it was time to move on. I had a son who loved hanging out with me. I felt so threatened and paranoid that I couldn't move without taking a million precautions. Lights in the house had to be turned on; gates to the yard needed to be locked. I felt like I had to barricade myself inside everywhere I went. So I started looking into alternatives.

A side venture began to look more promising. My mom and I had opened an arcade called the Game Room in a building she owned. Right across from a grammar school, its location guaranteed good income. Every morning she would swing by and open it up at 7:00 AM; at the end of the night I'd close things up at 2:00 AM. Earning between $1,000 and $2,000 a week, it seemed like an investment to pursue. I made a plan that would allow me to go legit. I figured that if I could save $200,000 from drug sales and then invest it all in arcades, I'd be able to create a different life. I was already purchasing new games. We'd open another Game Room, and then another. That was my long-term goal. I could already picture this new future. And everyone else was excited about it, too—Tiffany, my mother. The only person who opposed it was Eric, my cousin, who felt like I was abandoning our partnership and leaving him behind. After we split up and went our separate ways, I don't think he stopped being jealous.

Then, around 11:00 PM on June 3, 1988, I was driving with Tiffany and Ronnie Jr. when suddenly police lights flashed behind us. When I pulled over an officer of the gang crimes police squad got in my face with a search warrant for my house. Not wanting them to damage my door, I put up no resistance. I even told them where they could find my stash, about two hundred grams of cocaine in the freezer. I'm sure it was Eric who called the police on me. Even with the heat on me rising, even with a court date set, I had to keep hustling to earn that stake. So I kept on doing my thing. Thinking of the future, I was stashing money everywhere: in the ceiling of my mom's basement, at my grandmother's, in the back of the washing machine, in Ronnie Jr.'s closet.

Despite my cares, I managed to make the summer of 1988 memorable. Cash was coming in and girls were everywhere. My friends and I spent many late nights hanging out. The evening of July 26 was typical. A friend threw a birthday splash party for his daughter, who was turning three. Fifteen or twenty of us all met up at his mother's place, a few blocks from home, where they had an aboveground pool. My sister came around and we were all playing in the water with the kids. Till about 9:00 PM it was a family affair. We were swimming, throwing balls around, and pushing each other into the pool. Then Tiffany and the other moms picked up the toddlers, and the rest of us hung around listening to music until the early morning hours.

The most beautiful vision from that summer was this girl—my future wife—who stayed on South Lowe, a block away from me. I couldn't help but notice her when she came to visit with her family that year. The very first time I drove past, I slowed down the car and hollered at her, "Hey, wife!" And after that, every time I saw her, I'd call to her, "Hey, wife!" Finally, after a few times, she flagged me down and told me to stop, and that's when I heard her real name, Katina Carr. Before long, she and I were seeing each other almost every day. But that was a lone bright spot.

Other run-ins with police followed fast after that first drug bust. As the summer progressed my $200,000 goal always kept receding over the horizon. Finally, in late August, I decided enough was enough.

I counted up all the cash I had: it came in total to about $30,000. It was far short of my target, but I figured it might just be enough. I also had a narcotics inventory of nine ounces of cocaine and about six pounds of weed. "I'm through," I said to my mom. "As soon as I get rid of this stuff, I'm through."

The date was August 25, 1988. I still had some issues to work out, but I felt like a tremendous burden had just come off my mind. The future was looking so sweet, I was happy to stop by the corner store to pick up a roll of cookie dough for dessert that night.

3

THE CRYING YEARS

DAZED AND NUMB, I descended the stairs leading from Area 3
Violent Crimes—the hellhole where I had been tortured and kept
prisoner during the previous twenty-four hours. It was around seven
in the evening, on Friday, August 26, 1988. Cuffs bit into my wrists.
Officers walked on either side of me, propping me up if I staggered
or slipped. In their tight clutches, it almost looked like I was walking
normally. Exiting the building I suddenly found myself confronted by
a crowd of reporters. Camera teams from several local TV stations had
arrived to film my "perp walk," which would be broadcast for all to see
on the eleven o'clock news. I hardly noticed them. The whole episode
passed before I even registered it. My facial expression was blank and
distant—it was as if I were not even the person experiencing this. My
mind raced everywhere. I crossed the parking lot, limping ever so
slightly, to a waiting paddy wagon. Cops supported my arms and gave
me a boost by the elbow as I stumbled clumsily inside and took a seat.
The vehicle doors closed with a crash and the van jolted into gear.

Looking back, I realize that my body and mind were in shock. The
beatings and terror I had suffered at the hands of the detectives had

filled my system with adrenaline. From the moment they informed me that I was being charged with a quintuple homicide—the mass murder of two women and three children—an overwhelming surge of panic had flooded over me. From that instant on I had been too stunned to collect myself or even to understand what was happening. The sensation was similar to times in my life when I had been in a fight and hadn't been able to feel any pain until hours later. But this was on a whole different level. In the van, trying to keep it together, I was grateful to realize that Marvin was sitting next to me. I hadn't seen him since being arrested, though I'd been able to hear his screams from my interrogation room. He had a nasty black eye. I must have looked even worse. Throughout the drive he just kept repeating, "Hold on, hold on."

Over the course of the next twenty-four hours I would be transported in a crisscross pattern across large areas of the city, moved from one precinct to another, tossed in a holding cell over night before being transferred again in the morning, and finally arriving in the receiving area at Cook County Jail. The reason for all these movements was simple—it was to hide me. The detectives knew what they were doing. They had it down to a science, and they understood that the adrenaline would be wearing off soon. It would not serve their purpose for that to happen in a public place. I had to be out of sight so that my symptoms would not be part of my official record. Everyone was in on it: the drivers who shuffled me here and there, the officers who admitted me to the cells without asking any questions, the medical personnel who ignored my condition. For the system to work, many people had to be involved. That first night, in the lockup across town, my body finally started coming alive. The pain hit, the swelling began, bruises appeared. For hours I lay alone, moaning, screaming, and crying for help. And no one responded.

In the midst of this agony my mind wandered back to the ordeal I had just suffered. I had been in the clutches of the detectives. They had tortured me for hours and now they were pressuring me to sign the false confession. I had finally agreed to do so for the sake of my family. Ronnie Jr. was just a toddler, and Tiffany was pregnant with another baby. I was their sole provider. The police were going to kill me; I knew this in my heart. They were not going to let me walk out of that precinct alive. So I signed the confession thinking that I'd just go down for this in the moment, and then, with the help of my lawyer, I would clear things up. I didn't even know the people who were killed. I was never in that area. Beyond that, I would never do such a thing. The whole idea was preposterous. Obviously this was a big, messy, painful misunderstanding. The world would see my innocence and the charges would drop.

But already, just a few hours later, this plan was already in crisis. I had appeared in night court for a bond hearing. Bloody, swollen, unable to walk, I faced the night-court judge certain that just by looking at me, he would understand that something was not right. My public defender even pointed it out, saying, "You can clearly see he's been beaten up." No one in the court ever asked any questions about my condition. All they saw was a black dude who had killed innocent women and children. Somewhere between my pain and disbelief, my blind confidence in the system to recognize truth, and my sense of my place as a black man in a court of law, I couldn't find my own voice. The judge denied bond and did nothing for my medical needs. That was the first of many lessons I would learn in the coming years. People didn't want to know anything about me. They didn't want to hear my side of the story. To do so would mean they would have to consider the possibility that the police were lying. And in their eyes I was a monster already.

On Saturday morning I was deposited in the receiving area of Cook County Jail, a basement room crammed with scores of people waiting for their turn to be processed. The bullpen, as it was known, was jam-packed and filthy, filled with men waiting to be poked and prodded, to have the most private details of their lives recorded.

For ten hours I stayed there; for the few scattered moments when I was able to drift off to sleep, Marvin made sure to stand nearby and watch over me. Finally, when my turn came, I was called up to a long desk lined with computer terminals. Every second was excruciating for me. I couldn't walk. I was pissing blood. My scrotum was so swollen that I couldn't even touch my pants. The pain intensified moment by moment. But still I had to sit through an endless series of questions. *Was I gay? Did I have hepatitis? Did I have any STDs? Did I have tattoos or scars? Was I affiliated with a gang?* Next, a paramedic swabbed me for diseases and drew blood. He asked a list of questions about my medical history but took no notice of my current condition. I told him I needed help and described the beating I'd received. He ignored me, made no mention of it on his chart, and promised I'd be able to see a doctor soon.

Intake involved repeated interactions with officials. At every point along the way I asked for medical treatment. My injuries were on full display, but no one intervened, paid attention, or asked questions. Each time I was told I'd have to wait till the next stage. At last, they said the doctors would look at me when I got to my cell. The process took what seemed like forever. After all the paperwork was complete and signed, it was time to wait again. I sat in the bullpen with dozens of others. I was exhausted; my body was destroyed. I was issued my brown khaki Cook County Department of Corrections uniform and my housing assignment. When I asked for medical assistance after finally being brought to my cell, my final hope for treatment vanished. The officers there informed me I'd have to wait till the end of the weekend before a doctor would see me.

The detectives' reach stretched even behind bars. Rather than housing me among the general population, the guards put me in solitary confinement, an outcome usually reserved for disciplinary cases. Again, the purpose was to conceal me and hide my injuries from the wider world. It was Saturday night when I staggered down the 1R tier in Division VI of the jail. They called it "the Hole" for a reason. My cell seemed to have been chosen especially for its horridness; in fact, it might have been the worst one in the whole place. The light was broken and the sink had no running water. In the daytime I could enjoy some slivers of sunshine through the window, but it was so dark at night that I could not even see enough to find my way to the toilet. There were flying cockroaches in there that seemed to be the size of mice. A Bible—the only thing not affixed to the floor or the wall—lay on the steel bed.

I cried for hours that first night, feeling more alone than at any other moment in my life. All around me I could hear the shouts, moans, and screams of others in a similar predicament. For some this was a constant expression of pain. For many this was our only means of communication—shouting at each other through the walls. At one point, breaking through my own cries, I detected a familiar voice. Marvin was housed nearby. I could hear him calling out to me to make sure I was all right. I was grateful to hear his assurances, but I wasn't all right. I was lying in agony, in total darkness, desperate to understand how things had ended up going this far, and how, if ever, they would go right.

It wasn't until Monday, two full days after I'd been admitted to my cell, that my lawyer—by literally screaming at a captain in the jail—was able to arrange for a hearing. The judge took one look at Marvin and me and ordered our keepers to give us treatment. Photographs were taken of Marvin's face to document his bruises. I showed my ribs and the court ordered the sheriffs to provide us with health care. Even then there was a delay, but at last on Tuesday, August 30—nearly a full excruciating week after my beating—I was finally, grudgingly, allowed to see a doctor at Cermak Hospital, the medical center attached to the jail. For almost three hours, the ER staff gave me the care I had so desperately needed all this time. "Complains of groin pain," the doctors noted. "States that police hit in groin with night stick, knee & fist, lot of pain. Was swollen from Thursday till Tuesday. Passed blood Tuesday a.m. . . . . Pain to touch. Can't wear underwear with it." The doctors fitted me out with a scrotal support, which was a kind of sling, to support my private parts, and prescribed painkillers. I'd visit the hospital every day for the next month and a half for routine follow-ups as well as in emergency moments. Visiting the hospital, bleak and painful as it was, offered the only relief from life in solitary confinement.

The entire time I was receiving medical treatment I was still being housed in the filthiest hole in the jail—it was hardly a surprise that I developed infections and complications from my beating. A normal day for a prisoner in the Hole was supposed to include one hour to take a shower, use the phones, and watch TV. That was barely enough time to accomplish all the necessary tasks in the day. But for the first two or three weeks, I didn't even get that. They never let me out. I had almost no visitors. The only time I saw a human being was when the guard opened the chuck hole in the cell door to deliver my meals. Marvin would come down during the precious time he got away from his cell, slip me some juice to sip on, and talk me through the pain and depression. For the first few months I was in solitary, the guards treated me like shit. Mine was a high-profile case, my supposed crime was horrific, and the guards never let me forget it for a moment.

Though severely limited by the jail's restrictive rules, Marvin looked after me. Without him I wouldn't have made it. No way. He called my lawyer and my family and kept me up to date with the news. He went to the commissary for me and brought me food. Marvin was my lifeline. He was my grandmother's godson, so I had known him forever. But he was a good deal older than me—more like an uncle or big brother—and we didn't hang out. Of all the pains I felt, nothing cut as sharply as the knowledge that I was the one who had put him in this situation by signing the confession naming him as my accomplice. Marvin was never angry; he never blamed me. He knew what the police did. He heard my screams. He never showed me nothing but love. His family either. But I felt responsible. That was one of the lowest points in my life, knowing that I put Marvin in harm's way. Knowing that I took him away from his business, away from his family, away from his girlfriend, knowing that I was responsible for him being in this place, this hell.

I spent nearly two months in that dark pit on 1R. These were my forty days and forty nights, give or take a few—my test in the wilderness. And it was nearly enough time for me to lose my mind. Solitary confinement was lonely, but not a place for contemplation; the endless din of disturbed inmates in these segregated-housing units was like a circle of hell. There were so many sources of pain: my body, Marvin's fate, my children's future. Of them all, the thought that was hardest to endure was the knowledge of being innocent. I had always believed that only guilty people got locked up. To be treated like this with no evidence—no, I did not think I was going to survive that. Crazy thoughts, suicidal thoughts, drove me close to madness.

At night, the only light I could access was a paper-thin glimmer that snuck through the gaps in my cell door. I used to stand as close as possible in order to read my Bible. It was painful to keep myself in such a pose, craning my neck and getting on tiptoe. Sitting on the floor would have been infinitely more comfortable, but the cockroaches made that option unthinkable. In these months, my old beliefs came pouring back to me. I had been brought up in the church. Mama had made me put on a suit each Sunday and sing in the choir. It was a forced thing in my childhood, and as I had grown older, God had become less and less of a fixture in my life. But in this situation, in jail, I felt the need to call upon a being that I felt was more powerful than anything that I knew. I constantly prayed for the truth—for them to see that we were in here for a crime we didn't commit. I prayed for Marvin, for God to get him out. I'd be in peace knowing that he'd be out. I prayed a lot in that cell. I prayed and cried a lot. Prayed, cried, and thought about death.

I asked: *Why? Why would someone put me through this?* I knew cops were assholes. I knew they didn't miss an opportunity to fuck with me. I knew they could be dangerous and mess somebody up. But this was different. This was a whole other level. And something deep in me, just like something deep in most people in this country, felt the police wouldn't do something this horrific. The small cell, the steel door, the metal bed, the sparseness, and the filth. My brain really didn't sleep in those first months in solitary. The same thoughts turned in my mind, over and over. I stood, reading my Bible by the sliver of light from the hallway. I spent a lot of time in those first few months poised there by the door, crying and talking to God.

Of everything I drew on to stay strong, it was the Old Testament tale of Joseph that kept me going the most. That story pulled me through when nothing else could. Joseph was a promising young man whose life was marked for success. His brothers hated him and conspired to have him sold into slavery. Falsely accused of a crime he had not committed, Joseph was thrown into jail. Through his own talents he overcame every obstacle set in his path, rising to become a leader in Egypt. Joseph did not bear his brothers ill will but offered life-saving charity when their homeland sank into famine. Reunited after years of absence he assumed the triumphant role that had been foretold for him as head of the family and leader of his people. I read that story every night. Every night. I learned that story by heart.

———————

Between me and the city stood brick, concrete, steel, and a paramilitary force of sheriffs, correctional officers, and police. I lay confined in the bottom tier of the Cook County Jail's most isolated unit. From my tiny window I could see razor wire fences and machine-gun towers, all designed with the sole purpose of trapping me far away from the life I had known. Out there, where I was powerless, my future was being shaped.

The news media quickly ran with the story concocted by the detectives. Bits and pieces filtered to me inside over the coming days and weeks. Apparently, I was a household name by the night of August 26, when numerous TV reports showed me walking across the Area 3 parking lot. The morning newspapers offered further details of the story that the police and prosecutors were proudly presenting to the world. 2 ARE CHARGED IN DEATH OF 5, proclaimed that day's *Tribune*, atop mug shots of me and Marvin, looking guilty and defiant. 2 MEN SEIZED IN 5 KILLINGS, reported the *Sun-Times*. All of these reports were taken directly from the fiction that Kill and Burge had penned. It was the "confession" they had created for me, given added credibility with every repetition in the press.

Because of a drug debt of $1,225—so this story went—Marvin and I had gotten into his car on the night of Tuesday, July 27, driven across Western Avenue into a Latino neighborhood, and murdered two Mexican American women, Deborah Sepulveda and Rose Marie Rodriguez, and their kids in cold blood. "The motive was apparently money owed regarding a dope transaction," Lt. Burge explained. For this paltry sum—less than my arcade-game business brought me in a week—we were supposed to have beaten and strangled these women, and then suffocated their three young children, and finally, to mask our deeds, set fire to their house.

Our arrest was a huge local news story, as well as a major development in a case that had shocked the city for the previous month. The two dead young women had been well-liked members of the community, who had worked as beloved teacher's aides at a local school. Neighbors recalled fond memories of seeing them in the backyard playing with the kids, splashing in a pool and listening to music. Their murders—as well as the deaths of the children—had been a horrific and senseless tragedy. For the police department the investigation had been given special priority. Not only was it a sensational crime, but it was even more personal than that—one of the victims was the daughter of a Chicago cop.

Detectives had interviewed friends and relatives of the deceased but had failed to uncover or follow up on any clues or criminal motives. Investigators had come up completely empty, finding no evidence or witnesses. But they did not try very hard, or pursue the facts for very long. With mounting public pressure, and increasing frustrations over their lack of results, within two weeks Burge and his desperate underlings stopped trying to track down the actual perpetrators and began to look at other means of closing the case. They needed to find a fall guy—someone who fit the description of what Americans expected a cold-blooded killer to look like. For most white Americans, it wasn't even a question: black easily meant criminal. But just weeks after my arrest, black definitely meant criminal. Between George Bush's presidential campaign ads and the evening news, Willie Horton's name, face, and horrible acts were beamed into homes across the country. To millions, this convicted rapist and murderer represented all black men. But Chicago police didn't need an actual Willie Horton, they didn't have to look that hard. All they needed was a young black man with a less than perfect record. It wasn't hard for them to hone in on me.

Only those involved in fabricating the story know the truth. But I've spent years thinking through the puzzle, and it's clear to me that it was my cousin Eric who first put my name into the detectives' minds. Still nursing a grudge against me for ending our partnership in the drug business, there was no limit to his desire for revenge.

When police questioned him about us earlier that summer, when he tipped them off and they stopped me in June, he was all too eager to exaggerate our narcotics activities into something much darker and more evil. Eric, I suspect, was also the one who put them in touch with his brother-in-law, Willie Williams, a repeat petty criminal serving a three-year sentence in Vandalia prison for burglary. With these two accomplices working with them, Burge, Kill, and the others had all the material they needed to hatch their plot.

Someone in the department must have visited Willie in prison and mapped out the steps to take. The detectives instructed him to call my house in order to try to get some incriminating evidence from me. In early August, citing "reasonable cause," Burge received court approval to place a wiretap on my phone. Around that time, Tiffany and I began getting collect calls from Williams in prison. It only happened a few times, and I don't think I ever even accepted the charges. Why would I? I didn't know him and had nothing to say to him. We talked at most for just a few moments. It was a little strange. Tiffany found Williams to be creepy and unpleasant. But at the time I really didn't give it more than a second thought.

All the police had to do was add a few colorful details to lend the story some credibility. Thus, Burge and Kill came up with the $1,250 drug debt, a number specific enough to make it believable, and yet so small a sum as to make us appear especially cold and cruel—as if we placed almost no value on human life. Along the same lines, they had Willie testify that we had confessed to him about the deaths of "Mary" and "Debbie," casual nicknames for the victims that suggested we had known them well. In this, and numerous other ways, the police devised a narrative that had at least a chance of convincing someone who was already inclined to accept it.

Hard to believe as some of these details were, it would have been even harder to swallow the real truth: that everything in this story was a lie concocted by the police. That would require people to understand

and believe that *everyone* was in on the lie, and to accept that truth would mean that society itself had to be condemned. Suffice it to say, most Chicagoans in the late 1980s were not ready to take that leap. They were more than content to take a look at our mug shots while drinking their morning coffees, seeing just more evidence of the depravity and violence of young black men.

If anyone was paying attention, though, the media coverage should have raised at least some eyebrows. The newspaper articles that ran on Saturday, August 27, were filled with inconsistencies. Burge's account left far more questions than answers. The *Tribune* mentioned that the police wiretap had not provided any evidence. Reporters interviewed the victims' families and neighbors—everyone expressed shock and doubt about the police claims that the murdered women had been involved with drugs. Everything about the investigation, in short, was dubious from the outset. And this was freely admitted. But nobody noticed, or nobody cared, because no one had any reason to pause for even a second to wonder or even care whether we were innocent.

The scope of the police duplicity in this case was staggering. Too lazy and cynical to pursue promising leads, Burge and the others were more interested in closing the book on the case and getting a young black man off the street than they were in actually doing their jobs. Perhaps most sickening of all, they preferred to defame the dead— these two Mexican American young women—as drug dealers involved in a criminal syndicate, than to actually put in the legwork required to bring their killers to justice.

The "facts of the case" were not facts. They were lies. And knowing this gave me confidence. Not only had I never even been to the neighborhood where the murders had been committed, nor had any business dealings with people in the Mexican community, let alone ever met the victims, I had a rock-solid alibi for the night the crime had been committed. That was the evening I had spent at a splash party in my neighborhood. I had a dozen witnesses who were there with me that night. Anyone who knew me would know that this whole story about the murders was completely preposterous. Even if I couldn't, they would tell a judge and jury I was innocent. Although I didn't know it yet, the problem would be getting strangers to know me, to care enough about my life to listen to the real facts. Burge and his crew were already operating with that knowledge. They didn't worry about the little details, because they knew that the big lie—you might call it racism itself—was too deeply engrained in people's minds to allow any room for doubt.

Guards took me from my jail cell on visits to the hospital almost every day for months. My progress was difficult and unsteady. After a checkup on September 21 the doctors thought I was "doing fine," with "no swelling of testes anymore." But a week later I was back in the emergency room, "bleeding from groin area" this time, and in the grips of a painful infection. By mid-November, however, I was definitely on the mend. "No pain," the doctors noted, "no complaint . . . no pathology evident from external exam." When I had nearly healed from my injuries, coming up on my twenty-third birthday, I was finally moved out of solitary. Because my health remained fragile, I was not placed directly into general population. Instead, they threw me on tier 1N in Division VI. This was the "old man's deck," the level of the jail reserved for prisoners over forty years old.

Getting out of solitary was a godsend for my state of mind. But it came with new concerns. *This* was the Cook County Jail I'd heard about. It was overcrowded. There was a lot of violence, a lot of killings, a lot of gang activity. If you weren't plugged up with anybody, you were in trouble. A lot of fights in County were ten against one. Whatever mob you were in, somebody would pick a fight with you. My accommodations were more or less the same as in Seg, except now I had running water and lights—and a cellie. There was more to do, and more people to see, but it was still lonely. Everybody was in there—and desperate not to be there—for something: drugs, murder, rape. I couldn't socialize and think everyone in jail was a friend. There were plenty of guys in there like Willie Williams, and the last thing I wanted to do was to start a conversation with strangers. The thing about jail is your future is uncertain when you're there. You don't know what's coming, so you can't yet settle in and accept it. Most guys in there, like me, hadn't been tried or sentenced yet, and they might just be desperate enough to cut some kind of deal on somebody else's back if given the chance. Even on the old man's deck, the jail could be a dangerous place. Many of my new neighbors were tied to gangs, and they were deadly serious in their loyalties. The first time I walked down the tier, I passed a row of guys—one might be a Stone, another is a Vice Lord, a third is a Gangster Disciple—each one of them, as I walked by their cell, quizzed me about my affiliations. "What you is?" they shouted at me. "What you is?"

"I ain't shit," I yelled back. "I ain't nothing." Lots of people came into that jail claiming a gang; I was just claiming me. No pause. No hesitation. Me. That in itself was a statement. It was known that I would fight, that I would defend myself. It was just my frame of mind: I didn't take shit on the street, ain't no need to take it in jail. That made them pause. It sent the message that I was going to protect myself and not rely on anyone else to do that for me. They realized then that I wasn't scared. I wasn't going to let anybody talk crazy to me, and I sure enough wasn't going to let anyone put their hands on me. I didn't walk in thinking I was all tough, nor was I trying to be somebody I wasn't. I wasn't posturing. I wasn't looking for any trouble. But at the same time, if anyone got in my face I would have no problem fighting.

Luckily for me, I didn't really have to go it alone. People took to me. I made friends quickly with most of the guys on the tier. Ironically, it wasn't until I found myself in lockup—and had lost the freedom to live a social life—that I truly realized how many people I actually knew in the city of Chicago. Although I was two decades younger than the next youngest guy on the tier, I saw a lot of familiar faces: Popeye, Flintstone, Bootsy, Boogaloo. Some had skated at The Rink or hung around the Godfather. I had sold reefer to one guy's son. During the long periods of downtime that make up so much of life in jail, we would sit around and talk about the outside world. My cellies were always telling stories about people from the neighborhood. They would usually then turn to me and ask: *Do you know him? Do you know those dudes? Do you know her?* And the answer was always: *Yes, yes, yes.* I had gone everywhere and talked with everyone.

Just like on the outside, I had friends on all sides of the gang wars. Just like on the street, my personal connections let me get away with a lot that others might not have. There was a Vice Lord in jail at that time named Wild Bill who came to resent my independence. Other guys had to ask the gang for permission to use the telephone, but I just got on the phone when I wanted to. In general, within the limits of the institution's many rules, I did what I wanted to do because most of the prisoners liked me and gave me respect as a man. But, for some reason, it rubbed Wild Bill the wrong way. I heard he was complaining to his brothers, saying things about me like, "This bitch walking around thinking he's all this and that." One afternoon in the rec room he even went so far as to snatch the pool stick out of my hand. Things had gone far enough, and one of the other gang members asked him if he wanted to lock up with me and fight it out one-on-one.

"What about the Lords?" asked Bill.

"The Lords ain't got nothing against him," they replied. "You lock up with him alone and get it off your chest." Suffice it to say, that never happened. Without the backing of a gang, his determination to fight and put me in my place disappeared.

It's not bragging to say that people always told me I had a kind of a charismatic attitude. I didn't play games. I wasn't on no bullshit. Almost everyone recognized quickly that I wasn't going to start any trouble. In the penitentiary your reputation travels. If you let people extort from you—that's going to follow you. If you snitch—that's going to follow you. If they know you can fight—that's going to follow you. People who knew me from the streets knew that I was one little dude who was not scared to fight. If you put your hands on me, it's gonna be an ongoing thing. But some people can only learn shit the hard way.

The biggest troublemaker on the old man's deck was Kojak, an enormous and quick-tempered Gangster Disciple with a habit of getting on everyone's bad side. I was on the phone one day and saw him rummaging around in the cell of a friend of mine who was out at a court appearance. "Don't take nothing," I told him. "If anything's gone, I'm gonna tell." Sure enough, a pack of cigarettes was missing. And true to my word I told my buddy what had happened. The next morning I had just sat down for breakfast when suddenly Kojak stormed up, said something slick, and threw his tray at my face. This man was huge, and I was a welterweight, at best. He picked me straight up and lifted me right over his head. Flailing around in the air, desperate for some advantage, I jammed my thumbs fiercely into his eyes, forcing him to drop me to the floor. Before he could recover, I was on my feet beating him mercilessly over the head with my tray. Other guys jumped in, too—Kojak was universally despised—and before the guards finally broke it up, he was on the floor, subdued.

By the time the captain arrived ten prisoners were in handcuffs. Kojak pointed right at me and started hollering, "That's the guy! That's the little motherfucker right there! That's him right there!"

"Ronald," the captain shouted, "get your goddamned ass over here right now." He pointed to all the guys in cuffs and asked me: "Are you going to tell me who did it?" I looked him right in the eye and said,

"Damn right I did it. I did that to him." The guards all said I was too small to have been the perpetrator. But I pressed ahead, taking the whole rap on myself. "I beat his ass for stealing." Everyone cracked up laughing then, but the punch line wasn't so funny for me: I got fifty more days in the Hole for that fight.

———————

That kind of thing could make for a bit of excitement; it certainly kept everyone talking on the tier. But it was the real ties to lifelong friends and family that could keep you sane. For the first few months, Tiffany and Ronnie Jr. came often, and we talked frequently on the phone. My second son, Randall, was born in November of 1988, while I was incarcerated. I met him once, during a visit. But then it was too much for her. She didn't want the kids to come see me; she had problems even talking to me. Before too long they stopped visiting entirely. Other people who I thought would be there for me weren't. The friends I had, they stopped talking to me. Even my father, whose work as a county sheriff often stationed him inside the jail where I was housed, never came to see me or did anything to help out in any way. It was painful to realize that many of the people closest to me had taken the path of least resistance and actually believed that I had committed the crime I was accused of. At one point, I called my father's brother, to see if—as a Chicago police officer—he could do anything to assist me. Instead, he flat-out accused me of being guilty. "You did that shit," he said. "If they say you did it, then you did it." That's the thing, we're so willing to believe in the criminal, murderous capacity of young black men and, just as strongly, have faith in the incorruptibility of police, that even those who should know better have a hard time seeing the truth when it's in front of them.

The only person who came regularly for me was my mother, who showed up without fail—rain or shine—at every weekly visiting day.

These were no-contact visits; thick plate glass divided us. The partition was so filthy you could almost smell the breath of the person who had sat there before you, shouting his personal business loudly through the glass and over the noise of all the other conversations to his visitor sitting only inches away. At our first meeting I showed her my wounds; I pulled down my pants and she saw my newly prescribed sling covered in blood. We were supposed to get thirty minutes to talk, but often the vindictive guards chopped that down to fifteen. She was my biggest supporter. We talked on the phone every day, and she showed up at every court appearance I made. She understood who I was, where I had come from, and so she never stopped believing in me. I had seen so much violence—so much anger—in my short life before incarceration that I had come to the belief that every single one of us is capable of committing a murder. All it takes is for us to be pushed far enough. But not all of us would commit the same type of murder. And for me, a man raised by strong women, who honored his mother and grandmother above all others, who had never put hands on a woman, and who held fatherhood to be a sacred trust, the idea that I could have killed those two young women and their children was absolutely beyond the realm of possibility. Anybody who knew me, who really understood my character, would not doubt that fact for a second. My mother was at the top of this list. Because she knew I could never hurt a woman or a child, she knew with absolute certainty that I was an innocent man.

When I had signed the false confession at Area 3 Violent Crimes, my one thought had been to get out of the clutches of the detectives in order to find a judge and demonstrate my innocence. I knew I had some jail time coming because of my drug arrest, but I still believed that the murder charge could be cleared up quickly. In the lockup I'd talked to jailhouse lawyers who urged me to ask for a speedy trial, which would occur within 120 days. My first court appearance came in November 1988. It took only a matter of minutes to have the lawyers discuss the exchange of documents and for a new hearing to be set for the following month. The next time was just the same. Month after month, motion after motion, continuance after continuance, I got myself ready to face the judge only to find the case postponed again. The year 1989 passed by. Then most of 1990 came and went. Before I even had a chance to show my innocence, entire years of my life had been stolen. Much of my family had abandoned me. Everything had been taken away from me. I was dealing with the emotional toll of knowing I was in a place where I was not supposed to be. I had been snatched away from my life. These years were full of crying. These were my crying years.

For my defense I had retained Robert Edwards, the family lawyer, who had produced good results for me and my relatives in previous cases. Every time I spoke to him he insisted that I had a beatable case. "They have nothing on you," he told me. "We can win this." Looking back, though, I see there were warning signs that I should have paid attention to. He hired an investigator to pursue evidence on my behalf, but I only met with the man once. All in all, I don't think I met with Edwards in person more than three or four times. Instead of going out and finding witnesses to testify for me, he actually suggested that I do this part of the preparation myself—from my jail cell. I proposed that he subpoena the medical staff who had treated my injuries, but Edwards felt that would be a mistake because the doctors worked for the state and in his opinion would be unlikely to contradict the testimony of police officers. Instead of doing any real work, the lawyer just reassured me, saying the same thing over and over again, "We got it beat. We got it beat."

My moment of reckoning arrived in early September 1990. Finally, I would have the chance to tell my side of the story. I awoke at 4:00 AM on the first morning of my trial. I ate breakfast in my cell and changed into a suit and tie. Division VI of the Cook County Jail was all the way in the back of the sprawling complex. So it was a long walk through the tunnels toward the courthouse, especially in shackles. It had taken two years for me to finally get to tell my side of the story. Everything about those years had been depressing. The jail was depressing. Losing touch with family. The guilt of Marvin's fate. But the hardest part was knowing I was there for something I didn't do. Now, at last, I was going to get my day in court.

4

THE PEOPLE VS. RONALD KITCHEN

AT 10:00 AM on Monday, September 10, 1990, the clerk loudly announced, "People vs. Ronald Kitchen," and I was led into room number 704 in the Cook County Criminal Court building. I took my seat at the defense table and looked around. From a raised platform, Judge Vincent Bentivenga surveyed a chamber decorated with ornate railings and dark wooden benches. Large windows cast sunshine like spotlights across the actors in the drama. Everything was designed to create a sense of awe. But I wasn't impressed; I had been in too many courtrooms before. To me it looked like a Hollywood set, which I found comforting. I was reminded of scenes from old *Perry Mason* episodes, or the series *Matlock*, which aired on Tuesdays on channel 5. Those shows had shaped my vision of what would happen next. I fully expected my attorney to step in and display the kind of dramatic legal skills that I had seen on TV. In a climactic finale, he would unravel the district attorney's case, brilliantly revealing all its damning inconsistencies, and tear apart the detectives' web of lies.

I truly entered the chamber that morning in full confidence that an innocent man would not go to jail for something he never did.

That was an abstract idea. But my immediate response was much more physical. I knew this was no movie, this was me in here with my life on the line. Nerves set in. My stomach locked up with that familiar feeling of bubble gut that I used to get while robbing the freight yards. Hell, hadn't Hollywood also made at least one movie about an innocent guy going to prison for life? I was already locked up by the time it played in Chicago, but I knew *The Thin Blue Line* was a 1988 blockbuster. My mind was reeling, my emotions on a rollercoaster ride. Moments of coolness quickly gave way to anxiety, and then I found my confidence only to be betrayed by physical nerves. As I settled in, the lawyers huddled with the presiding judge in a preliminary discussion. This was the first moment of the trial— prospective jurors had not even arrived yet—and already there were signs of the serious issues that would follow. My attorney, Robert Edwards, had provided the state with a list of witnesses and their addresses. According to the prosecutors none of the information was accurate. "One is a factory," the state's attorney complained, "one is a vacant lot, and there's other addresses that just aren't there." In part, this was a result of time and the unsettled nature of life on the South Side. Two years had passed since my arrest. People had moved. Houses had been torn down. But it also stemmed from carelessness on behalf of my defense team—a seemingly minor point that would loom large as the proceedings continued.

Because of the importance of the moment I had come in looking my best, wearing an Armani silk suit with gray alligator loafers. Edwards took a look at me and panicked. "Don't come in looking like that any more," he hissed. "The prosecution is going to try to make you out as a shot caller, the lieutenant of a major drug enterprise, and you are dressed perfectly for the part." He insisted I have my mother bring me in more casual clothing—gym shoes, T-shirts, and a jacket—to wear for the rest of the trial.

The first batch of jurors filed in. As they took their seats the judge addressed them from on high, outlining general points of the criminal statutes. "The defendant under the law, he is presumed to be innocent of the charges in the indictment," Bentivenga explained. "This presumption remains throughout the trial with the defendant until you have been satisfied by the evidence in the case beyond a reasonable doubt as to the guilt of this defendant." Then he began to read the charges against me. It took almost ten full minutes just to read them aloud. As he continued, the atmosphere in the room grew more and more somber. After hearing the words "first degree murder" and "aggravated arson" repeated over and over again—especially against women and children—it was easy to see that the presumption of my innocence was already in jeopardy. Finally, the judge concluded with this ominous pronouncement: "In this state the death penalty is one of the possible penalties which may be given to an individual convicted of a crime of murder."

It took nearly two entire days and well over fifty candidates to choose a jury. For the most part I sensed they were decent everyday men and women, a few lawyers and professionals, but generally working-class Chicagoans, many unemployed and retired. These were the people who would decide my fate, so I closely scanned their faces as they discussed themselves and their feelings about justice. I tried my best, but it was impossible to look across a room and get a feel for people answering yes and no questions. For their part, the jurors seemed unwilling to make eye contact with me. Whenever I put my head down on the desk I'd feel them all watching me, trying to see if I was the kind of man who could do the things I was accused of doing. But when I lifted up my head, they would all turn anxiously away.

As the interviews continued I was dismayed to realize that some of the most sympathetic candidates would not be given a chance to serve—anyone who expressed opposition to the death penalty was automatically excused. Others were rejected for different reasons. Several people reported being unable to act impartially in a case involving a crime against children—a feeling I completely comprehended. One man informed the court that he had recently been robbed at gunpoint, and that I bore "a slight resemblance" to his assailant. Reminded that I had been in jail for the previous two years—and thus could not possibly have been the perpetrator—the man still said he did not feel he could be sympathetic to me.

About a third of the potential jurors were African American but almost every time one appeared, he or she was rejected by the prosecuting attorneys. Even someone who otherwise would have been a good fit for their case—for instance, a woman who had herself been a victim of a crime and who had no objection to the death penalty—was still kept off the jury because of her race. Of the prosecutors' twelve challenges, six had been used on African Americans and another on a Latino. Their justifications for rejecting these individuals were hardly convincing. One was dismissed simply because the lawyers didn't like "the way he was acting and looking." My lawyer objected vigorously, even calling for a mistrial due to systematic exclusion of black jurors, but the judge rejected his appeals. At the end of the process, the jury consisted of eight whites, three blacks, and a Latino. But that surface diversity masked a systematic effort by the state's lawyers to bar as many people of color as they could.

———

Opening statements commenced late in the afternoon of the second day. "This case is about the gruesome and brutal murders of two mothers and their three young children," began the state's attorney.

"You will learn from the evidence that you are about to begin hearing today how those five human beings were beat, strangled, suffocated. And after they were dead their bodies lit on fire and burned." He then repeated the fabrications that Burge and Kill had concocted, including the story of the victims' drug debt and the narrative of my murderous visit to their home. For the prosecution, it was critical to introduce Willie Williams as a credible figure. He would serve as their chief witness—and he was the only theoretical connection between me and the crime. The lawyer told the jurors that Willie had been my lifelong friend and a close business associate. Willie, he acknowledged, was "an individual who's been in trouble with the law a couple of times in his life himself." He spoke of Williams's conviction for burglary a few weeks before the crime, and how he'd been sentenced to three years in prison. According to this lawyer, Willie had called me from jail and I had freely confessed to him of going out to murder the women because they owed us money. "We killed those bitches," I supposedly told him, sounding like a hardened gangster. "If I had to do it again, I would do it."

Then it was our turn. Robert Edwards got off to a strong start, pointing out the complete lack of evidence to show that the murdered women had any connection to drugs—or to me. He went on to describe my experience of torture at the hands of the police that had led to my false confession, given for the sole purpose of escaping their clutches. He mentioned the fact that I was at a splash party on the night of the murders and—more important—that I had numerous witnesses to prove it. But even when he was dead-on with the facts, Edwards had an uncertain way of speaking. He fumbled the address of the pool party. He mispronounced names, admitted to being unsure of certain things, and in general demonstrated a lack of preparation. "The mere charge and allegations of counsel means nothing," he concluded, regaining something of his stride. "You must weigh the evidence in this case before you come up to a conclusion in your mind beyond a reasonable doubt. . . . With that, ladies and gentleman, let's get to the trial."

The prosecution's strategy became clear as soon as the state called its first witnesses. One by one, relatives of the murdered women and children took the stand. Playing on heartstrings, the district attorneys would attempt to overwhelm the courtroom with details about the tragedy. As the jurors wept in sympathy with the dead, and their demand for justice swelled, they would be moved by their emotions to hold someone—me—responsible, and to punish me to the full extent of the law. Our challenge, then, was to show sympathy for the victims while demonstrating the flimsiness of the polce evidence linking me to the crime. We had to survive the sob stories, and then convincingly counter the lies without being so aggressive that we alienated the jury. It would require nerve, preparation, and sensitivity to pull it off.

I had not known the women and children who had died, but I wouldn't be human if I didn't feel for them and their families. I had kids of my own and visions of the fate of those babies had kept me up at night for years. Not one day had passed by since my arrest that I hadn't thought about them, or the person who had gone in there and wiped out three innocent kids. But now I was hearing the families' stories in detail. The first witness was Debbie's mother. In heartbreaking detail, she told of having lunch with her daughter, who had seemed "happy and normal" on the day before her death. Then she choked up remembering the moment she'd received the phone call telling her that the family had all died in the fire. "I couldn't believe they were dead," she recalled. "I don't know why. I went into the house and it was burned. And, but, I had to go through . . . it was all burned." Everything in her testimony was painful, perfectly calculated by the prosecution to heighten the grief in the room.

And, oh God, did it work. I could see the jurors nearly in tears themselves as the bereaved mother told her tragic tale. Pedro Sepulveda, husband of one of the murdered women, sat in court every day, paying extremely close attention to the proceedings, watching it all with an inscrutable air of concentration. The presence of these relations and all the testimony served to build sympathy for the victims, to make the jurors want to avenge them. But as effective as it was, nothing linked the women to illegal drugs, or—for that matter—to me. That was the weak spot of the case, and Edwards went for it hard.

"You and your daughter was very close, is that correct?" he asked.

"My children and I are close," the woman replied.

"Did you know was your daughter a trafficker in narcotics?"

"Pardon me, sir?"

"Did your daughter deal in narcotics?"

"Absolutely not."

"Did you ever see strangers coming in and buying narcotics from your daughter?"

"Of course not. No."

Pressing the advantage, Edwards asked if she had known me, seen me around, or ever heard her daughter speak of me. Of course, the answer was no. She testified that the first time she had ever laid eyes on me had been at my bond hearing. Cross-examining the neighbors later that day, Edwards had another breakthrough moment, asking, "Now, would you tell the ladies and gentlemen of the jury . . . whether or not you saw Debbie with black people coming to her home?"

"No," the neighbor replied, "I never seen it." She had no black friends, and though there were some African Americans in the neighborhood, she had never talked to any of them. After hours of emotionally charged testimony, the prosecution had failed to reveal any evidence linking the victims of the fire to drugs, or to me. The only—highly circumstantial—connection was the testimony of a fourteen-year-old kid who claimed to have seen a car like Marvin's parked in front of his house on the day of the fire. It was preposterous to believe that this child would have remembered this one car two years after the event, and Edwards eagerly pursued the witness on this point.

Though things seemed to be going our way, Edwards continually showed a knack for confusion at the worst possible moments. Whenever he'd be gaining momentum, his missteps would trip him up. He got dates wrong, mispronounced words, and repeatedly flip-flopped names. Edwards's mistakes always seemed to occur right when he was on the verge of scoring a major point. For instance, when he was pursuing the witness about the car, his confusion over details grew so convoluted, that the judge himself issued an objection, pleading, "Please let's get the dates straight!" After that, any benefits from Edwards's questioning were largely erased.

When the relatives had finished, the state presented experts from the police and fire departments, as well as the medical examiners office, to describe the crime scene in technical detail. Here, Edwards scored a key point—and this time it went smoothly—during his cross-examination of an autopsy doctor.

"Your examination of the blood in terms of adults," Edwards asked, "it was negative for opiates, correct?"

"That is correct."

"Negative for alcohol?"

"Yes, sir."

"And there was nothing of a controlled substance nature in the blood, right?"

"None, none."

A police officer with the canine unit testified that his dog could detect cocaine ninety-nine out of one hundred times. At the scene of the fire, this animal had reacted to a scent but had not actually turned up any discoverable narcotics. Again, no actual evidence existed to support Burge's story that the women were involved in drugs. Other witnesses described the flimsiest of evidence. One detective testified to discovering empty gasoline and lighter-fluid canisters in Marvin's car; another mentioned seeing boxes of empty envelopes—the kind drug dealers used for selling dope—in the house after the fire. Not only were these findings circumstantial in themselves there was also no way to show that they hadn't been planted by police. All in all, as the days dragged on, we had some reason for confidence. If Edwards had made a few missteps, he had also scored some key successes. The state had done basically nothing to connect me to the crime.

And then it came Willie Williams' turn to testify. First, he spelled his last name for the court reporter, "W-i-l-l-i-a-m-s." Then he said he was twenty-seven years old and listed off the names and ages of his kids. After that, basically every word out of his mouth was a lie.

Though in reality we were just distant acquaintances, Willie told the court that he had seen me every day for the previous twelve years, and that he had acted as my chauffeur, driving me to all my major drug deals. In great detail he recounted a series of meetings between me, Debbie, and Rosemarie. With obvious coaching, he described the women's appearance and then—no surprise—identified them correctly in photos provided by the prosecution. He established a scenario in which I sold the women an ounce of cocaine each month for a year, traveling directly to the crime-scene house on multiple occasions. The level of detail at times was almost comical. He seemed to be able to remember the exact route of every drive we ever took; he described the decorations on the front of the house, even the layout of the furniture. Of course, it was smooth. It had all been rehearsed in advance.

I didn't know Willie very well, but I know people, and I could see him get pleasure from the lies he was telling. You can't build on the truth, it's going to stay what it is, but you can get excitement out of a lie. Each time Willie opened his mouth more bullshit came out. Every location in his story was a public place that had since closed down. There was no way to verify any of it. He never had nothing to back his story up. Every meeting took place in a Mexican neighborhood—never in a black area where people might have known me and could dispute his version of events. I kept telling Edwards, "He's lying, he's lying, he's lying." Willie was shooting me looks, and the jury was eating up every word. It was unbearable. As the performance went on, I began to feel something like an out-of-body experience. It was as if gravity was pulling me out of my chair and forcing me up to the stand in order to confront him. I fought myself with all my power to stay seated. My lawyer literally had to grab my hand to keep me from leaping to my feet and attacking this two-faced witness in front of everybody.

Because Willie's own criminal past could damage his credibility as a witness, the prosecution encouraged him to describe his various legal troubles, including his latest trial and sentencing. Willie told the court about calling me from prison and hearing my confession. According to him, we had spoken on the phone every other day the whole time he was locked up. The lawyers noted that Willie's sentence had since been reduced; just a few weeks after my arrest he had been released from prison and placed on parole. But they did not want the court to conclude that a deal had been struck. "Have you been promised anything or given anything in exchange for you testifying to the truth in this case?" the lawyers asked.

"No," Willie responded, perjuring himself yet again.

Edwards began his cross-examnation—perhaps the most important moment of the trial—with a series of flubs: he confused the names of the victims, misstated the address where they had died, and then even got Willie's name wrong, too. I sat there cringing, while the prosecutors must have been thanking their good fortunes. Edwards spent significant effort trying to pin down Willie's use of collect calls. The details were confusing and mostly irrelevant to the main facts of the case. Edwards pointed out that the records only showed three calls, while Willie claimed to have spoken to me more frequently. But Williams was able to wriggle out of this discrepancy—he had a slippery answer for everything—claiming to have talked to me at other people's homes, saying that the phone numbers had changed several times, and that he had since forgotten them. After that, the prosecution redirected. A few more squabbles ensued over technical issues, and then Willie was off the stand—and off the hook. One more huge opportunity had slipped by.

Day three began with the testimony of detectives from Area 3 Violent Crimes. These were serious men, each with decades of experience on the police force. They had seen everything and conveyed a sense of professionalism and competence in every word they spoke. And none could match Detective Michael Kill for drama. Thin-lipped and pale, he had a sneering face that looked to me to be filled with hate, but he certainly knew how to make an impression. He painted a picture of me as alternately cruel and confused. One moment, the wiry detective said, I was stammering and lost, staring at my shoes in guilt and remorse. Then, in his version of the story, he had showed me pictures of the dead bodies, and I had responded with a heartless "So what?"

He claimed that I was not handcuffed in the interview room when he initially appeared at 1:00 AM, and that the first thing he had done was read me my Miranda rights. At that time, I refused to talk. But then, Kill said, when he had returned to the room four hours later, I'd undergone a dramatic and inexplicable change of heart and decided to confess to everything. Of course no mention was made of the hours of torture I had undergone in the meantime—much of it at his hands. Kill then repeated the concocted tale of my murderous trip to the West Side. A skilled actor, he told a colorful story, complete with sounds, smells, and visual details. I watched with mounting concern as the jury hung on his every word.

Our cross-examination of Kill was crucial. It needed to establish the fact that I had been tortured, that my rights had been violated, and that the entire story connecting me to the crime was a fabrication.

Edwards began by asking if I'd had access to a telephone. "He had the opportunity," Kill responded.

"Mr. Kitchen was handcuffed to a rail, was he not?" Edwards asked.

"No, he was not," Kill lied.

"Now, did Mr. Kitchen at any time ask you during the time that you were with him to have an opportunity to consult with a lawyer?"

"No, he never wanted to speak with an attorney at any time I was there."

"He never asked you?"

"Never."

It was infuriating. Edwards asked about my abuse, legal and physical, and Kill calmly denied everything.

"Didn't you strike Mr. Kitchen with a telephone book on the head and in between his legs during the period of time that you conducted this so called interview?" Edwards asked.

"No, sir."

Kill was obviously a practiced liar. His blatant misrepresentation of my experience in the hell of the Area 3 lockup poured from his mouth smoothly and without an instant's hesitation. The jury swallowed it whole. After Kill finished, the state rested its case. Prosecutors had called a crowd of witnesses representing the victims' families, neighbors, law enforcement officers, and investigators. They had introduced fifty-five separate exhibits as evidence. It was a mass of information, designed to confuse the jurors, play on their sympathies, and mask the deficiencies of their case.

On Friday morning, we launched our defense. For two years I had been gearing up for this. For two years all I had thought about was *How did this shit happen to me? Where did it come from?* I wanted to get down to the whys: *Why did they target me? Why did they lie about me?* Now it was my turn to fight back, head-on. For a whole week I had been worked into a state of nervous exhaustion by the trial. It was a lot of pressure, but at that time in some way and fashion I still believed somewhere deep in me that the truth was going to come out in this courtroom. And now the time had finally come. But it did not get off to a promising start. Despite having all the time in the world to prepare, Edwards had failed to line up anybody to come to court that day. The judge was frankly baffled, asking, "So you are saying you have no witnesses available right now?"

"That is right, Judge," Edwards was forced to reply.

"Is there any possibility, Mr. Edwards, some of your witnesses may be arriving, but perhaps late?"

"Very slim possibility, Judge. Very slim possibility."

The judge suggested that I testify, but we felt that for me to go first without any preparations would have been highly prejudicial to our case. The prosecution sneeringly suggested that we close, ending our case before even having gotten started. In the end, an entire day was wasted. The case adjourned till Monday. We had made a bad first impression.

Our first defense witness was my cousin Eric Wilson. The irony was obvious—he was the very person who had put me in this situation in the first place. But Eric had been in Area 3 with me on the night of my arrest; he had also been beaten by detectives, and we figured that if he testified to that experience, he would—for once—do more good than harm. Eric told about the abuse he suffered at the hands, elbows, and knees of Detective Kill. He described hearing my screams coming through the walls from another room. But the jury seemed disinterested. This was a trend that would continue. They had taken careful notes while all the prosecution's witnesses had spoken, but now that people were telling my side of the story they just stared distractedly into space.

I tried everything to reverse the trend. Throughout the trial I served as a kind of unofficial second chair to Edwards, taking notes and offering suggestions and advice—not that he was capable of making the most of it. Looking back, it's obvious that he was interested in getting paid while making as little effort as possible. He billed my family $100,000 for his services. But when it came down to actually doing the legwork necessary to win the case, he did not bother. On the very first day, the state's attorneys had entered the courtroom accompanied by boxes and boxes of material, no doubt in part to impress the jury. Edwards had strutted in with a single file folder one-inch thick. An old family friend, who had handled some cases for me in the past, he had known me since I was a kid. But it was obvious that he had no business trying a murder case. He was out of his depth. He repeatedly drew the judge's anger; chewing gum, racing off for breaks before a recess had been called, failing to line up witnesses on time. I could have switched attorneys, but he was reporting to my mother and grandmother that things were going well and I didn't want to do anything to upset them. On top of that, the practicality of it was overwhelming. It would be impossible to find someone else at this stage who could do a decent job. The jury would see any change as an admission of, at least, a guilty conscience. No, it was best to stick with Edwards.

I had given him the names of almost a dozen guards at Cook County who had seen me arrive at the jail in my wounded state. They all said they would testify on my behalf. But Edwards had only roused himself to call one of these officers to the courtroom. Raymond Roscoe had been working the Hole in Division Six when I limped in for the first time in August 1988. Perhaps it was because the witness was a uniformed officer, and his testimony would carry weight with the jury, but the prosecution objected to almost everything he said. And every time they objected, the judge sustained. Despite their efforts, Officer Roscoe did manage to testify and he told the truth about my condition: that I was limping and in constant agony. But the opposition also accomplished their task of confusing the issue enough to take away some of the impact of his evidence.

Edwards managed to get a representative of Illinois Bell to discuss the question of the phone calls. We had subpoenaed my home phone records, which revealed that I had received no collect calls from Vandalia on the days when Willie claimed he'd talked to me. This seemed like a strong point, but our victory didn't last. The prosecution was ready and quickly argued that collect calls billed to other numbers would not show up on my bill. Nothing could have been easier than to have subpoenaed the other numbers that Willie had claimed he had billed the calls to. But Edwards did not bother.

Another crucial oversight involved my alibi. I had been at a splash party surrounded by friends the entire night on the evening when the murders had taken place. This should have been a slam dunk for our side. But Edwards had not bothered to visit the scene of the party, to interview the woman who owned the home, nor to take photographs of the pool. Considering the amount of movement of people in the neighborhood this would turn out to be—almost literally—a fatal mistake.

As the realization of my lawyer's incompetence grew, I understood the true weight that would fall on my own testimony. It would mean everything. I needed to be well rested and totally prepared. But, of course, Edwards had not taken the time to work with me even once to ready me for the experience, or to strategize about how to answer questions from the prosecution. Also, I had not been able to sleep the entire time I was going to trial. I could not rest. A million and one things ran nonstop through my mind.

Every morning it was the same routine: Wake up at 4:00 AM to get ready, then take the long walk, handcuffed, to the courthouse. I'd wait in the bullpen for the judge to call me and then be escorted into the courtroom itself. During the midday recess I'd be brought back downstairs to eat a brown bag lunch. Every day my hope faded a little bit. But one thing kept me going: the knowledge that I would get to testify. I still believed that once the people in the court heard me speak, they would realize I was telling the truth.

Being in the courtroom filled me with panic. One time, while standing at the defendant's table, I had to grab hold of the desk to keep myself from falling over. I worried constantly that I would faint. At times I wanted to break down and cry, or to shout out to the jury and the judge, "I didn't do it. They're lying about me. They set me up." But I didn't. The prosecution would have loved it, helping them paint me as an angry black guy who didn't follow the rules. No, I stayed quiet and determined to prevail. I refused to show weakness—not out of any sense of pride, or anything. I was being resilient for my mom and my grandmother, who sat in that courtroom the whole time. I kept a strong face in public, and then I lost it behind closed doors. At night I'd cry my eyes out in my cell.

It was all on me as I finally made my way to the witness stand. I took my oath and sat down. Edwards told me to turn and face the jury to tell them the truth of my story. Almost as one, all the members of the jury turned their heads and looked away. In that single moment I realized the futility of my testimony. The people who would judge me had already made up their mind—and they had not even waited for me to open up my mouth. Still, I did the best I could. In my own words I explained that everything Willie had said was a lie. Accurate with dates, names, and addresses—unlike my attorney—I detailed my alibi, described the beatings I suffered from the detectives, the numerous attempts I had made to contact a lawyer, and set the record straight in a hundred different ways. I talked for hours. The climax of my story was my description of the decision to sign the confession. After hours and hours of Kill's violence, I'd had enough.

"I told him I will do what he wanted me to do."

"Why did you say that?" Edwards asked.

"Because I was tired."

"Tired of what?"

"He was beating me up. I was tired of him hitting on me and stuff."

When I finished, the cross-examination did everything to impeach my version of events. Prosecutors pushed me about the confession, and I kept repeating the truth, that the words in this document were not my own. "Like I said," I explained yet again, "most everything that the statement says, Detective Kill said that is what I told Willie Williams over the phone."

"So, what you're saying, sir, it is Detective Kill's idea?"

"Yes, it is."

And this was the truth, that senior police officials, in collusion with Eric and Willie, had concocted the whole story. I knew how hard it would be for this jury to comprehend—let alone accept—the enormity of that fact. But I did my best to explain the reality to them.

After the defense rested, the prosecution brought back the detectives one after another to once again deny, deny, deny that they had tortured me. This was crucial for their case, as was casting doubt on my alibi.

Officer Dowling, the local beat cop in our neighborhood, took on both challenges. First, he declared that the home at 825 West Fiftieth Place—the address Edwards had given for the splash party—had never had a pool. He produced half a dozen photographs clearly showing that there was no pool, nor any space to install one. This seemed to cast my whole story into doubt, but it was actually due to a simple confusion. It was the wrong address. The splash party had occurred at 815, not 825, West Fiftieth Place. The two addresses were about five houses apart on the street. The party had started at one house and then moved to another, both of which belonged to the same family. It wasn't a dramatic mistake but combined with Edwards's other blunders it seemed to be worse than it was.

After the day's session finished, Edwards went over to the correct address and took a bunch of pictures of his own. Introduced into evidence the next day, these photos showed some weeds, a fence with lights, and the spot where the pool had been. The homeowner had left in the previous year, taking the portable pool—or, as the judge had taken to calling it, "the nonexistent pool"—along with her. As a result of Edwards's lack of initiative a major piece of my defense was called into question.

Along with the pool fiasco came questions about my injuries. Bailiffs set up a VCR and Officer Dowling played news footage of me walking from Area 3 to the paddy wagon. In truth, I didn't even remember this moment. I had been in total shock. The physical agony of my beating still had not kicked in yet, and so I actually was able to walk across the parking lot with the appearance of ease. None of my friends or family would ever mistake the limping gait in the video with my natural stride, but the prosecutors used it to convince the jurors that no one who had suffered as I said I had would be able to walk on their own power. This just showed that the detectives knew what they were doing. All of their torture techniques were designed to leave no trace; any obvious wounds would ruin their plans.

As further proof of my well-being, an EMT from the Cook County Jail hospital came to court to claim I had shown no signs of injuries during his intake exam, and that I had not asked for medical assistance. These lies could have been easily refuted if Edwards had subpoenaed my doctors or records at Cermak hospital. But this never happened. Instead my testimony was all we presented to the jury as evidence of my wounds, my treatment, and the months of painful recovery I went through.

In closing arguments, the prosecution—predictably—spent the bulk of its allotted time rehashing the tragic details of the case, showing pictures of the victims, and playing on the jury's heartstrings. "This is shockingly evil," the counsel said, gesturing to the images. "And this man sitting here, Ronald Kitchen, is an evil person, because he is the one responsible for committing these crimes." The attorneys rushed past the bulk of their supposedly corroborating evidence—Willie's testimony, the gas cans in Marvin's trunk, the "trace" signs of drugs, envelopes in the basement, the neighborhood kid who claimed he recognized our car—before getting back to the appeal of their case: the brutal deaths of the family.

They made the most of the creative touches in the detectives' story. "As you heard," said the lawyer, "this was over a drug debt of $1,225. Life was worth $245 each to Ronald Kitchen. Life sure isn't worth much these days." A detail conjured by Kill from thin air now in the courtroom served as a crucial tool for the prosecution to paint me as a sinister and heartless killer. And, finally, Edwards's careless and incompetent mistakes were magnified into supposed proof of malfeasance, with the prosecutor speaking of "this trumped up alibi party where he can't even get the right house."

When the summations were done, the judge gave his final instructions and I watched the jurors file out of the room. It was 6:30 PM, Wednesday, September 19. The trial had lasted for eight full days. Now, three and a half more hours went by. At 10:00 PM, I was told that a decision had been reached. Everyone filed back into court and the judge admonished the audience not to react when the verdict was read. The foreman stood up. For me there was really no suspense: all five counts of first-degree murder—guilty.

After the guilty verdict, sheriffs led me to a bench in a holding cell connected to the judge's chambers. I had barely started to digest the news before the two prosecuting attorneys sauntered in wearing big smirks on their faces. They were really feeling themselves. *We got you*, they boasted. *Now, we're going to make you testify against Marvin.*

"You can't make me do a goddamned thing," I shouted back. "I just got found guilty and you're seeking death on me. There's nothing more you can do."

They kept talking crazy, going on and on. Every time they said something I made a little coughing noise. I got off the bench—*cough, cough*—and walked closer to the bars. With every little throat-clearing sound I worked a bit more spittle into my mouth. When I had gotten right to the bars, and they were in the midst of their rant, I hocked a giant wad of saliva and green phlegm at them. It landed right on their faces, landing with the sound of a wet tissue smacking against a wall. You should have heard them then.

"You motherfucker! You motherfucker! You're going to pay for that!"

"Fine," I said, cracking up. "If you're man enough, come back here. If you're man enough open the cell doors and we'll settle it now."

"We're gonna press charges! You motherfucker!"

They sputtered and fumed until the judge came back and sent them on their way. I laughed my head off, perhaps needing the release, but it was only a moment's satisfaction. Within a minute, the larger reality of my fate hit me again.

With the verdict rendered, we proceeded to the sentencing hearings. This, too, was more or less a formality. The prosecutors were seeking death and the jurors had already decided I was a monster. Another day of testimony—even the voice of my own mother defending my character—was going to do little to change their minds. After the last witnesses had spoken and the final motions were filed, there was another recess for deliberation—shorter than the previous one—and then we all returned to court. I watched the foreman of the jury stand up and heard him speak the fatal words: "We, the jury, unanimously

find that there are no mitigating factors sufficient to preclude impo-
sition of a death sentence. The Court shall sentence the defendant,
Ronald Kitchen, to death."

Did I gasp for air when I was sentenced to death? I don't remember exactly. Everything went hazy after that. I could hear my mama
as she cried, cried, cried. The officers carried me from the courtroom
down to a cell. My execution date was set for December 7, 1990. I
had six weeks left to live.

5

A KILLING SPREE

A S THE JUDGE ordered my execution, I remember him looking down at me from on high and saying, "May God have mercy on your soul."

"God may have mercy," I thought at that instant, "but you don't."

For a few terrible hours after I received the sentence of death I believed that only a matter of weeks stood between me and my demise. I was an emotional shell, in a feeling of shock. And my mother was in an even worse state. The guards transferred me from my old cell to the lowest tier in Division I of the Cook County Jail. Once again I was in the Hole, which in this part of the institution was classified as F-I, the location for Chicago's most serious high-risk offenders. I had a one-man cell in the oldest part of the building, and it was infested with rats—I mean infested. You had to keep your food in the bed with you; anyone who accidentally left their commissary on the floor would wake in the morning to find their bags torn to shreds by vermin.

There was, however, one positive for me in this arrangement. Visitors to F-I were allowed to come right on to the deck where I was being held. My mother was down to see me on the day after my sentencing. She was in hysterics, and I wasn't much better. Upon seeing us, two men on the tier—Dino Titone and Murray Hooper—came up to their bars and schooled us in the reality of Illinois's execution process. "Don't worry," they said. "He's gonna be all right." I had appeals coming, they explained, years and years of appeals. I had my direct appeal, then a post-conviction petition, and then I'd file for a writ of habeas corpus at the federal level. If the feds denied that motion then that would be it for me. But that was twenty years down the line. It wasn't much comfort. But at that point of desperation, this news was as welcome as anything we could have heard. The cloud of death hanging over us cleared up, just a little bit.

It was not a deep relief, and it didn't last. The fact that I was about to go on death row—just knowing that this was what in store for me—made it impossible to feel any lasting sense of calm. I had too many hours alone to think. Life was flashing before my eyes: everything I had ever done, everything I wished I had done differently. I agonized about life without my family, not seeing my two sons, or my mother and grandmother, who were both suffering from health issues and needed me more than ever. And the same old burning questions were constantly in my mind: *How did I get caught up in this bullshit? Why did they choose me out of all the other black men from the South Side? Who was behind it? Why?*

At that time, I had nothing but my thoughts. I had no trial transcripts, legal books, or court records to pore over. My lawyer, of course, had done nothing to assist me with the appeals process. But I did have Dino and Murray. They weren't jailhouse lawyers, but they were death row inmates—both men were in Cook County lockup at the time for appeals hearings—and they helped me get my mind right for what lay ahead, recommending a rigorous course of study. "If you can't read," they told me, "learn to read. If you can't write, learn to write. If you don't know anything about the law, get to know the law."

I hardly needed their advice. My experience with the police, courts, and jails had already taught me to see the world differently than I had as a young man in the streets. Then, I had paid little attention to politics or civil rights. Martin Luther King Jr., Harold Washington, and the thousands of protesters and activists who had tried to integrate and reform Chicago's schools and neighborhoods—I understood these efforts were important to society, but somehow they had never seemed relevant to me personally. Now I knew differently. My situation made me feel—for the first time—that I was part of the larger narrative of black history. I started reading hungrily. I can't tell you how many books I read, consuming one after another. In particular I remember reading about Martin Luther King, Medgar Evers, and Jesse Jackson. Their stories and my story all became part of a larger truth. In a way, it was like reading the same book over and over again. Before my conviction, I'd held this naive belief that innocent people didn't get charged with things they didn't do. My own life had shown me the folly of this idea, and reading up on history made me realize that I was far from the first black man in America who'd had to learn this the hard way.

On the morning of my transfer just a few weeks later, in November, I was awakened at 4:00 AM, and taken—groggy and stunned—to receiving, where I was shackled and loaded onto a crowded bus. Here I saw another mechanism of the machine, as I joined dozens of guys—mostly black and Latino—who were being sent out from the county jail to serve long-term sentences at one of the state's penitentiaries. Our first stop was Joliet Prison, forty-five minutes southwest down the interstate from Chicago. Some would remain here, while the rest of us would undergo blood testing, psychological evaluations, and then get sorted and shipped out to our final destinations.

At Joliet, we were funneled into a large auditorium. Passengers from other buses were herded into the room, until about three hundred prisoners—all in green D.O.C. uniforms—were sitting around, slouching in the seats, waiting around for someone to call out their names. There was almost a sense of camaraderie. Guys were joking around. We were all in this together. Everyone was excited to get away from the horrors of the county lockup. And then I heard the words, "Ronald Kitchen, step out!"

I walked up to the front of the auditorium, as all the other men had done, but suddenly I found myself surrounded by guards. They led me into a cage at the side of the room. Inside, I was shackled hand and foot to the bars. It was like being an animal in a zoo. As groups of prisoners walked by I heard them saying to each other, "Yo, what he do?" And the answer would come back, "Man, he going to death row." Then the guys would start cracking up, pointing and laughing. "He dead," they snorted. "He ain't never comin' back. That nigger dead."

A few minutes earlier I had just been one of the hundreds of men in the room, all of us tied up in the criminal justice system. But now, suddenly, I found myself separated even from them. I was branded as the worst of the worst by everyone—by society, the system, even guys serving time. Somehow this made my situation feel real and serious in a way that nothing had done so far. I felt a rising panic and heartache. Tears welled up in my eyes. A sympathetic correction officer noticed and tried to calm me down. "Just be cool," he said. "Everything's going to be all right."

But for the moment I could not be consoled. "These fuckers are laughing at me because I'm going to death row," I blurted out. "They don't understand that I didn't do this shit. I don't belong here." Finally, preparing for the next leg of the journey, I was led out of the cage. By then I had realized something about these guys who found my predicament so hilarious: they didn't understand that the situation was about as serious for them as it was for me. This could have happened just as easily to any of them.

––––––––––––––

Cold and already feeling defeated, I trudged in the heavy metal shackles onto the next bus, which would carry me to death row. The transfer was handled with all the protocol of an action film. I was driven in the prison van with a lead car in front and a chase car behind, and we flew down the highway on the hour-long trip to Pontiac. Completely surrounded, yet wholly alone. I looked out the window at a sparse midwestern prairie on a frigid November day. We passed between rows of fences topped with coils of barbed concertina wire.

Inside, the van was motioned through to an intimidating red brick building. The Pontiac Correctional Center was one of Illinois's oldest and most notorious prisons. Almost two thousand people inhabited cell blocks designed for about half that number. The institution was overrun with drugs, weapons, violence, and corruption. The first impression was terrifying, and it just got worse after that. Death row was in the North Cell House. It was freezing out when I arrived on that gray autumn day in 1990. "Oh my God!" I thought, the moment I saw it. "Oh my God."

I was hungry, literally starving, by the time I was finally brought to cell number 419, my first address on death row. It had been hours since I'd had my last bite of food. So for a moment, I was excited to see that someone had left candy bars and other snacks on my bed. Then I got nervous real quick. I recalled seeing a scene in some movie: Guys arrive at the penitentiary and find candy bars or sodas and donuts on their beds. After the newcomer had eaten them, some other inmate comes up and says, "Hey, did you eat the candy bar?" Then he asked for it back. But of course he didn't have any commissary credit yet. Then there was serious trouble.

"So," asked the man in the next cell. "Are you going to eat that?" I could see him in a mirror he had sticking out through the bars. He was a big dude: six-foot-two, three hundred pounds. I'm thinking—*Noooooo! I just went from catching five murders, and now I've barely arrived on death row and I got to tussle with this silverback?* I feared there was about to be another murder. "I'm not hungry," I said, and handed him the untouched food through the bars on the door. He must have seen the look in my eyes, because he said, "Ronnie, it's me, Renaldo. Don't you remember me?"

And then the tension broke. Renaldo Hudson was one of my uncle's friends, just a couple years older than me. I had even gone to visit him a couple years earlier in Cook County Jail. So much had happened since then that I'd forgotten all about it. The memory flooded back as I talked to him; he and Earl had been on the very tier in the jail that I had just left. Never in a million lifetimes could I have imagined then that I would end up in exactly the same position he was in. I wolfed down the candy bar as we chatted.

My reaction to this friendly gesture showed the kind of things you had to worry about. In the county jail I had woken up on guard every morning. On death row I would gradually develop a different mindset. My concerns were not focused so sharply on the little day-to-day worries, but instead I obsessed over *the day*—years down the road—when my time would be up. I knew we'd keep fighting, kicking that day further down the line, but I feared the end of the road would come far too soon. I never knew when my latest appeal would be denied. It was like fighting on double time in an ongoing battle. You go to sleep with it on your mind and wake with it on your mind.

When you were on death row, and began to look into your prospects and seek out possible ways to save yourself, you quickly became an amateur historian of the death penalty. I learned that before the 1990s, Illinois's last execution had occurred in 1962. Death sentences had disappeared nationwide in the late 1960s and early 1970s as the

US Supreme Court weighed numerous challenges to state laws governing capital punishment. As urban decay, rising crime, and economic hardships received greater attention, executing offenders once again became a popular political stance. In the mid-1970s newly crafted legislation in Illinois once more allowed for the death penalty. Although the American Civil Liberties Union and the National Association for the Advancement of Colored People continued to argue the racism and ineffectiveness of state-sanctioned murders, public opinion polls consistently showed that a large majority of Americans favored them as a way to get tough on crime.

As more people started receiving capital sentences, the rundown, old death row at Menard prison had quickly filled beyond capacity, forcing Illinois to house some of its condemned men out of state. Desperate for more space, the corrections department spent tens of thousands of dollars to reconfigure a maximum-security housing unit at Pontiac, walling it off from other parts of the prison and eventually constructing four galleries of cells to serve as a new death row, more than twice as large as its predecessor. It opened in late 1982 and within months the ACLU had already sued the state, claiming that conditions inside constituted cruel and unusual punishment. Nevertheless, a dozen new arrivals or so appeared each year, meaning that long before I arrived the addition itself was already at capacity.

On September 12, 1990, right as my trial was getting started, Illinois executed its first prisoner in twenty-eight years. No one knew it yet, but this marked the beginning of a state-sponsored killing spree that would continue for more than a decade. There were, at that time, 125 men on death row. The new unit was packed. When I arrived, and in all my time there—as far as I can recall—every cell had a body in it. Each individual compartment measured eight feet by thirteen feet, the size of a typical apartment bathroom, with no room on the floor to do sit-ups or push-ups. You could lie on your bed and rest your feet on the far wall.

Although it was less than a decade old when I arrived, death row was already dilapidated and crawling with cockroaches. The white cinderblock walls had become stained a dull yellow. Like at Cook County, the beds, toilets, and sink were all steel. Across the corridor was a blank wall. But unlike the jail, the galleries were designed so that prisoners could never communicate directly. Three sides of each cell were blank concrete, the fourth had bars running floor to ceiling. The result of this design was chaos. Unable to communicate with one another, the residents of death row used mirrors just to glimpse their neighbors, and every conversation had to be carried out at top volume. A dozen different radio and TV stations were always booming simultaneously at top volume. Men would be arguing, talking, playing chess or checkers by calling out moves over the gallery. Then, on rare moments, the discord would disappear and some crucial piece of news would get passed from one end to the other in a matter of seconds. But in any event, our whole life was just hollering and screaming. That was all you heard in the morning time—shouting—and you went to sleep listening to the same music.

Our mirrors were our eyes—to check on our neighbors, to see face-to-face, to make eye contact. But even these were considered by some guards to be contraband. If they saw one out, it was confiscated, a ticket was written up on that person, and the little privilege that we did have was taken away. We also weren't technically allowed to pass anything to one another—that was considered trading and trafficking and could get you a month or two of seg time. These rules weren't always enforced, but sometimes they were—you couldn't get too comfortable.

My typical day began before 7:00 AM when the guards on the day shift stormed onto the gallery rattling the bars with their nightsticks and waking everybody up. Six days a week we did "twenty-two and two" in these tiny spaces—twenty-two hours inside, with only two out for showers and recreation. Showers were at 7:30 or 9:30 in the morning and lasted ten minutes, although some of the more kind-hearted guards might stretch it to fifteen. We were carefully segregated from other prisoners. Fearing, I guess, that the inhabitants of death row might be desperate enough to cause trouble in general population, the guards were adamant that we never mix with the two thousand or so other men also living at Pontiac. That's how they ran it. I went to the yard, or the rec room, or the law library, with the same people. I played basketball or chess, or worked out, always with the same people. Breakfast, lunch, and dinner were brought to us on individual trays. On Sundays, and in our long lockdown hours, we just sat in our cells, reading, writing letters, doing legal work, or watching TV. There was no lights out on death row. The lights in the corridor were always on. The bulb in your cell went out when you turned it out, or when they killed you. At the end of the evening, each night after bed check, a loud factory horn would sound over the community, informing the good people in the town of Pontiac, Illinois, that every inmate had been accounted for.

This daily routine gave rise to a lot of despair and a lot of drama, but I tried my best to focus on steering clear of the nonsense. I did not intentionally set out to keep my distance from the others. A few guys I bonded with; I made some friends for life on death row. But my main thing was survival. I was just trying to survive. Books were a godsend for me. My mom bought books and sent them to me; supporters and death-penalty opponents supplied me with more. Dozens of books passed through my hands; the shelves in my cell were always filled. I'd finish one and send it back, or give it to friends on the row, where we had an active lending library.

One book had more impact on me than any other. It was an old paperback in a guy's cell that caught my eye one day—a collection of writings by great philosophers. "Let me check it out," I asked. Though many of the chapters seemed irrelevant to my life, I discovered one section inside that would shape my outlook for the rest of my time on death row: Plato's "Myth of the Cave." In that story, a group of captives or slaves was trapped inside a cave for their entire lives. Restrained with chains, they could only face one direction—staring at the blank, far wall of the chamber. Unable to turn their heads, without a mirror that might allow them to view left and right, all they knew were the shadows that passed along the wall. Even though they were just seeing reflections of objects and people, to them the reflections were the reality. Eventually, one of the prisoners managed to escape. Once outside, he was finally able to see the world for the first time, but he found that knowledge terrifying. His horror was so strong that he had himself recaptured and returned to the cave, where he could live amid the comfort of his delusions.

That was how I read this myth, and it was as if it had been crafted just for me to describe my plight. For many of the guys inside, death row became their real life and the outside no longer existed. They had nothing left in the world out there. This was it for them. Criminologists call this the revolving door syndrome, referring to offenders who keep committing crimes that land them in jail again. People came out, realized they could no longer function in the free world, and did some crazy shit to go back because being inside was all they could handle. People around me were like that. And for guys on death row, maybe it was a little less painful if you just focused on being inside and forgot about anything outside. But that was not for me. It would never be me. My point of view was that this cell—this cave—with its shadows and myths was not going to be all I knew.

Whatever could make me free, whether mentally, physically, or judicially, that's what I devoted my energy to. Anything that would be a distraction, I avoided at all costs. Other than the pile of books on my shelves, I did nothing to decorate the space I inhabited. I didn't want to get comfortable. Most of my neighbors had family photos and other knickknacks hanging on their walls. Some had brought in carpets and put up colorful decorations. But me—no. To me, putting up pictures was the equivalent of saying, *This is my home.* When you create a house for yourself and personalize it with all your belongings you are making a statement that implies you are going to be there forever. And I was not planning on being in that cell forever. I kept my cell clean. I kept it in order. I kept it white and gray. But I did not try to make it my own.

To free myself mentally I embraced the practice of fasting during Ramadan. With my newfound interest in black history, I viewed this Islamic ritual as a way of getting back to my roots. But—like my refusal to decorate the cell—it was also a way for me to exert control in a powerless situation. By fasting from sunrise to sunset I felt like I was getting a grip, imposing some distance between my mind and my physical surroundings, and increasing my ability to think about my options with clarity. Cleansing the mind, body, and soul, Ramadan was a time of self-reflection and intense devotion to God.

My uncles and my little brother practiced Islam before I went to jail. They were always trying to get me to do it, but I thought I was better than that. It wasn't until I was locked up in Cook County that I started reading the Koran, along with the Bible, and realized it was on a whole different page. A lot of the guys in prison were in the Nation of Islam, and they listened to tapes of Farrakhan's sermons. Not me. I didn't listen to him. I didn't follow Elijah Muhammad. I didn't agree with his preaching or his teaching. See, the Nation of Islam says that white folks are the devil. I didn't agree with that. Shit, it wasn't just white guys who put me here, it was a black dude. Don't tell me that the devil is white; in my eyes, he was many shades. I became Sunni. And Ramadan is the most holy of times. It was an added bonus that the Ramadan trays always featured the best food we would receive all year. For breakfast we had sunnyside-up eggs, turkey bacon, biscuits, and coffee cake. At night, the evening meal had so many dishes in it—lamb, chicken, pies—that the guards would have to bring it in piled up on two separate trays.

Not that anyone should imagine for a second that being on death row was an easy ride. Being in the penitentiary is never easy, and death row was no exception—especially for people who know they don't belong there. Every day I was around murderers. And I'm not talking about heat-of-the-moment crimes of passion or gangster jobs either. In my years there, Illinois had numerous serial killers on death row. The most notorious was John Wayne Gacy, but he was at Menard and I never laid eyes on him. Among my neighbors in Pontiac were people just as sick. They said they were guilty, and they lived like they were guilty. I listened to them talking about butchery, about cutting people's heads off, and I'd think, *What am I doing here?* I knew I was different from them. That knowledge allowed me to keep my mind strong. I laughed and joked with them when it was time to laugh and joke—in the rec room or while we were working out. But otherwise I stayed with my books and spent time with the people who wanted to get out.

Nothing sharpened my resolve for freedom like visits with family and supporters. For my first two years on death row I was able to see Marvin, who had gone through his own messed up trial and received five concurrent life sentences. He was housed in general population at Pontiac—just a few hundred yards from where I was staying but a world away. Somehow the prison authorities were under the impression we were related, and we never corrected them, so he and I got to have "brother visits," which otherwise would have been completely prohibited. For a couple hours on the first or last day of each month, he would come by with a pizza and a case of sodas and give me a hundred dollars in coupons. Although we had not been close before our ordeal, Marvin and I had become brothers in spirit through our experiences of the previous years. Thanks to the Area 3 detectives our lives would be tied together forever.

In the old days on the South Side, my grandmother had hosted lavish family feasts on the weekends. Those times were over, but even on death row we managed to salvage a version of that tradition. My mother made the two-hour drive every Sunday, often bringing my sisters, nieces, and nephews along with her. We were only allowed three or four visitors at a time, so if she told me in advance that a larger group was coming, we'd have some of the party call down other inmates from death row. In the visiting area cafeteria we could sit around without bars, eating hamburgers, chicken, and ice cream and resurrecting some of the fellowship of family life. On crowded weekends we might be limited to a scant few hours, but if no one else needed the table, a visit could last all day. Later on, the regulations were tightened up. We were cuffed and could only talk to our visitor—not to people at neighboring tables. And most of the food went away. It was not home, of course, and never could be, especially because of the people who were absent. My grandmother came down one time, and that was it. She just couldn't handle seeing me in this place. For a few years my mother was able to occasionally sneak my two sons, Ronnie and Randell, in with her. Tiffany—their mom—did not want me to have any contact with them, but she would sometimes leave them with my family on a weekend, and then my mother would bring them to see me. But soon enough Tiffany got wind of these activities and from then on she forbade the boys from seeing anyone on my side of the family.

The telephone was my lifeline. I spoke with my mother as often as I could. My grandmother and I spoke every week, on Wednesdays. Then one Wednesday my cousin picked up the phone, and she was crying. Geraldine was dead. She had passed away in her sleep the previous night. That's how I found out. It was heartbreaking, but I didn't shed a tear. By that time I had compartmentalized the outside world, or at least I had tried my best to do so. Whatever was going on out there, I couldn't let it affect me inside. I couldn't allow myself to be broken. I had to put a wall up to survive.

As time passed in prison I developed a fear of the calendar. I looked forward to moments in the day, and I eagerly anticipated my family's weekly visits, but as far as marking time went, on death row I came to despise milestones and anniversaries. They took me further from life and closer to death. I learned to hate birthdays. I came to dread Christmas time. There was no way I was going to throw myself a party or celebrate any joyous occasion while inside. It was part of my commitment to never get comfortable in this reality. The only way for me to survive was to take my life as a day-by-day thing. Each morning, when the guards rattled the bars, I prayed, *Let me get through this.* And every night as the shouts rocked the galleries and the all-clear sounded, I had the same thought: *Let me get out of here.*

The first two executions in my time at Pontiac occurred within an hour of one another, in the early morning of March 22, 1995. By that time, nearly three hundred people had been executed in the United States since 1976, when the Supreme Court had allowed the resumption of the practice. Capital punishment was becoming so common that people were starting to feel blasé about it. But it didn't feel ordinary to us. The two men killed had been on death row for almost twenty years and had exhausted all of their appeals. One was black and the other white, and many of us wondered whether Illinois had chosen to kill them at the same time to demonstrate some twisted evidence of its racial colorblindness.

I remember like it was yesterday. There had been a somber attitude on death row that whole week. The two intended victims seemed, outwardly at least, to be more or less resigned to their fates. Many of the other inmates planned to turn off their radios and TVs and mark a moment of silence for the two departed men. No one I knew thought that the administering of lethal injection by the state served as some form of justice. It was simply the merciless operation of a deeply flawed system. When the time came for them to depart, they were taken by helicopter to the execution chamber, which was housed at Stateville Correctional Center in Joliet, about an hour away.

These first two deaths served as another reality check for me. I had been at Pontiac for almost four and a half years by that time. Life would never be normal in that setting—and I didn't ever want it to be—but the monotony of the daily routine meant that at moments it was almost possible to forget why you were there. Now I was suddenly reminded of the stakes—of the ending that awaited every single one of us on death row. The feeling was like being in a horror story, where one by one, or two by two, the characters were picked off. We spent every minute with a very small crowd of human beings; then, in an instant, certain members of that group would disappear.

The execution chamber itself was a barebones cinder-block enclosure, about ten feet square, that looked like an operating room in some mental hospital. The same space that had once housed the electric chair was now used for lethal injections. Naked spotlights shone directly on the victim, who lay strapped on his back on a steel gurney. A phone on the wall was reserved for the possible last-minute call of reprieve that might—but almost never did—come from the governor's office. Journalists and other representatives of the public could sit on plastic chairs in the attached theater and watch the proceedings through a giant picture window. In the viewing area the floors sloped so that any vomit could be easily drained away.

On many nights I would lie on my cot and picture the execution that awaited me. My mother was standing outside the prison walls. Hundreds of activists waited with her, wearing yellow armbands, singing protest songs, and holding up their flickering candles against the night. Inside, the guards took off my shackles. I stung from the humiliation of strapping on a diaper. I felt the pressure as the doctors belted me to the gurney. I could imagine every texture and detail:

the cold vinyl of the bed, the thin fabric of the gown. They wheeled me down the corridor. Lying on my back I watched the ceiling lights flicker past my eyes.

Although I had never seen the death house at Stateville penitentiary I had pictured this destination a thousand times. The small room was bare except for the bed. Shiny tiled walls and terrazzo floors, clean white sheets, and the staff of doctors all combined to present the vision of an operating room: sterile, rational, scientific. But there was nothing reasonable about this place. No, it was a theater for spectacle. I lay on the bed and stared up into a row of spotlights. A hungry audience watched me through a two-way mirror. At 12:01 AM—execution time in Illinois—the specialists would mix a potion of toxins. Three drugs would flood down through the tubes into my veins: the first to put me to sleep, the second to quiet my breathing, the third to stop my heart. Each day passed by like a dream in the prison, but this one scene always stayed clear and fixed, more real than our reality.

None of us had ever seen the room in person. Or, to be accurate, no one on death row who saw it ever returned to Pontiac to describe what he had seen. The possibility always existed that you would be the next person to make that trip, and so it loomed large as a dark place in our imaginations. It was not a thought that could be ignored or set aside. For me, it was a danger that had to be held close. Once you blocked it out you would lose your sense of purpose. So, as scary as it was, I imagined the reality of that ending as often as I could stand it. But if I was obsessed with it, my mother was haunted. She would tell people that she had visions, waking and dreaming, of seeing me strapped to the gurney and facing imminent execution.

———————

Change on death row was gradual, but at the same time the guards made sure never to let you get too comfortable. I started out in cell number 419 and was eventually moved to 313 on the lower level. That lasted six or seven years. From there I moved to 204, and then 218, and finally 216. When I first arrived, I'd estimate that more than half of the guards were African American. Not wanting to be around the most heinous criminals—desperate men with nothing to lose—white guards, who tended to have more seniority in the prison system, handed off this assignment to their black colleagues. Yet, even this racial balance still didn't match the stark demographics of the prisoners—blacks outnumbered whites on Illinois's death row by a ratio of about two to one. As the years passed, the outlook and makeup of the guards changed. With us, jailers actually interacted less directly because we spent almost all our time locked down in our cells. Although we had been convicted of capital offenses, our day-to-day lives were less hectic than the gang-dominated atmosphere in general population. Belatedly realizing that death row was something of a haven amid chaos, white officers steadily took over. Before long, there wasn't a single black guard to be found.

Some of the other guys would kid around and crack jokes with the guards. That was a taboo for me. Any time inmates saw another prisoner in a cell talking with the authorities there would always be some suspicion that he was telling something about the rest of us. More than that, though, it was part of my determination not to get comfortable, not to make the row feel like home. If the authorities had something to ask me they could come and get me, and that was that. I was not there to socialize. The guards would come in three shifts: morning, evening, and midnight. We saw the same faces for years. Some of them treated this task as a job. They were getting paid, and all they asked was to go home each night in the same condition they had arrived in. Other guards—white and black—were on some bullshit. These officers seemed to think that their responsibilities included not just maintaining order and providing us with essentials but also contributing to our punishment. For me, that crossed a line.

My punishment was being in the penitentiary—and living with the constant threat of death—and it was not the guards' duty to pile injury and insult on top of that. In fact, as I used to tell them: *If it wasn't for me being in here, you wouldn't even have a job. So, in a sense, you work for me.*

They didn't like that. And one of the white jailers, in particular, seemed to take up a grudge against me. He was part of the first shift of the day, and every morning before 7:00 AM he came up to my cell and rattled the fuck out of my bars with his nightstick. Just mine. He walked past all the other guys and did this only to me.

"What's your problem?" I asked him one morning, jumping up off the cot.

"This is my job," he replied.

"I don't see you do this shit to anyone else," I pointed out.

This continued to happen almost every single morning. It was the kind of thing that could—and did—really mess with your head. And I knew I had to make it stop. I complained to the sergeant. He told me to take it up with the lieutenant. The lieutenant suggested I mention it to the captain. When I finally got his ear, he told me that it was good that I had brought this to attention. "If you have an issue," he said, "take it up with me." But the guard continued on as he had been doing, waking me each day with an earsplitting, headache-making racket. I called for the captain and then waited for hours, watching the hallway with my mirror to see when he arrived, but he never came. That's when I remembered his advice to *take it up* with him. "I got you," I said to myself. "No problem."

Knowing he wouldn't respond to my request, I had the man in the next cell over call the captain down to speak to him. Then I put a pot of water to boil on my little hotplate. I left it there for two hours, waiting. Finally, the captain came down to speak to my neighbor.

"Yo, Captain!" I called as he walked past my cell.

"Yes?" he asked, turning to look at me.

And that's when I hurled the entire pot of scalding hot water through the bars straight at him. As he collapsed, screaming in pain and grabbing at his face, I said, "You told me if I had an issue, I should take it up with you. I guess I did just like you asked me to do."

After that, I went to seg for a little bit. This was an extreme action to take, but it was an extreme situation. Our serious grievances received no attention, and no functional avenues existed for legitimate protest and complaint. When I was done in solitary confinement I came back to my cell. I was pleased to see that the bar-rattling had stopped. In fact, the guard who had started all the trouble in the first place had been transferred off the unit for good.

That guard, he was just one guy. There were plenty of others who seemed to enjoy making life difficult and could always justify withholding privileges as a matter of security. In a letter to a friend in January 2000, I inventoried everything they had taken away from us in the previous year. After the hot water, they took away all the hot cereals, foods, and drinks, like grits, cream of wheat, oatmeal, rice, noodles, coffee, tea, and hot chocolate. Then they came and took all can goods—chili, stews, Campbell's soups—because they said we could use the cans as weapons. Next came soaps, shampoo, underwear, T-shirts, socks, thermals, blue jeans, jackets, bath robes, shoes, bath towels, watches, rings, chains, eyeglasses, tapes, headphones, extension cords, night lamps, cups, books, pens, cleaning supplies, art supplies, crocheting needles and yarn, blankets, and hair trimmers. Then they started fooling around with the temperature in the visitor room as well as on the unit, keeping it real cold. And when someone would say anything they'd move him—or put him in segregation. That's how they did things: they took control with no questions asked. And if you did ask, they had something for you.

Anyone who was on death row or who served hard time and says that they never thought about suicide is a goddamned liar. Every person who has been through something like this has thought about it. Guys I played basketball with, strong as shit, went back to their cells and had heart attacks or killed themselves. The most tragic case was an inmate in his late forties, Frankie Redd. He started showing signs of depression and psychosis but the prison administration ignored the warnings. After one suicide attempt, instead of providing psychological care, the guards put Redd in a cage for three days, butt naked for everyone to see, and then sent him back to his cell without any follow-up treatment. Not surprisingly, he spiraled out of control. I could hear him screaming, "They're coming to get me!" We desperately tried to secure assistance for him, but the lieutenant who finally stopped by blithely said nothing was wrong. A few hours later, Frankie Redd managed to twist his pants and shirt into a noose, tie one end to an air vent, and hanged himself. "There was no suicide note, no warning signs," the prison authorities reported in a heartlessly false statement. I penned an obituary for him in a prison activism newsletter. "Frankie Redd was me," I wrote, "a man here on Death Row. He was a man who needed help, but none came to his aid. I'm so sorry, dear brother Frankie. To them, he was nothing. To me, he was a man and a friend."

No aid came to Frank Bounds, either. He was an incredible guy, a real peacekeeper among the guys. On October 10, 1998, he died alone in a prison hospital room from untreated lung cancer. The Illinois Supreme Court had just thrown out his death sentence, but the neglectful treatment he received inside made that reprieve meaningless. It was hard to see him go from being healthy, energetic, and playful to being so sick, to being nothing. It felt like it happened overnight. One day, he stopped going out. He lost all his teeth. He couldn't hold any food down. Suddenly, his clothes didn't fit him any more. He was like a skeleton with skin.

Every day on death row was like having a gun held to your head. You were not really living, just breathing. And then, one day, you weren't. As men dropped around me, I never knew whether or not I was going to survive. Execution hung over me every second of every day. I suffered panic attacks. I couldn't sleep. My hands shook out of control. I poured with sweat. I couldn't promise myself that I wasn't eventually going to go crazy, or snap, or act on my suicidal thoughts. My thing was: I was going to fight. I wasn't going to give it up easy.

When the time came for one of the guys on death row to finally take that journey, it was a big event. With a brutal repetitiveness—one in 1994, five in 1995, one in 1996, two in 1997, one each in 1998 and 1999—men would be snatched off death row and spirited to the execution chamber. Among this number there were those who were heinously guilty, and others who were certainly innocent. More than one had been convicted—like me—almost solely on the basis of a coerced confession. All told, Illinois executed a dozen people in the years after 1999. Half of these had been housed at Pontiac. They were men I knew and lived with in the closest proximity. On the night of their departure, the guards at Pontiac would relax discipline to let the man walk freely through the galleries, saying one last good-bye to his friends. I could hear approaching footsteps and the forced cheerfulness of the other prisoners. Tinny laughter and hollow jokes, that's the way it sounded to me. We were all condemned men, and this was the routine.

That's why I had nothing to say to those six men who came passing through on their way to the reality of that final scene. These were men I spent every day with. Some of them I genuinely liked. They were my friends. A few of them were certainly innocent of the horrific crimes for which they died. But I had nothing to offer any of them. I could not say those empty, meaningless pleasantries, "Have a safe journey," or "I'll see ya when I see ya." There was none of that. I didn't want them to stop by my cell. As they approached, I'd switch the TV set off, hit the lights, and play like I was the hardest sleeping guy in the world.

6

THE DEATH ROW TEN

SIX MONTHS AFTER I entered death row at Pontiac, a large box, heavy as hell, arrived in my cell. It was filled with the documents from my case: trial and grand jury transcripts, motions, continuances, arrest records—everything. The guard smacked the carton down on the concrete floor. And it stayed right there for days. I wanted nothing to do with those files. To tell the truth, I didn't even dare to touch them. Only the hectoring from Renaldo Hudson, in the neighboring cell, eventually convinced me to crack the seal on the accounts of my conviction. "You have to read it," he said. "Dive in. You need to see what mistakes were made."

As soon as I started examining the records, I found myself transported to the time of the trial. I was reliving it. It was riveting, like a good book. I was back in that courtroom again. The very first thing I did was to flip directly to the testimony given by Willie Williams. There were details in the files that I had never seen before—interviews, telephone records from the phone taps the police had run on my house—and none of it showed any evidence that I had been involved. This explained why prosecutors had never used any of it in court, preferring to mention it while not actually playing tapes for the jury or entering them formally into evidence. The more I read, the more my hatred for Willie returned. My resentment at the judge, my frustrations with my lawyer, my sadness for my mom, it all came flooding back.

My time in jail had instilled in me a love of reading, but it had not transformed me into a natural student. Learning the law did not come easily. Inspecting the transcript was one thing—that was like reading a legal thriller—but when it came to hunting down case numbers, cross-referencing citations, and double-checking the precedents invoked by the attorneys, that was—to me—a kind of torture. But I knew Renaldo was right; diving in was the only way to ever get out.

Other guys brewed coffee and puffed cigarettes to keep focused on their studies. My thing was to put on headphones and tune into a twenty-four-hour jazz radio station. There were times when I would sit at my desk for days on end, not even sleeping for two or three nights in a row. I wouldn't go outside for my rec time. When they ran the showers, I just stayed put, reading and scribbling down notes. I would order ten legal pads at a time and fill them all up. I typed out memos and motions on the electric typewriter I had purchased at the commissary, burning through ribbons so frequently that I had to ask my visitors to supply me with a constant series of replacements. And every second of it was a struggle. To became a legal expert without the benefit of a law degree, or any formal training, with limited access to consult my lawyers, and with only the prison law library and the knowledge of other prisoners to rely on—this was the challenge I set myself. Being in the penitentiary is an experience that has two effects on people: it can turn you into a man or it can take your manhood from you. I went in there with a teenager's mentality, and through hard work I transformed myself into a man who knew and understood the law.

Pontiac prison transformed innocence and guilt into the slipperiest of categories. One common refrain I heard from detectives, jailers, and prosecutors alike was "Everybody in prison says they're innocent." These words belittled our pleas for justice and ignored our claims to redress. But I had a standard response for anyone who spoke like this to me: "No, you people know perfectly well who's innocent and who's guilty." Detectives worked hand in hand with the state's attorneys to frame people for crimes they did not commit. At the end of the day, the only ones who knew the truth were us, God, and the officials who put the prisoners behind bars. The innocent ones—like me—had been driven here by the premeditated conspiracies of agents within the criminal justice system. To my mind, those supposed law-enforcement officers who had colluded to place me in Pontiac with an execution date looming were as guilty of murder as almost any of my neighbors on death row.

Still, relations among inmates were always complicated. Prison culture fostered rules and customs limiting what could and could not be said to one another. "Don't talk to anyone about your case"—that was one of the first things my lawyers told me as I was headed into jail, and everyone else had heard more or less the same from their attorneys. The other guys all wanted to go home just as much as I did, and many would not have hesitated to use information—any information—about me as a means to shorten their sentences. If you said the wrong thing in the wrong crowd, someone might just call the state's attorney and tell them you'd confessed. There was another issue, as well, for me and some of the other guys. We didn't really admit it to anyone—even ourselves—but deep down many of us couldn't help blaming ourselves for signing our confessions. It felt like proof that we weren't tough enough, that we were cowards. That shame and embarrassment kept us from wanting to think about the ordeal, let alone discuss it. Because of these reasons, years passed before I ever talked about my case with anyone around me. And that's exactly what Burge and his coconspirators had counted on.

I worked on my case, instead, with a succession of lawyers. Edwards put in my motion for a direct appeal right after the trial ended, and—fortunately—that was the last of our connection. The court appointed an attorney named John Hanlon to take over. I took full advantage of the opportunity to use the prison law library, and I spent my time drafting motions on my typewriter. When I needed Hanlon to look something over he would come down to the prison to double-check my efforts, but he never went out of his way to assist me. I was the one doing all the research and legwork. It took more than a year to prepare my direct appeal. In this round we did not introduce new evidence but focused on highlighting improper aspects of the trial. It was my first sustained foray into the legal process, but I still was not really acting on my own behalf. For the most part I followed the leads suggested by my lawyer. When we filed the legal documents, I felt satisfied that I had raised a series of issues in my case that no impartial authority could entirely ignore.

Beginning with my strongest and most focused arguments and then proceeding to throw some Hail Marys against the system itself, the brief touched on every aspect of the case. I described the racial profiling used by prosecutors in selecting a jury, detailing each individual juror that the lawyers had excluded and tearing apart the state's supposedly "race-neutral" explanations for barring them. Next, I challenged the quality of the case against me by pointing out the lack of physical evidence linking me to the crime and showing the inconsistencies in Willie Williams's testimony. As a third major point I argued that I had not received the "effective assistance of counsel." Edwards had failed on many counts, but in particular I suggested that by serving as my lawyer he had made it impossible for him to testify on my behalf. He had seen me after my beating at the precinct house and could have described my injuries. His testimony as a witness might have swayed the case. Instead, he chose to take my money and run. For my last—but crucial—argument I stated that Illinois's death-penalty statute itself was unconstitutional and had to be overturned.

In March 1994, Hanlon called to tell me that the Illinois Supreme Court—by a five to two majority—had denied my appeal. This was not a shock. Of course I'd harbored some aspirations of hope, but I was not naive. Back then, the courts were hard. Overturned convictions were extremely rare. I understood at the intellectual level that rejection was more or less guaranteed. I knew I had a fight on my hands, and that the fight had just begun.

I received the official court decision and read it cover to cover, hoping to identify the specific details the court had used to reject my claims. On each point, the majority had discovered some small detail allowing them to skirt an issue or refute an argument. I realized that their opinion was predetermined; all they were doing was finding legal excuses and plugging them in to justify their preexisting attitudes. It was painful to realize that the same lies and errors were still harming my case; despite my arguments, the justices had lacked the vision to see through to the issues. In particular, I had not yet been able to elude the long reach of the detectives' lies. The appeals judges took Kill and Burge at their word. My alibi could not be true, they said, because Kill testified that I had not mentioned it to him. I could not have been tortured by police because the police themselves avowed that I was fine. As long as the Chicago police detectives maintained their credibility as witnesses, my claims would continue to go unheeded. Thinking logically, the importance of this was clear, and frightening: society needed to change before I would be freed. A movement would have to arise dedicated to the transformation of Chicagoans' fundamental trust in their own institutions.

It was difficult to think logically, or to stay positive, while staring death in the face. At the end of the majority decision, I read the following words:

> For the reasons set forth above, we affirm defendant's con-
> victions and death sentence. We direct the clerk of this court
> to enter an order setting Wednesday, May 11, 1994, as the
> date on which the sentence of death, entered by the circuit
> court of Cook County, shall be carried out.

Once again, I faced an execution date; this one less than two months away.

Acting quickly to move ahead with the next stage of my appeal, I made another determination. Looking over all the documentation, I realized that it was adequate but hardly enough to overcome the odds I faced. My lawyer had been helpful, but he had not gone to any special lengths to assist me. I made a pledge to myself at this moment. Moving forward, I was going to take more responsibility for my case. We filed another appeal and had the execution date postponed. From then on I'd redouble my commitment to learning the statutes and legal codes. I was not going to let another lawyer fuck me over. I wanted to know everything that was going on. Whatever decision needed to be made about me, I wanted to be the one to make it. I would be the senior partner in my future.

While I pursued my legal studies inside death row, people on the outside whom I had not yet met were finally starting to discover traces of the police department's deception. These were the revelations that could—with determination and hard work—bring about the revolution in consciousness that would save my life. Although Jon Burge and his cronies had been at it since the 1970s, early suspicions had only begun to reach the public in 1989—while I was languishing in Cook County Jail awaiting trial. That year Andrew Wilson, a torture victim serving a life sentence for murder, sued Burge and the City of

Chicago for damages. If there had been many who had long suspected the existence of police brutality, Wilson's case—argued by lawyers for the People's Law Office—would now make that fact a matter of public record. In the course of legal arguments, the attorneys learned of the existence of other men with similar stories. In ones and twos, at first, the names began to pile up.

This was proof—unimpeachable evidence—that a conspiracy of racial violence was ongoing among the city's detectives. In January 1990, John Conroy, a reporter for the *Chicago Reader,* wrote an article entitled "House of Screams," listing victims' claims and hinting at the existence of a scandal and cover-up. But if activists had hoped that exposure would lead to reforms, including the punishment of guilty officers, they were disappointed. Mounting evidence and connections to the highest reaches of power did little to spur change. In 1993 Burge was fired from the department, but it appeared that the city fathers were prepared to let him serve as scapegoat; no further actions were planned. Burge himself was allowed to keep his full pension. Three years later Conroy wrote a follow-up article, "Town Without Pity," examining the reaction—or lack thereof—to police torture. "The courts know about it, the media know about it, and chances are you know about it. So," he asked, "why aren't we doing anything about it?"

After losing my direct appeal I had sworn never to let another attorney run my defense without my input. Having worked with a series of lawyers, none of whom had ever gone the extra mile for me, I had seen little to soften my skepticism about the profession. Then, sometime in 1995 or 1996, Dick Cunningham walked into the visiting room at Pontiac prison. A hero among my fellow inmates, Cunningham was already defending half a dozen other guys on death row. He was wearing a baggy suit and had white hair, a snowy beard, and jolly red cheeks. He looked like Santa Claus to me. The first thing he told me was that he had just come from talking to my mother. In all these years, no other attorney had ever done anything like that. He was the first to actually show some initiative. That right there gave me a little bit of trust. The more we worked together, the more we started to click. Cunningham had a style of litigating. He looked at the situation with the outlook of a fighter, and he and I both realized that our bout with the justice system was just getting started.

One of the first things he did was to bring down a binder filled with pictures of policemen. We sat together in the visiting room with all these photos spread out around the table. I flipped through the images and pointed out all the people I saw who had put hands on me. I identified Kill and Dowling. Then I saw the pudgy, red-haired officer and pointed to him. Cunningham almost jumped out of his chair. He told me the man's name was Jon Burge. It was 1996, and this was the first time that I had ever heard that name or had ever pointed him out to anyone.

This identification would become a crucial new argument in my post-conviction appeal. Edwards had failed to make the connection between my claims of torture and the already notorious practices of Burge and his henchmen. Back in 1988, during my ordeal in Area 3, there had been a moment when a tall, heavyset commanding officer had charged into the interrogation room, removed the nameplate on his white uniform shirt, and started brutally kicking me in the back, ribs, and groin. At the time, I had no idea who he was. I was able to accurately describe his physical attributes but was badly mistaken about his professional status. In conversations with Edwards—and in my trial testimony—I had always described him as a sergeant. With no experience with military rank insignia, I'd had no way of knowing that I was, in fact, in the presence of a commander.

Between the time I had been arrested and the start of my trial, Burge's name had begun to frequently appear in the newspapers with

allegations of torture and misconduct. All of this had happened without me knowing it, while I was in Cook County Jail. But my attorney
should have been aware of the significance of these reports. Even
though I had not known his identity, Burge's name clearly appeared on
police reports and had been listed among the potential witnesses proposed by the prosecution. It had somehow never occurred to Edwards
that the "sergeant" I had seen that night might have been Burge; had
he just shown me one photo of the notorious police commander I
could have instantly identified him.

As it happened, we had missed another opportunity, too. I remember being brought into the courthouse during my trial and passing a
group of protesters. Through security, one of them managed to press
a flyer into my cuffed hands. There—on the handout—was a picture
of Jon Burge. "That's him!" I told Edwards, "That's the fat sergeant!"
But somehow—even then—my attorney didn't realize how important
this was; in any case, he never did the legwork necessary to make
the connection stick. As a result we didn't use this evidence in the
trial—Burge's name was never mentioned. Not taking these simple
steps had severely prejudiced my defense, and—as I would argue in
my appeal—this blundering amounted to "conduct that fell below
a minimum standard of professional competence in a capital case."

———————

Torture was becoming a topic of conversation in Chicago. Due to the
culture of silence in prison, years passed before I started opening up
to the others on death row about the particulars of my case. I didn't
talk about my business with just anyone, of course, but gradually I
was able to identify the people—like Renaldo and some of the guys
Cunningham represented—who seemed worthy of trust. Beyond cau-
tion, or practicality, there was just a simple psychological fact—the
emotions were too powerful to rein in, I had to talk to someone about

it. Apparently, others felt the same way. Once the conversations started they got real intense, real quickly. We would all start dialoguing in the prison law library, move on to a detailed discussion in the rec room, and follow that up with a heated debate out in the yard.

Some were guilty and said so; some of us unquestionably innocent. But death row was a horrible place for all of us and getting out of there was top on our agenda. For that, we had to dive deep into our cases and find the legal missteps and issues that might find some kind of favor with the courts. In the mid 1990s we structured these informal chats into an organized law class that began meeting twice a week. Through chance and error we eventually settled on a format that worked for us: mock trials. Beginning in 1996, each of us got a chance—one by one—to have our cases reenacted. We were all assigned a part to play, with some guys acting as defense attorneys, others serving as prosecutors, witnesses, jury members, and the judge. The only role that didn't change was the defendant. Every one of us had to relive our own trial trauma, once again, in the guise of the accused.

We took this shit seriously, too. Every one who participated—and often as many as fifteen guys could be involved in a case—completely immersed himself in his part of the drama. We made copies of all the files and took them back to our cells to study and internalize the characters, settings, and arguments of the case. We tried to stick to the script, but it was hard when you were arguing a point—this was your trial now, you took ownership of it. In the end we ended up staying as close to what happened as possible, while adding arguments now and then that we thought might make a difference. When the system was really working, guys would add their own arguments onto what was in the script, so that the performance took on a life of its own. You wanted to win the case and so you had to do what you had to do. In the course of these mock trials, I played a defense attorney once, the prosecutor another time, and even served as bailiff. Everyone got

I was literally born in the projects. My mother had been one of the first to move into the Robert Taylor Homes. For my family—which had just arrived in the North from the Deep South—it seemed like a dream come true. These weren't "the projects" to us—they were "the high-rises." *National Archives*

My grandmother, Geraldine Howard, was a pillar of our South Side community. For her, the neighborhood wasn't streets and houses, it was people and community. *Family photo*

My mother, Louva Grace Bell, did everything for me and my brothers and sisters. She wanted us to be better and to do better. *Family photo*

While African American families were able to buy homes in many areas on the South and West sides, the Chicago enclave of Bridgeport clung stubbornly to segregation. It was also the home of an ambitious young Vietnam vet named Jon Burge. We never went near there if we had the choice. *Photo by Joan Radtke*

Left: On the evening of August 25, 1988, I was taken to the Chicago Police Department's Area 3 Headquarters, where Commander Jon Burge and a group of his detectives tortured me for hours, until finally I agreed to confess—falsely—to committing a tragic murder. I had no choice. *Family photo*

Right: Family visits were rare—and precious—in the years when I was on death row in Pontiac Prison. My mom was my most frequent visitor. When we got a chance to hug, my joy was always lessened by the fact that I was wearing handcuffs. *Family photo*

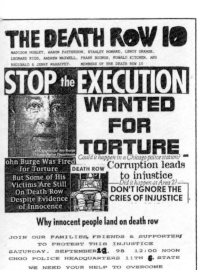

When we founded the Death Row Ten the first thing we did was create a handmade flyer, calling for a demonstration in support of victims of the Chicago Police Department. We mailed these out in the hopes that a small rally would begin to build momentum around our cause. *Death Row Ten*

y mother was out there fighting
or me every single day, every
hich way she could. Louva Grace
ell, she was my soldier. She had
ne spirit of ten thousand angels
nd the roar of a lioness. *Campaign
 End the Death Penalty*

On New Year's Eve 2000, Reverend Jesse Jackson made a surprise visit to Pontiac's death row, along with several of our mothers and supporters. Jackson stands behind my mother. Next to Louva is Stanley Howard's mother, Jeanette Johnson. Beside her is Alice Kim, activist with Campaign to End the Death Penalty. And beside her is Costella Cannon, Frank Bounds's mother. *Campaign to End the Death Penalty*

Illinois governor George Ryan, a Republican who campaigned on a firm pro-death penalty platform, had a change of heart once he became responsible for ordering executions. Years later I would write Ryan a heartfelt letter. *Creative Commons/Flickr user spsarge*

On January 10, 2003, Go nor George Ryan announ the pardons of four mem of the Death Row Ten. I hoped to be among then but my name was not ca The next day, the campa against the death penalty I'd dedicated myself to fo years won a stunning vict Ryan commuted all death sentence to life. *Terence A James/Chicago Tribune/TNS*

After leaving death row, I was transferred into general population at Stateville, a massive institution hidden behind imposing stone and concrete walls. At the center of the grounds stood "F House," the last circular cellblock left in operation in the world. *U.S. Federal Government*

On July 7, 2009, I walked out of the Cook County courthouse a free man. This was my freedom day, my Lazarus day, the day I was reborn. Surrounded by a huge crowd of friends, lawyers, family, and the media, I took a moment to take it all in. The warm summer air. The sunlight. I was breathing, filling my lungs with freedom, sensing the lightness of my soul. I couldn't stop smiling. But I also had a message to tell the press. "For someone to finally see and understand that we have been telling the truth for twenty-one years is great," I told reporters. "But as long as Jon Burge is free the fight has to continue. And that's that." *Abel Uribe/Chicago Tribune/TNS*

After being arrested together and serving twenty-one years in prison together, Marvin Reeves and I walked out together as free men on the same day—just as I always promised myself we would. *Bluhm Legal Clinic Northwestern University*

Celebrating my freedom with Carolyn Frazier and Tom Geraghty. Carolyn had been a third-year law student when we first met. She and Tom had never stopped working on my case. After years of delay, Illinois finally conceded that the state could not "sustain its burden of proof." All charges were dropped, and I was awarded a certificate of innocence. *Bluhm Legal Clinic Northwestern University*

Seeing South Aberdeen Street, and my other old blocks, for the first time after prison gave me one of the biggest shocks of my life. Almost everything was abandoned. I drove around town to find landmarks from my youth, but discovered only empty spaces. *Family photo*

Fired from the Chicago Police Department in 1993, Commander Jon Burge finally was brought to trial in 2010. Although hundreds of us could have testified about being tortured, he was accused of the lesser crime of perjury. In his trial, he appeared to be a frail old man. It was almost impossible—unless you had suffered the grave misfortune of having seen him in action—to imagine this pudgy retiree as the mastermind behind the Midnight Crew. But then the victims began to speak. In the end, Jon Burge—who has been linked to the torture of more than a hundred men and women—would only serve a four and a half sentence in a minimum security prison. *Terrence Antonio James/Chicago Tribune/TNS*

Former Chicago Police Detective Michael Kill continued to deny that he participated in torture as a feared member of Burge's Midnight Crew. "I didn't see anyone get beat, electrocuted, electrified, set on fire, thrown out any windows, all the accusations you're making today," he testified under oath. "None of that happened." But I will never forget the hate in this man's eyes as he pounded on me, hour after hour. *Terrence Antonio James/Chicago Tribune/TNS*

Along with my attorneys—Locke Bowman (left) and Flint Taylor (center)—I called a press conference at Northwestern University Law School campus on July 1, 2010. To a room full of reporters we announced that I would be bringing a sweeping civil lawsuit against Burge and the other detectives, as well as Mayor Daley, Dick Devine, and Cook County. *Alex Garcia/Chicago Tribune/TNS*

was driving the first time I met Tina arr, back in 1988. I slowed down the car d hollered at her, "Hey, wife!" It took most thirty years, but in 2014, she and I ere married. *Family photo*

My daughter, Madison Grace, was born in 2011. Madison is my chance at redemption. *Family photo*

Almost a decade after our release, Marvin and I still speak on the phone every single day. *Family photo*

Since my release I've finally been able to spend quality time with my two sons, Randell and Ronnie Jr., as well as making up for lost time with my father. *Family photo*

I am grateful to make it through every day with Maddy and Tina, even though there are times when having a family feels more difficult than any other type of labor I've ever done. My most fervent hope is for her never to go through anything like what I had to suffer. I hope that for all my kids—for everyone's children. This is what I live for. This is the whole point of telling my story, to let my experiences be a lesson. To let my life be a stepping stone. *Family photo*

a fair trial—which was more than could be said of the Illinois court system—but it was no cakewalk. Lots of guys went through the pain of re-experiencing their days in court only to be found guilty for a second time.

It was with a mixture of excitement and nerves that I greeted the approach of my own case on the docket. Renaldo Hudson would be the judge; Mario Flores was state's attorney. Stanley Howard was chosen to serve as my defense attorney. Talking strategy with him before the opening gavel, I realized that the two of us had actually met more frequently and taken things more seriously than my actual lawyer had done back in the 1980s, when it really would have mattered. The mock trial lasted several weeks, taking up multiple legal classes and dominating our thoughts and conversations in the intervening days. During arguments, things got heated. When Stanley and Mario took a sidebar with the judge I wanted to get out of my chair and join in.

The emotions came close to getting out of control, but this was a good sign. This level of investment said everything about how we felt. Sometimes, when we had acted out previous trials, there had not been any passion; we just went through the motions with no big fights or disputes. At the end of these proceedings, the defendants were inevitably found guilty. In my case, everyone was on edge, ready to go to any length to explain and defend their positions. For me, it was pure stress. I was reliving one of the most painful events of my life. Watching a jailhouse lawyer do a better job than my actual attorney had done, seeing him and the prosecutor objecting to obscure points of law—these experiences were exhilarating and frustrating at the same time. Renaldo did his best to keep order, staying true to his role as judge. Everyone tried to stay in character; we had people reenacting the testimony of the police department witnesses and even had someone playing Willie Williams.

It was a helluva trial, culminating in Stanley's thrilling closing argument, where he went completely off script, hammering away at the failings in the state's case—the telephone calls, Willie's claims about our drug business, my airtight alibi, and all the other inconsistencies. Lines of argument that might not have swayed a jury of strangers with no direct knowledge of life on the streets, served as irrefutable proof here among guys with local knowledge about how the game really worked. For instance, the idea that any Mexicans would ever sell drugs for an African American was a preposterous assertion, as anyone who had ever lived on the South Side with their eyes open could tell you. This was our trial strategy in the venue of Pontiac, to throw logic on top of law. And it worked. When my peers announced the verdict of not guilty, the first thing I said was, "Damn, why couldn't this shit have been for real?"

It should have been us in that courtroom. We used the same materials that had been there at the original trial. The same stuff. But out there I had been burdened with a judge who wanted a conviction more than the truth and a jury dazzled by flashing lights. Out there I had a lawyer who was more interested in a paycheck than in getting his hands dirty. Here on death row we didn't have any of the regalia or show of the legal system, but we at least had the advantage of an honest chance.

By the time my mock trial was over, we had all become experts on one another's cases. Reading through the transcripts we kept discovering similarities coming up over and over again—the same detectives who had tortured me testified in many of the others' trials. The same methods, the same threats, the same abuses—the same people: Jon Burge, Michael Kill, and others.

We realized that about a dozen of us had been tortured into false confessions—all at the hands of this one group of officers. There it was, plain as day. Whatever the reason, whatever the motivation, we were living proof of a racialized police torture scandal that reached all the way up in city politics. It was Stanley Howard's idea to form a group and dub ourselves the Death Row Ten. The actual membership would fluctuate—eleven, twelve, thirteen—but we knew instinctively that the number ten had a special ring to it.*

Together we were stronger than the sum of our parts. Just jelling as a group was a major boost to our morale. With the inspiration upon us, we dove in and got to work. Although we had cracked the case, we knew there was only so much we could do from our cellblock; we had to get news to the outside. The first thing that we did was cut up letters and words from magazines and newspapers to create a handmade flyer, calling for a demonstration in support of victims of the Chicago police. We mailed these out to loved ones in the hopes that they could put together a small rally and generate at least some momentum to begin building a movement around our situation. Stanley Howard had written to an organization called the Campaign to End the Death Penalty, which had been formed as part of the anti-capital-punishment movement in response to the case of Mumia Abu-Jamal. He wanted the group to serve as our spokespeople and allies on the outside. My mother brought our flyer over to the Campaign's offices to see if they might spread the word about our idea for a little demonstration. With the Campaign and our families involved, our small rally ballooned into something far larger than we had ever hoped for. Eighty people showed up for that first protest. And from there it just blew up bigger than any of us had imagined.

———————

Alice Kim was still in graduate school in 1995 when she began to organize with the Campaign. A passionate activist, she felt it was important to put herself in uncomfortable places and spaces. My mother, who was living in an apartment complex on Eighty-Seventh Street at the

*The original members of the Death Row Ten were: Frank Bounds, Madison Hobley, Stanley Howard, Grayland Johnson, Leonard Kidd, Ronald Kitchen, Jerry Mahaffey, Reginald Mahaffey, Andrew Maxwell, Leroy Orange, and Aaron Patterson.

time, met her first, and before long Alice and I were talking on the telephone with regularity. Soon she made her initial trip to Pontiac, accompanied by my mom. I was called down to the visiting room, where we met face to face for the first time. While we talked, my mom sat at the next table, visiting with Stanley. As I recall, Alice arrived with an academic approach. As a young activist she had a vision of what her political work should look like. Wanting to keep our relationship professional and objective, she started our conversation by reciting a list of wouldn'ts and don'ts: She wouldn't send money to inmates, she didn't send pictures, and she wouldn't accept an inmate's personal phone calls. "I don't care about any of that," I responded. "I don't need your money. I don't need your pictures. I don't need you to accept no phone calls. All I want you is for you to do the job you say you are going to do."

That was the first of many visits; Alice and I soon became the best of friends. She sent me books every month—everything from James Baldwin to the Harry Potter series, poems by Langston Hughes, memoirs by Hurricane Carter and Stanley Tookie Williams, and history books about the civil rights and the Black Power movement—and would come down to Pontiac and spend hours playing cards, catching up on news, and strategizing about the campaign. Alice's friends would always ask her if it was depressing to go to death row so much. She explained that her visits, even in such a dire setting—the sterile room, the ever-present guard, and the shackles—were dominated by the warmth and humanity of our conversations. Things could seem so normal that she sometimes had to remind herself that the threat of death hung over everything we did. When it was time to leave she would always ask in her mind, *Why can't they just walk out with me?*

Back in Chicago, Alice, my mother, and the dozens of other organizers working on our behalf found themselves facing hostility and ignorance. In the late 1990s most people still believed strongly in the death penalty. Activists holding signs on the city's streets would have hate spewed at them. The Campaign held rallies in the Loop and outside the governor's office, on frigid winter afternoons and in the midst of torrid heat waves. Sometimes they drew a handful of people; on other days several hundred might show up.

As the organizing gained momentum, we kept fighting from the inside. Everyone in the Death Row Ten brought something special to the table. Stanley had been picked out of a lineup and convicted of murder. He was a smart, natural leader, determined to keep it real, no matter the situation. Stanley always had a clear understanding of the stakes of our battle. Talking about his quest for innocence, he liked to say, "It's gonna be a party, or it's gonna be a funeral. It's just that simple." The man had a sense of humor; he used to always complain that I was being too serious. No one had come to death row under more tragic circumstances than Madison Hobley. Hobley was a star athlete with no criminal record who was tortured into confessing to arson—of a fire that had killed seven people, including his own wife and child. Madison stayed angry with the system that had entrapped him, but he also kept a deep faith in his eventual release. He was skilled at building networks and making connections. Most of all he was strong enough to show the world how much his experience had hurt him. Aaron Patterson had been a known activist in the streets, which is why the police had targeted him in the first place. He truly carried himself as a political prisoner. No one was quicker to protest an injustice committed by a guard or the administration.

I wrote articles and did interviews. Because my case was so obviously flawed, we made sure to point attention to it whenever possible. Just like in the streets, I always had a knack for strategy and for thinking ahead. I took to politics like a natural. But I guess my main strength was my speaking skill. The Campaign to End the Death Penalty hosted Live from Death Row events all over the country, where people in prison were able to speak to a crowd of folks on the outside. It's easy now to forget how complicated these were to organize. Prison phone privileges were always contested, and authorities had a vested interest in keeping us silent. Speaking at these events certainly violated the traditional norms of prison communication and potentially broke all kinds of regulations. We had to make sure that whoever was on call to speak at a Live from Death Row could get the phone at the right time. But we managed to get messages to each other, sometimes by shouting across our cells and other times by entrusting another prisoner to get word to someone else. We would do a three-way call. There had to be someone to accept the charges, and then they would forward the call to the event. The event venue had to have a special speaker system set up, and there was the cost; phone companies put high premiums on collect calls from prison phones. It was always a challenge.

Alice told me about my first Live event about a week or two in advance, leaving me plenty of time to agonize over it. This would be my first time ever talking to a bunch of people at once. And it was a terrifying prospect. While I read up and prepared my speech, Alice, my mom, and some others at the Campaign, had to book a meeting hall, handle publicity, and arrange a host of other details. Finally, the day for my first talk arrived. At the appointed time that I'd requested it, the guard brought the phone to my cell. I dialed the number, my stomach churning with bubble gut. On the other side of the line, Alice picked up the call. She told me that there were five hundred people in the room. In the background I could hear them chanting, "Free Ronald Kitchen! Free Ronald Kitchen!"

Then I heard a special voice. "Hey, Ronnie," said my mother.

"Hey, beautiful," I replied.

I talked for about ten minutes, describing the Death Row Ten, retelling the story of my case, and placing my experience of torture in the larger context of politics in the Bush and Cheney years. It was just like being in person and talking to a friend one on one. Once I got started, I got the hang of it pretty quickly. The trick was to not put too much detail in it when you were talking to a crowd about your case, because you never knew when there might be a state's attorney in the audience. I spoke about torture and focused on the ones who put their hands on me. "I can visualize the whole thing," I said, in a typical speech. "It's something I have to live with every day. Being handcuffed to a wall and being beaten up by people while hollering for help is something that you can always visualize. It's going to be a part of me forever and even today I wake up in a cold sweat, angry."

Later events were held all over the country. The University Church in Chicago's Hyde Park neighborhood was the home base for the Campaign, but we organized Live from Death Row calls in New York, Texas, and dozens of other sites. Crowds ranged from intimate gatherings to fifty, a hundred, or a few hundred people. The best ones were those where my mother was in the audience. It was a treat to talk to her and our love for each other came through in a way that the audience could understand. She would brighten up. There would be momentary joy. And everybody was witness to it. It was real, and also politically powerful. My mother hosted one of these events at her own church, where campaign activists—who were often white college students—could interact and organize with African American community members. The movement was multigenerational, interracial, invigorating—and it was working. The publicity brought faces and names to the Death Row Ten. It brought some humanity back to us, forcing the world to recognize that these are human beings, these are men, who had been tortured by a gestapo police force.

My personal freedom struggle advanced along multiple fronts. While my mother and the Campaign helped to create a mass movement, Richard Cunningham and I pursued my formal legal appeals. Over the course of several years, we found ourselves bouncing between

Springfield and Chicago, supreme court and circuit court, even coming up again before Judge Bentivenga, the man who had put me on death row in the first place. Suffice it to say he was in no hurry to reverse his own earlier rulings. Doing what no previous attorney had ever done for me, Cunningham doggedly pursued leads. At the trial, the police had referred to the phone recordings between me and Willie Williams, but neither the defense team or the jury had ever actually listened to the tapes. Cunningham forced the state to produce them. Some of the calls the prosecutors had discussed didn't even exist, while the recordings that actually had been made had no relevant evidence in them.

Moving beyond the flawed nature of the trial itself, Cunningham and I then attempted to subpoena internal police disciplinary records in an effort to uncover evidence supporting our claims of torture. These documents, had we succeeded in obtaining them, would have been damning—not just of Burge and his cronies, but of Chicago politics at the highest level. Among the people whose names would have been exposed in those files were Dick Devine, the state's attorney at the time who had been a prominent prosecutor in the 1980s— and, even more shocking, Mayor Richard Daley, who had served as state's attorney during the height of Burge's reign of terror. Desperate to keep these archives closed, the appellate court had taken the extraordinary step of suddenly dismissing our entire appeal during a hearing in which we were supposed to be merely arguing over a point of procedure. This was an obvious overstep, and in 2000 the Illinois Supreme Court reversed that decision with a strongly worded censure stating that the lower court's action had amounted to a denial of my constitutional rights.

In any other context, this would have been a narrow victory. Considering the fact that police torture was a proven fact—Burge himself had been fired half a decade earlier—I, and every other member of the Death Row Ten, should have automatically received new hearings long since. Nevertheless, Cunningham was elated by the outcome. The door had opened a crack, and the smallest technicality could eventually lead to a full reexamination of my case. My mother abandoned herself to hope. Even I allowed myself to feel some optimism. "I can see some light shining through now," I told the Campaign. "It's a small win, but it's a win."

One of the worst parts about being inside was our lack of control over events. I found it inspiring and maddening, in turns, to watch a mass movement arise on my behalf and yet remain always beyond my ability to directly influence it. This was literally a matter of life or death to me, and I felt grateful to the activists who were choosing to commit their time and energies to organizing against the death penalty. But at the same time they could never do enough. I found myself constantly urging them to do more, to sacrifice more, because that's what I was doing, and it was what I desperately needed from them. Nevertheless, I understood that they had their own lives and could only do so much. Activists came and went. People moved on from the movement and focused on other things. I had to accept it.

There was just one person who could always be counted on to do everything I would have done, and more—my mother. She was out there fighting for me every single day, every which way she could. It wasn't easy. She used to tell me about how the police intimidated her. At rallies they told her that I was a murderer, that she was fighting for a child-killer. She watched them throw a brick through her car window. In spite of her fear, she felt my fight was one she had to continue. My mother had an unbelievable strength that came from the love she had for her son. Her strength came from me, just as my strength came from her. While I was fighting inside she was going to keep up the fight on the outside. If she was rallying in front of the supreme court, I was in the prison law library researching my appeals. We were each other's strength. Louva Grace Bell, she was my soldier. My mom was a superwoman. She had the spirit of ten thousand angels and the roar of a lioness.

Nothing hurt me more than knowing I couldn't be there to support her. She worked as a home caregiver, doing the backbreaking work of taking care of sick people in their homes. And after caring for her clients, she'd head to meetings, make phone calls, petition on the streets for my case. Before finding the Campaign she had felt so alone in this fight. She was made to feel ashamed that her son was on death row. Being involved in the movement allowed her to "hold her head up high" for the first time in years. She made a new set of friends. In particular, two other Death Row Ten mothers—Costella Cannon, Frank Bounds's mother, and Jeanette Johnson, whose son, Stanley Howard, was one of my closest friends—kept her spirits up. They called themselves the Three Musketeers, and their energy kept things moving.

People knew my mother and many loved her. They respected the work she was doing. Others—men and women who played key roles in my ordeal—dreaded the sight of her and the other mothers. She followed Dick Devine and Richard Daley; whenever they made a public appearance, the Three Musketeers would be in the audience ready to ask pointed questions about my case. They went to Washington, DC, to hold a press conference in support of legislation proposing a national moratorium on the death penalty. I saw her on the TV in my cell. There was my mother on the evening news. Her name was spreading, just like mine was. And that's when I really knew that things were starting to take off. Only in my wildest dreams had I imagined the possibility that our little campaign, beginning with the flyer we pasted together behind bars, would blow up the way it did.

For years, we had worn ourselves out trying to connect with so-called black leaders. I cannot tell you how many times we wrote to Jesse Jackson without ever receiving a response. We were truly surprised, really taken aback, when Minister Louis Farrakhan responded to one of our letters saying that the Nation of Islam didn't consider us true believers because we had become Muslims only after we were in prison. Other prominent African American politicians dismissed us the second they realized we were locked up. No brothers wanted any part of the death penalty issue. After years of trying, we had all but given up hope that politicians would ever take up our cause. And, with all the work that we were doing, it really didn't feel like we even needed them anyway.

As the outside world prepared to welcome the arrival of the year 2001, I felt I had nothing to cheer for. A decade on death row was no cause for celebration. While parties and fireworks blared outside, my cell at Pontiac would be a somber and quiet place. To survive the madness of my situation I had long made it a policy not to observe holidays in the penitentiary. New Year's Eve was no different. All around me, at midnight, all hell would break loose as the other prisoners banged away on the bars and cell walls with anything that would make a racket. I didn't do anything special. It was just another passing day for me. I covered up my ears and tried to get some sleep. As far as I was concerned there would be no seasons of rejoicing until I was celebrating my exoneration and release.

On the evening of December 31, 2000, the guards came to my cell to inform me that I had a surprise visitor. At this hour it couldn't be anything good.

"I ain't going," I informed them, imagining that some state's attorney had come to try to coax information out of me or ask a string of useless questions.

"You're not coming down to see your visitor?"

"Nuh-uh, no way."

Finally, the guard admitted that it was my mother who had come for a New Year's surprise, and that members of the Campaign were here, too. I was transferred along with other Death Row Ten members. When we arrived at the visiting room, the guards did something they had never done before: they took off our cuffs and shackles. I would be welcoming guests unchained for the first time since arriving on death row.

When I entered the room, the first person I saw was Rev. Jesse Jackson. After years of ignoring our correspondence, he must have sensed that our campaign was picking up momentum. In my opinion he was just hopping on a bandwagon—the anti-death-penalty movement was now a celebrity cause, and we were his local connection. He had arranged for this special reception, though, and had even convinced the guards to take off our restraints. He stood in the room, arms outstretched like Jesus Christ, as if I was supposed to hug him. But I went straight to my mother, instead. For the first time in ten years I hugged her tight, without cuffs, with both arms around her body.

7

CLEARING THE ROW

OF ALL MY friendships on death row, none was more unlikely than the one that developed in the late 1990s with a fellow condemned man named Andrew Kokoraleis. A white guy with a shaved head and a goatee, Andrew looked like a racist biker—definitely someone to avoid. And that was even before you learned about his backstory. He had suffered through a rough childhood, and in the early 1980s had joined in more than a dozen satanic-style killings. It was horrific, brutal, disgusting stuff. But by the time I got to know him, nearly twenty years later, he had grown into a mild-mannered man in middle age, deeply repentant for what he'd done as a teenager. I considered him an OK dude who never gave anybody any problems. He and I played ball and worked out together. His cell was directly below mine, so we talked back and forth every day.

Kokoraleis had been on death row since 1987, and by 1999 his appeals had finally run out. For several weeks, his lawyers worked desperately to postpone his execution. A last-second plea had passed from a county judge, to the Illinois Supreme Court, and finally—on the appointed day—the issue was sent all the way up to the US Supreme

Court. Out in the yard that morning, Andrew was in an optimistic mood. He told us his lawyers had just informed him that a stay of execution had been arranged. Then, that afternoon—around two or three o'clock—I heard the guards come knocking on his cell bars and telling him it was time to go. Kokoraleis was flown by helicopter to Tamms, the state's brand-new maximum-security prison. He made a final statement, offering condolences to the families of his victims. Then, at 12:30 AM on the morning of March 15, lethal poison was injected into his arm. For four minutes he shook, whispering verses from the Bible, and then my flawed friend Andrew was gone.

On the TV news the next day we learned that the US Supreme Court had refused to hear the case, throwing the question of postponement back to the newly elected Republican governor of Illinois, George Ryan. Ryan had campaigned on a firm pro-death-penalty platform. But when he was suddenly faced with having to decide Kokoraleis's fate, he realized the difference between abstract issues and holding the power of life or death over a flesh-and-blood human being. Ryan shared his feelings widely. The Kokoraleis case had forced him to examine the growing debate over capital punishment. "It was probably the worst experience I have had in my life," he told the media. "And I spent a lot of time agonizing over it."

Ryan's anxieties stemmed from an exposé of the death penalty that had recently been published in the *Chicago Tribune*. We eagerly read the stories as they appeared. The newspaper's review of roughly three hundred capital cases in Illinois since 1977 revealed an undeniable system-wide failure of the justice system. More than two-thirds of us sent to death row were African American. Thirty-five of the African American defendants were convicted or sentenced to death by all-white juries. And forty-six of us were convicted on the basis of testimony from jailhouse informants. Thirty-three of us had been represented at trial by an attorney who was later disbarred or suspended from practicing law. Fully half of the capital cases in the state had been reversed for a new trial or resentencing. Ryan expressed shock and confusion upon learning these figures and reviewing the cases. "How does that happen?" he asked. "How in God's name does that happen? I'm not a lawyer, so somebody explain it to me."

In the yard the morning after Andrew's death, everyone was discussing the governor's statements. Two other death row inmates—Mario Flores and Nate Fields—remarked that there might be an opportunity in what we had all just witnessed. If Governor Ryan was so unsure of his action in Kokoraleis's case—in which some legal technicalities existed, but where there was no doubt about the man's actual guilt—then perhaps he would consider some type of general executive action on the death penalty itself. We proposed that Governor Ryan issue a moratorium, halting all executions in the state until problems in the system had been fixed. The whole Death Row Ten took up the idea. In law class it was the only thing we talked about for days. Guys discussed the precise wording we should use, and we all hammered out the details together.

To be honest, I was not particularly optimistic about it. The other guys allowed themselves to get excited about the idea, but personally I didn't really think it was going to take flight. I agreed to it and thought it would be a good thing if it actually came off, but I wasn't exactly giddy about the whole project. By then, however, I had learned that this was how political organizing worked. You never turned away an idea. You tried this and you tried that. It was like throwing grass seed on the ground. Some of it gets eaten by birds. Some gets eaten by worms. But some of it's going to grow. The lawyers took our draft moratorium, gussied it up and added legal language, then the activists helped spread the word and build public support for it, but we were the ones who put it together.

About nine months later, these efforts paid off. On the evening of January 31, 2000, death row exploded with excitement. Guys were hollering, "Turn on channel two! Turn on the news!" I could hear televisions buzzing to life, one after another, as everyone switched on their sets and started watching an incredible scene.

George Ryan stood at a podium in front of a dark curtain. Reporters and cameramen crowded around him. He spoke hesitantly and from the heart. "I now favor a moratorium," he began—and, at his words, my own heart started to beat faster—"because I have grave concerns about our state's shameful record of convicting innocent people and putting them on death row." The governor went on to announce that he was enacting an official moratorium—a ten-year hiatus—on executions in the state. From all sides of me came cheers, shouts, outbursts of surprise and amazement. I could only barely hear the rest of the speech as Ryan explained his rationale for the decision. "Until I can be sure that everyone sentenced to death in Illinois is truly guilty," he said, "until I can be sure with moral certainty that no innocent man or woman is facing a lethal injection, no one will meet that fate."

Each waking and dreaming minute of every day and night for the previous decade, the threat of death had lingered over me, sometimes only weeks away. Now, with a few brief words, Governor Ryan had removed it—not forever, but for the moment. Years of activism—phone calls, leaflets, study, writing, strategizing, and protests, demonstrations and travel for those outside—had just yielded our first major victory. Ryan's moratorium was the first of its kind. No other state had ever done such a thing, had looked at its own criminal-justice history and decided that it could not be trusted to decide matters of life and death. That drastic admission, that complete turnaround from the status quo that had existed when I was railroaded onto death row, was a direct result of the work we had orchestrated from inside our cells. We had needed a revolution in consciousness, and now, with Ryan's speech, we were beginning to see what that might look like.

Less than a year after Andrew's execution, the moratorium had become a reality. Like so much of the anti-death-penalty movement itself, the idea had begun right here at Pontiac prison. Because of this success, the threat of execution had withdrawn a bit, but the reality was that I was still sitting in the same place. I had ten years of life, at least, but those were ten years on death row, and that was not a life I could stand to live much longer. Death row was still death row, the same horrible thing. I didn't want to be stuck there for another ten minutes. The moratorium came into effect and some guys celebrated like all our problems were solved. But for me the feeling was more like "back to business," because I was still trapped in a place where I didn't belong. I remained in survival mode. If you take a wild animal out of its environment and put it in another environment, it is still going to be wild, and still going to try to get out of there. The moratorium didn't make me cool off. It made me want to fight harder.

───────────

Jailhouse doors slam shut. Blues music plays evocatively in the background. Barbed wire fences flash by. A series of quick images appear: syringes, leg restraints chained to a gurney, a lethal injection chamber, prisoners in handcuffs. An announcer says, "This is an *NBC News* special Geraldo Rivera Reports." It was early September 2000, six months after Governor Ryan's moratorium announcement, and the Death Row Ten was about to go prime time. We watched from our cells as Geraldo himself appeared on screen. "The death penalty," he began. "The old debate that's back in the news. You may think you've heard it all and know where you stand. But before you turn away, no matter how you feel about capital punishment, think about this: Is a confession to police always good enough to send a man to death row? Is the testimony of a jailhouse snitch good enough to condemn a man to die? Is one eyewitness on a dark night good enough to base an execution on? And should every prisoner have the right to a simple scientific test, one that could prove guilt or innocence? Tonight we focus not on whether capital punishment is right or wrong, but on whether the system works the way it is supposed to."

These were our issues—my issues. Geraldo was hitting all the talking points, conveying to the public the precise message we'd been honing for years. About halfway into the program, he turned his attention to Illinois. Standing on the shores of Lake Michigan, he described Jon Burge and his detectives as "a renegade group of Chicago cops." The very same men who a decade earlier had boasted such unimpeachable credentials were now—at last—finding their own names dragged down to the level where they belonged. In the next shot Geraldo appeared, all in black, standing in front of the old Area 2 police precinct. He described how neighbors used to hear screams coming from behind the walls and how the department was facing allegations of torture. "Ten men on death row had hauntingly similar accounts of how confessions had been forced out of them," Geraldo reported, "claims of brutal police interrogations using everything from lit cigarettes to electric cattle prods." As he spoke, our Death Row Ten pamphlet flashed onto the screen. No moment could have better demonstrated how far we had come: the original publicity document that we had pasted together in the rec room at Pontiac had just been beamed out to an audience of millions.

And then heartbreak. Suddenly, my mother's face was on the screen. She was literally gasping with emotion, speaking indistinctly between sobs. "I hurt," she barely managed to say, "because, it's like, I'm waiting. I don't know when they are going to take my child away from me for something he didn't do." The Geraldo special was just one in a blitz of national prime time exposure for our cases. My mom was taking calls from all the networks. Every time we spoke on the phone she had new appearances in the works. But we didn't prep for any of these shows. We never went over what she had to say, because when you are going on TV to say your son is innocent, you never want to sound rehearsed. It had to be live and unscripted. That was the best way. This was not a play, not a motion picture, this was real. No one who saw my mother on Geraldo could have ever doubted her pain, not for a single second.

Newspapers and magazines from around the world covered the issue. We were handling a string of interviews from death row. Ted Koppel and ABC's *Nightline* dedicated four nights to an investigative report on capital punishment across the country. After years of brushing us off, *The Oprah Winfrey Show* filmed an emotional episode on the death penalty with three wrongfully convicted men as guests, including a man who had served time on Illinois's death row. As media from around the world circled the story, nationwide polls showed that support for the death penalty was declining, and opposition to it was growing. People's minds were actually beginning to change.

For some, engaging in such lofty debates might have been a thrill. But I was having none of that. My thing was: I'm sitting on death row. Politics was the last thing on my mind. I was not about being a TV star or a media darling. I was trying to think about how to come up from under this, in order to not be the next person to walk to his death. The main challenge for me was staying focused. That was my number-one day-to-day concern. I exercised my mind by reading my Koran, my body by playing ball outside. I made sure to talk to the lawyers every day, to Alice Kim and the other activists with the Campaign to End the Death Penalty. I gripped these tasks with an iron hand because it was easy—so easy—to let it all slip away and get lost in the horror and despair of death row. I had to stay mentally strong in the face of a constant onslaught of depression and mortal fear on the one hand, and tiny annoyances on the other. And always there were the daily annoyances and provocations of the guards and administrators. One slip up and my chances to get out could be badly diminished. They knew it, and I knew it. They relentlessly tested me. But I refused to let them throw me off. Momentum was growing and for the first time it was dawning on me that I had a real opportunity of getting out of here. I had to stay focused. My mama was working too hard for me to mess around with her work as well as mine. I just had to keep fighting.

Although the media attention was proving effective, I was also working daily on my case. Dick Cunningham and I were in constant contact as we developed arguments and tracked down precedents for my post-conviction appeal. Our latest motion was based around the discovery of new evidence—things we had discovered that had not been featured in my original trial. We demanded access to Willie Williams's full prison files, and all the relevant phone records, as well as the police department's internal affairs reports on Burge and Kill. Going over the files in my cell I had also got wind of another piece of crucial evidence that had been withheld: reading the materials carefully, I spotted for the first time a mention that the detectives had conducted polygraph tests on Pedro and Arturo Sepulveda—husband and brother to one of the murder victims. According to clues in the records, I realized that these men had failed the tests, making them— by any standard other than that used by Burge and his Midnight Crew—prime suspects in the case. With these demands, Cunningham and I felt confident in our case, even though the judge we'd be facing would be the same man—Vincent Bentivenga—who had railroaded me to death row in the first place.

Cunningham was more than just a lawyer to me. He was an ally and a friend. Like my mother he was someone who would go anywhere and do anything for my cause. He was in the streets protesting and marching; he was building a legal team to help out; he attended almost every single Live from Death Row that I ever participated in. He sent birthday cards and money orders for Christmas. His letters often ended with a militant and encouraging note: "Keep being strong, man," or "Yours in Struggle." No other lawyer before him had ever come close to this level of commitment. I was more than a just a client to him, and he was more than just a lawyer to me; we had a genuine friendship. I loved the fact that he believed in me. He was fighting for a just cause and his work showed that fact. Whenever my mother had one of her recurring visions of seeing me strapped onto a gurney and wheeled toward the death chamber, she would call him up and he would console her. "It's going to be all right, Louva," he'd say. "We're going to get Ronnie out of there." With both of them in my corner, along with the campaign and my comrades in the Death Row Ten, I was starting to feel like I had put together a team that could win.

Word traveled fast on death row, but rarely did a story fly through the tier like it did on March 2, 2001. One guy switched to the news that morning, and suddenly he started hollering, "Turn to channel five! Turn to channel five!" I flipped on the television and watched with horror as the facts were revealed: Dick Cunningham had been murdered, viciously stabbed to death almost twenty times by his own son, who suffered from schizophrenia. A compassionate defense attorney to the last, with his dying breaths Cunningham had asked the doctor to make sure his son received the best legal help possible.

I could not process this news. It was inconceivable to accept that violence could reach out like this and strike down such a committed man and attorney. Cunningham had just turned fifty-six; he had never seemed so vital or had worked so well for the cause. He had six clients on death row; I wasn't the only one affected. In shock, I refused to believe it. Only after I spoke with Alice, my mother, and Dick's widow did I finally begin to accept the reality of what had occurred. Then, my thoughts were for my mother. Cunningham had been the strongest support during her crisis, and her best hope for the future. After his death, she couldn't stop wondering: "Who's going to be there now for me and Ronnie?"

We had no way of knowing it at the time, but just before his death Cunningham had already started to reach out to other attorneys for assistance. Realizing he needed backup, he had invited lawyers at Northwestern University's Center on Wrongful Convictions to join him on his death row cases. Thanks to his foresight my mother and I did not have to waste precious energy seeking out new legal help. I'd be fighting side by side with the faculty at Northwestern, led by Tom Geraghty, and a series of amazingly idealistic and dedicated law students for years to come.

On death row, where almost every day had the same exact rhythm, and even the passing seasons hardly registered, time often felt timeless and change felt close to unimaginable. But every so often I witnessed events that I instantly knew had profound historic significance. One of those moments came for me on a Tuesday morning, in early September 2001. On that day I was in Cook County Jail waiting for an appeals hearing. Sitting in my cell, I could hear an unusual clamor from the hallway. Shouting and chaos were typical, but this was something different. This wasn't the regular din from down the hall. I walked to the door of my cell and saw a group of guards gathered around the TV, watching a most incredible scene: an airplane flew through a skyscraper, which then collapsed into dust.

"That's some action movie you all are watching," I said.

"It's not a movie," a guard replied. "This is happening in New York City." We watched live coverage of the 9/11 attacks. At one point a white guard said, "I gotta move to a black neighborhood. Terrorists don't attack black neighborhoods." That was a statement I could not let stand as fact.

"Oh yes they do," I replied. "Terrorism occurs every day in black communities—domestic terrorism perpetrated by the police."

The global ties linking the War on Terror abroad with the sustained assault on black bodies at home—ideas that would occur to scholars and historians about a decade later—could hardly have been more apparent to me from my position on death row at the start of the new millennium. "Jon Burge was our al-Qaeda," I used to say. "He was our bin Laden in our neighborhood." I wasn't surprised to watch as President George W. Bush guided the country with a blind moral certainty toward military involvement in the Middle East. This was the same man, after all, who—in his six years as governor of Texas—had presided over 152 executions, more than any other governor in history.

I pondered these connections in my cell: DC and Chicago, Burge and Bush. Cynical conspiracies of racism were everywhere. "A man no one elected sits in the White House," I wrote a few months after 9/11. "The media can turn and look the other way if they want and the pundits can keep trying to sell their lies by repeating them so often that they start seeming true, but we millions of Americans are not going to fall for the deception." The Middle East conflict was another layer. Foreign terrorism was just a distraction from the war at home; we couldn't be suckered by the sideshow. "The fight must continue," I concluded. "We cannot, we must not slack off in our effort to abolish the death penalty and get justice for the Death Row Ten. We may have won a battle or two—however, the war goes on."

As I studied to make sense of my life it was clear to me that these wars were all related. From the day-to-day grind on death row, to the politics of mass incarceration in America, to the global war on terror. Racism and white supremacy, control of resources by a small elite, violence and fear as tools of the trade—these existed at every level. And I had no choice but to keep the struggle going.

I had to even confess that I, too, had been personally involved in terrorizing my community. It was right around that time, in 2001, that I saw something that made me seriously reconsider many of my own choices as a young man. Passing through Cook County Jail for a court appearance, I found myself in the bullpen area of the receiving department. This was a massive holding cell, with dozens of people crammed against concrete walls or chain fencing and one toilet for all to share. Nearly one hundred thousand people passed through this bleak space every year. The walls were covered in graffiti. I had been here before, of course, but during this visit I noticed something different. I was surrounded by young people suffering from extreme symptoms of addiction and withdrawal. They were sixteen, seventeen, eighteen years old—young guys and girls—and they were shitting on themselves, pissing, puking. They were balled up in pain. I had never seen anything like it before. This was the crack epidemic. It was sickening. Back in the 1980s, I had never sold drugs to people this young, but I had sold cocaine to their moms, daddies, aunties, and grandmamas. Looking at the impact these drugs were having I had to admit to myself that at one time I had been a part of this. The long trail of pain and suffering that had driven deep into black communities had, to a small degree, passed through me myself.

Governor Ryan had faced a rocky time in office. His actions on the death penalty had earned him many friends, as well as international acclaim. He had received telephone calls of encouragement from President Nelson Mandela and had even been nominated for the Nobel Peace Prize. But these same choices had simultaneously alienated much of his traditional Republican base. Further, his administration had been marred by a series of scandals that eventually convinced him it would be fruitless to pursue reelection. When I saw him announce that he would not run again for office, I counted it as yet another in a series of disappointments. But I soon realized that this, at least, might have a positive outcome. Unburdened by the need to campaign for votes, Ryan as a lame duck would be more or less free to follow his moral instincts. In fact, as I pored over the text of his speech in the newspaper I started to think that his words were hinting at precisely this outcome. "The governorship should not become mired in the political divisions of a campaign year," Ryan had said. "And that's why over the next seventeen months I will . . . devote every ounce of my abilities to the challenges that Illinois faces and the duties of higher office that you've hired me to do."

It was clear the governor was trying to find a way to take action on the death penalty. But he struggled to find the best method. A series of commissions and investigations followed one after the other during the final year and a half of his time in office. The stakes were high on each of these initiatives. But none was more important than Governor Ryan's decision in October 2002 to order individual clemency reviews for almost every pending capital sentence in the state.

In all, the Illinois Prisoner Review Board would examine more than 140 cases in a frantic ten-day marathon session. It would be a spectacle as well as a legal proceeding that would attract media—and protesters—from around the world. After years of retrials, newspaper exposés, and television specials, it was common knowledge that the state's capital punishment apparatus was a mess. There were issues with almost every case. But for Ryan, a small percentage deserved special attention. "The governor is aware that there are a few cases out there where lawyers are actively pursuing appeals to prove actual innocence," a spokesman said. "That is a thing that deeply concerns him." Since 1977, twelve prisoners had been executed. Thirteen had been exonerated. This dire statistic spoke volumes. As the executive in charge, he was determined not to order the death of any other potentially innocent man.

The solution Governor Ryan seemed to prefer was to grant a blanket clemency to everyone on death row, freeing some—we hoped— and commuting the sentences of the rest from death to life without parole. This would have been an unprecedented decision, and he did not take it lightly. Though he wielded enormous powers, and his time in office was running out, he still had to confront certain realities of politics. Prosecutors, police organizations, and the relatives of victims inundated the statehouse with letters protesting any drastic action. Many of the most powerful people in the state remained determined to resist to the last. Chicago mayor Richard M. Daley, in particular, and state's attorney Dick Devine—both of whom had been all too close to the original policing scandals—were far more interested in stalling the tide of further disclosures than they were in seeing any real justice done. For me and my team, however, it was time to shine light on the situation. "A number of cases the board will hear rest upon unreliable evidence," Tom Geraghty, my new lawyer from Northwestern, told reporters. And my own experience of torture would be Exhibit A in that endeavor. A poll released as the hearings were set to begin showed that Illinois voters were about evenly split on the proposal to offer clemency for all death row prisoners. We wanted to push opinion even further in our favor.

The proceedings occurred in Chicago and Springfield. My case came up on the first day. I was not permitted to attend, but Geraghty was there on my behalf, and I heard vivid reports of the scene from my mom. It was standing-room only in the chamber that day, as TV cameras, law students, and audience members crowded in. Geraghty focused on Willie Williams. He made the case that this informant could have used newspaper articles to easily discover all the supposedly secret details he told the detectives he had learned personally from me. Using dramatic techniques, Geraghty set up a series of large blow-ups of the headlines and news stories about the murders and displayed them on two easels in the hearing room.

My hearing went well. We were starting to feel optimistic about my chances of clemency. But my case had been featured on the first day, and the mood in the proceedings began to change drastically. Interested excitement quickly gave way to horror, as prosecutors and police, released from courtroom restrictions, indulged in a kind of grisly sensationalism—including graphic reenactments of the crimes—while victims' family members wept and wailed. These performances made Geraghty's large-format newspaper articles seem downright tame. The prosecutors dramatically overshadowed the subtler points of law on which defense attorneys had to rely. For those of us who were truly innocent, the melodrama of the hearing was a public-relations disaster. Media outlets focused solely on the pathos: 142 CLEMENCY HEARINGS IN ILLINOIS ALSO REVIVE 142 CASES OF HORROR, screamed a headline in the *New York Times*, while the *Tribune* ran one that read, TEARS SEND A MESSAGE.

No one—neither the governor's office, nor the lawyers, nor the Campaign to End the Death Penalty—had anticipated just how damaging these emotional scenes would be to the cause. "I would have to admit that we probably underestimated it," said one of the Northwestern attorneys. "It's pretty much overpowering." Polls at the start of the hearings had shown a close divide among the electorate, but the victims' stories—and the sympathetic coverage they received in the press—had rapidly swung opinion against our cause: suddenly almost 60 percent of voters opposed a clemency. More damaging to our prospects was the apparent attitude of the board members. It was just like my original trial all over again. They swallowed whole the arguments of the prosecutors and were visibly swayed by the family members' grief. Meanwhile, they appeared unconvinced and skeptical of everything our lawyers had to offer. "They've shown their minds are made up," one of my Northwestern attorneys said, "and they're not going to give defense presentations any credence whatsoever."

It would be several months before the board would issue its recommendations. But the immediate result was clear: Ryan's risky attempt to generate sympathy for reform had backfired. Lawyers agreed that the chief executive possessed the legal authority to grant clemency to all 160 or so people on death row in Illinois. But he now stated repeatedly that such an action would probably not occur. Ryan spent his final months in deep reflection. He met with the families of murder victims and with people who had relatives on death row. He heard every opinion and listened to everyone. It was his decision to make. All we could do was wait.

The clock ticked down toward Ryan's departure from office. January 13, 2003, would be his last day as governor. In the final week or so developments came quickly. As we had feared, the board had not been persuaded by defense arguments. Counseling against blanket clemencies, the members instead recommended pardons for fewer than ten cases. Then we began hearing that the number was reduced to five. My lawyers called me up to give me some confidential news: a source had leaked the names to them, and I was going to be the fifth on the list.

On January 10, Ryan was scheduled to hold a press conference. TV news broadcasters were listing potential amnesty recipients. My photograph kept popping up on the screen. The mood on death row was giddy and almost exuberant. All televisions were on and blaring as the governor stepped up to the microphone. One by one he announced the names of men who would be receiving pardons: Madison Hobley, Stanley Howard, Leroy Orange, Aaron Patterson. And then he stopped. I waited to be called, staring blankly at the television and then exploding in a blind anger. Shouts of joy erupted all around me. Still, Ryan didn't say my name. He wasn't going to say it. In my cell I felt torn between despair and rage. I tore apart my possessions and then cried wildly into my arms. Aaron and the others talked me down, saying, "Be cool, be cool. Your time is coming, too." For my mother, in her new home in Augusta, Georgia, the moment was even worse. It took my family three hours just to begin to calm her down after she heard the news.

All of the freed men were members of the Death Row Ten. I could feel elation for them, even while mourning my own fate. That same afternoon, three of them walked free out of Pontiac Correctional Center. Stanley Howard was off death row but stuck serving out the rest of a sentence for another crime. When I talked to my lawyers, I learned the shocking truth behind my disappointment. Convinced that Ryan would not be granting pardons, Geraghty had not even bothered to submit one on my behalf. If he had done so I would have been a free man that very day. At the time, it seemed like a heartbreaking oversight, an unforgivable mistake.

The next day—January 11—Ryan scheduled a second press conference, this one to be held at Northwestern University Law School itself, the center of anti-death-penalty legal activism. A packed auditorium buzzed with anticipation. Newspaper journalists and TV crews crammed the aisles. Cable news reporters roved the crowd interviewing people. Ryan looked determined and a little somber as he approached the podium. "Today," he began, "about two and a half days before my term ends as governor, I stand before you to explain my frustrations and deep concerns about both the administration and the penalty of death." The room was intensely silent. "The legislature couldn't reform it, lawmakers won't repeal it, and I won't stand for it—I must act." Hundreds of people in the audience sat—literally—at the edge of their seats, straining to hear every syllable. Then Ryan spoke the words they had all come to hear. "I am commuting the sentence of all death row inmates—167 of them . . ." Before he could even finished his sentence, the auditorium exploded in cheers. Lawyers, students, activists, and many formerly incarcerated people—including Aaron Patterson, less than twenty-four hours removed from death row—stood, weeping and hugging their neighbors. A sustained standing ovation poured down on the governor.

Amazingly, this otherwise bland and unremarkable Midwestern politician—an all-too-human bureaucrat soon to be incarcerated himself for his own corrupt dealings—had just completed a truly heroic and moral action. The audience grappled with shock, and he seemed as surprised as anyone else in the room. Acknowledging that there would be many critics of his decision to grant a blanket clemency, he insisted that he possessed the power by law to take action. "Even if the exercise of my power becomes my burden, I'll bear it," he concluded, in a summation that inspired yet another energetic ovation. The entire speech had lasted only a little more than three minutes.

On death row pandemonium ruled. It was like a party. Men were clapping and cheering, smiling, and crying tears of joy. There were guys who were out of appeals, who were on their last legs, and for whom the fast-expiring moratorium was the only thing standing between life and the death warrant. Clemency meant permanent relief for them. And they celebrated it in style. As for me, for the second time in two days I faced a painful case of mixed emotions. The specter of death had been lifted, not just from above me but from over many others for whom I'd developed real brotherly feelings. A political campaign that I had been working on for years had just achieved its most stunning victory. Alice Kim and the other activists were celebrating. And rightly so, they had earned the chance to cheer. "We won!" Alice wrote in the campaign newspaper. "Four pardons for members of the Death Row 10 and a blanket commutation of all those on Illinois's death row. . . . And we can proudly say that activism made a critical difference in winning this important victory."

No one had more reason or right to rejoice than me. All of this was a direct result of that original "Justice for the Death Row Ten" flyer that I had helped to paste and staple together back in the 1990s. I was not going free, but I would be taking a step away from the brink of execution. And yet I didn't cheer or scream in joy. No. Me, I lay on my bed flat on my back, the television turned off, a pillow covering my face. I didn't feel like I had anything to celebrate.

Like it or not, however, change was coming. It took a while before the prison administrators could recover from their surprise and begin to reassign us. But within a week or so, the first inmates began to be shifted off the tiers of Pontiac's death row. The moves occurred in batches of ten to twenty at a time, over the course of several days.

We were divided up between Stateville and Menard. Suddenly, after years and years of stasis, every single one of us was facing a new and frankly unsettling reality—life in general population. Anxieties were so high that extra therapists and counselors were assigned to watch us for cases of dramatic mood swings or depression.

The most stress-filled period of my life was coming to a surreal ending. Every day a few more of my neighbors were transferred out. I had come to death row as a young man in my early twenties. A few days after Ryan announced the commutations, I marked my thirty-seventh birthday. The best years of my life had been stolen from me by the justice system. In my heart I had always believed I would have been free before this time. My younger son turned seventeen, got a driver's license, and came to see me—fulfilling a promise he had made years earlier. Because of the governor's ruling we no longer had to wear shackles in the visiting room, but here I was, still inside, and there was no end in sight to my long ordeal. I could hug my son, but I couldn't be there for him as he grew into manhood.

From the time when I had arrived on death row I had transformed myself into a stronger character. I had learned to trust people, including some of my other fellow inmates, but also the activists from the campaign as well as Cunningham and the lawyers from Northwestern. The experience hadn't necessarily transformed me. People ask me if I had somehow become a better person on death row. It would be more truthful to say it reinforced my priorities in life. For more than a decade it had taken my entire supply of willpower just to stay true to myself. That's what I had wanted to do, and I accomplished it. But nothing could undo the bitterness I felt just from knowing I was in a place like that for something I didn't do.

The other men kept disappearing until the tier was nearly emptied. I was in the last group of prisoners to be transferred out. Leaving death row was a momentous occasion, but to be honest I don't remember none of it. I can't even tell you what I was thinking or how I felt. My mind was still stuck on the missed chance of release. I simply could not get past the fact that a pardon had been sitting there for the asking, and we had missed the opportunity to grab it. This was a time when I truly lost my composure, when I lost myself. I was supposed to have been number five—the fifth man out of the cage—and it hadn't happened. My mind was all over the place and it took a long time to recover. They moved me out of death row; the gate slammed shut for good behind me. Those things happened, but I don't remember them at all.

8

GENERAL POPULATION

————

OF THE MANY, many, priceless pieces of advice that my mother gave me over the years, few had been as key to my survival as her suggestion that I start a journal to record my thoughts while in prison. She had shared this idea with me right at the very beginning of my long nightmare—all the way back in 1992—and I had heeded her call. During all the following years, I had steadily added to this record of my sufferings and triumphs. It was a diary of my feelings and experiences, a serious document. No doodles or pictures, just words, written furiously and with passion. Some thoughts came so fast that I could hardly make sense of them the next day. Other sections offered observations on my philosophy of life. I put my emotions down, how I felt, what was going through my mind. If I had a talk with my cellie, or heard something memorable out in the yard, I wrote it down. If I had a revelation about religion or society, I wrote it down. If I was feeling desperate to see my family and loved ones, I wrote it down. That's what it was, my emotions and actions on these pages.

It wasn't a book, it was just me putting my thoughts on paper. Notebook paper, legal pads, typing paper. It didn't make a difference.

Whatever I had, I grabbed it. When I filled one up, I grabbed another. After fifteen years or so, this document had grown to something like two thousand pages. I had made sure to never personalize my space in prison; I didn't want any part of me pinned to those walls. But this journal was my one exception. Filling three manila envelopes fit to bursting, it was my most prized possession. I guarded it. When I got sent to seg, I made sure they brought it to me. When I was moved from cell to cell, or from institution to institution, it was always the first item I checked to be certain it was safe.

Without this journal I never could have kept myself together during my ordeal.

————————

When the guards transferred me from my cell on death row in Pontiac, they came, put me in shackles, and loaded me on to an old-ass bus. Its seats were worn and tattered and the windows were blackened, so it was impossible to see any scenery outside. Choking fumes filled the air as we started off. I was still in a haze. It was surreal, like a movie script. Just a week earlier I had been on death row awaiting inevitable execution, and now I was suddenly taking a bone-rattling ride to serve a sentence of natural life. Inasmuch as I could concentrate at all, I was trying to think about what the next chapter of my ordeal would be like.

It took a little more than an hour driving north on I-55 to get from Pontiac to my new address—Stateville Correctional Center. Still in chains I climbed awkwardly down off the bus, craning my neck to get a view of the infamous prison. I had visited incarcerated family members here as a teenager, but that had been decades earlier. I had seen TV shows and films shot on location on the prison grounds, but otherwise I'd never seen the facility firsthand. Even before I could get a good look, though, I started hearing dudes hollering my name out.

It was loud. A lot of guys were yelling to me: "Ronnie! Yo Ronnie! Ronnie Kitchen!"

The guard turned to me in surprise and said, "I thought you said you was on death row for the past thirteen years, Kitchen. How do all these people know you?"

"Shit!" I responded, looking around. "You got my whole damn neighborhood in here locked up."

It was a head trip to hear my name called out like that in a new place where I had never been. A lot of people still knew my name and remembered me from Englewood, Back of the Yards, and the other Chicago neighborhoods where I had lived as a young man. But more than that it was a sign of the era. I had been locked away in isolation from the early 1990s until the early 2000s. In that time, a whole generation of black men had been taken from their lives, their families, their jobs, and locked up for long, trumped-up sentences.

I had lost touch with the people from my old neighborhood. But I kept informed about events from my cell by reading the *Chicago Defender*, the city's famed black newspaper, which had always been around in my grandmother's house as a kid. Activists in Chicago looked at the thirty-five years that had passed since the death of Martin Luther King Jr., and they saw few clear signs of progress. In fact, if King had lived to see the city in the early 2000s, he would have been heartbroken to find the same inequality and segregation that he had struggled against in the 1960s. Fighting against the racist criminal justice system would have been King's top priority. By the first years of the new millennium, the United States had the highest incarceration rate in the history of the world, and the imprisoned population was overwhelmingly black and brown. Illinois offered a local version of the larger story. Across the state, twenty-seven massive facilities housed almost fifty thousand inmates: two-thirds of these were African Americans, mostly from Chicago.

Even these statistics told only part of the story. There was plenty of crime and violence in Chicago, but these numbers didn't result from some crime wave. Instead they came from harsher penalties for violent acts as well as longer terms for nonviolent drug offenses, mandatory sentences for relatively minor infractions, and the increased jailing of parole violators. Imprisoned black males had been snatched from their families, a situation I knew personally and all too well, making it difficult for those left behind on the streets to maintain economic stability. In our work with the Campaign we had come to memorize these facts. The number of black men in prison and the number of African American households on welfare were nearly identical. Thousands more black men in Illinois were in state prisons than in state colleges. Parolees and others who made it out of their cells returned home to neighborhoods with few opportunities for advancement; about half found themselves back inside within a few years of their release.

These larger trends had begun in the late 1980s, coinciding almost exactly with my arrest and torture. They had peaked during the 1990s and early 2000s, when I had been locked away on death row. And now, as I stepped out of the bus at Stateville, I was seeing its effects for the first time. For everyone else this had happened gradually over the years. They had watched the process play out in one incident after another, as sons, brothers, fathers, and—increasingly—mothers and daughters, were taken away. But it hit me all at once in the very first instant when I emerged from my forced isolation. Here was my entire neighborhood. Good guys from Fifty-First Street that I never thought I'd see behind bars, people who had bright futures ahead of them. All those opportunities had been lost. It was not just my neighborhood either. Every black neighborhood, every poverty-stricken neighborhood, had the same issue, the same thing. Sure, people have choices, but let's be clear, not everyone has the same choices. Chicago politicians made some choices too: they chose to completely abandon—sometimes actively destroy—the city's poor neighborhoods only to turn around and point the finger at the people living in them.

Scholars, journalists, and activists coined a phrase to describe this phenomenon. By the early 2000s it was beginning to be on people's lips a lot: "mass incarceration." We who were inside the penitentiary had a different word for it. We called it "warehousing." We saw people being housed like cattle and sheep and pigs, to no good purpose or clear end. It certainly wasn't solving the problem of crime, gangs, and violence on the street. Every block in every prison was stacked up; every one-man cell had two people in it, and every two-man cell housed four or five. The useless and reckless caging of men and women like animals—that was warehousing.

My introduction to Stateville was proceeding through the usual steps that were used to turn an individual into a faceless member of the prison community. I went through receiving and personal property— where I gratefully retrieved the box containing my precious journals and books—and then we hit a snag. The sudden clemency and transfer of all the men on death row had caught prison officials flatfooted. Even with a week or so to adjust they still had not figured out exactly where my new housing assignment would be. It was a Friday. With the weekend coming up there were going to be further delays. So I'd be spending the next few days in F House.

Stateville is an enormous complex, featuring multiple buildings and structures all hidden behind imposing stone and concrete walls. More than eighty years old at that time, it was falling to pieces and about half of the buildings in the complex had been abandoned. At the center of the grounds stood the iconic—infamous, rather—F House, the last circular cellblock left in operation in the world. The dream of some mad philosopher, it had been an innovation in its day, but the experiment had failed. From the outside it looked kind of like an old-fashioned theater. Inside, five levels of cells clung to the outer walls while the inner space was entirely open to view. A raised guard post towered in the center of the chamber, like the spindle that sticks up through the middle of a record on a turntable.

This design—in theory—meant that a single guard could have a complete, unobstructed, 360-degree view of all the cells. Not only would this allow a smaller staff to manage the facility, but the inmates would be aware that their actions were being monitored at all times. It was supposed to enforce a kind of self-discipline among the prisoners: feeling the watchful eyes of our captors on us, we would inevitably see the light and reform our behavior. This was the theory, remember. In practice, it was a disaster. The designers had forgotten some crucial details—namely, that even though the guard could watch the prisoners, the prisoners could also watch the guard, and surveillance worked both ways. Also, there were a lot more of us, and no one was gonna just sit in the cage quietly for years. No. The roundhouse served as an echo chamber. It was a huge building, teeming with people, in which there were no secrets. The noise was as deafening as a college basketball arena in crunch time. As I was led in, I entered this big old circle, and every person in the cells all around me was talking, screaming, banging, laughing, crying, fighting, whatever—you constantly heard all of this.

With my head still spinning after the hurried exit from death row, I probably would not have been able to organize my thoughts even in the most serene place. But in this maddening setting, it was impossible to concentrate. All of my energy was directed toward getting oriented in this new institution, coping with the pain of still being incarcerated, and keeping an eye out for the next threat. I had a bunch of stuff going through my head. I couldn't pinpoint on one thing, or focus on one emotion or feeling I had during this moment of transition—I was all over the map.

One concern topped all others. As thoughts spun around my brain, this was the fear and the wish that kept emerging with the most clarity: hoping against hope that I wasn't stuck with some crazy cellie. The cells in Stateville were similar to those on death row. On death row, however, I'd been alone. That made the meager square-footage a paradise compared to what I now faced. With a cellie, a five-by-eight cell became a box, a trap. And a difficult roommate could turn claustrophobia into a living nightmare. I'd heard horror stories of cellies thieving and bickering, fighting and killing each other. I wasn't afraid of having to fight—my fear was that I'd be forced to do something that would end up landing me right back on death row.

On Monday morning, I was escorted out of F House to a different building and into cell 929. I was ready for anything, except for what actually happened. My new roommate looked at me and then welcomed me inside. He reached for a box and offered me food from his supply. "Whatever you want, Cellie," he said, kindly, "take it."

"I won't have commissary privileges for a week," I told him. "Are you sure?"

"I don't care, man," he replied. "If you hungry, take it. Don't worry about getting me back."

That was what good cellies could do. They made your life easier with an attitude of "If I don't have, he got—if he don't got, I have." Finding myself lucky in this regard, I looked around the room for the first time. I glanced at my bunk and saw that my things had arrived safely—including my journal. And then I steeled myself for the new life ahead.

There would be challenges in general population—that was for sure—but it meant life instead of death. I was amazed to hear about some of the others from death row who actually lobbied to get sent back. These people would have traded the chance to live for the small daily comforts afforded them—ironically enough—by the restrictions people lived with on death row. I never could understand that attitude. Their reasons were beyond any comprehension to me. If you were on death row and your appeals failed, or the moratorium expired, then you'd be dead. As long as you have life you can fight. A dead man can't fight. Nevertheless, it was an adjustment for everyone. The administration was leery of us. For the longest time, they didn't allow us to hold jobs. I was sent to a counselor each month who wanted to talk to me and see my state of mind. He asked if I was depressed, or if my cellie was acting right. They treated us very differently. They saw us as dangerous, a threat to stability. In the mind of the warden, we had gotten off death row not due to any merit in our cases—or because we might have been innocent—but only through what he saw as Governor Ryan's misguided executive action.

I felt different, and it showed. Strangers inside were always surprised to hear what I had been through. I clearly remember one of these conversations from around the time I arrived in Stateville.

"Man, you from off death row?" one guy asked.

"Yeah."

"Damn," he said. "You don't look like the rest of them. You don't look like you was there."

"What you mean?" I asked.

"The rest of the death row guys look like they went through hell back there," he told me. "You don't look like that."

I'd heard the same thing in Cook County Jail when I would pass through for hearings. "You don't carry yourself like you see the other guys who come off death row," several inmates told me. "They have some type of aura about them. They act different or look different. You don't look like you from off death row." I can't really say exactly what set me apart, or why it was apparent to so many different people. Maybe I looked the way I looked because I stayed focused on what I had to stay focused on. I prayed. I read every type of book I could get in my hands. Reading those books took me away; while I was on death row, I went to every place in the world through books. I never made death row my home or my reality, and I worked hard to keep my mind free. As a result, maybe, the experience didn't scar me as deeply as it did some of the others.

———————

The typical day started early in Stateville. Around five or six in the morning I'd hear the noisy rattling of the breakfast trays being slammed into the cell bars. I'd stay wrapped in my blanket a while longer—the food wasn't anything to hop out of bed for. There were scrambled eggs, and then a variety of things depending on the day of the week: oatmeal on Monday, gravy and biscuit on Tuesday or Wednesday, coffeecake on Thursday, boiled eggs on Friday, grits on Sunday, pancakes and waffles. That may sound all right, but nobody could make those prison breakfasts look good. I choked mine down, and even enjoyed some of the offerings at first as a novelty, but it could never be confused for home cooking.

After getting out of bed I'd wash out my mouth, brush my teeth, and use the toilet. We got to shower three times a week—on Monday, Wednesday, and Friday. If we had a visitor then we could also shower on the weekends. Much of the morning was spent tidying up the cell. Of the various places I lived in, none—except, possibly, Cook County Jail—could compete with Stateville for grime. It was the pits of all of them, beyond nasty. Roaches scuttled across the walls, rats scurried around the floors and pipes, birds perched on the bars—it was just a filthy institution. A huge amount of time and energy just went into keeping my cell livable. That was my private space and it had to be pristine. I didn't have any special tools to keep things tidy, except for a broom and some washing powder that I picked up from commissary. Every day I went through the same ritual, cleaning the toilet stool and emptying the water. Filling plastic bags with warm water and soap, I would get on my hands and knees and wipe down the floor with towels. When I finished that I washed the bars. Twice a week, at least, I wiped down the walls, too, until the whole cell glistened and my eyes were stinging from the soap fumes.

And then, almost like clockwork, as soon as I had completed my chores, a bird would flutter down to land on the bars and take a shit. All this work, of course, only improved conditions in my own private space. The moment I stepped out of the cell I was back in a disgusting environment. You couldn't control that; all you could control was your own cell and mine stayed clean. But still it was just a cell. Other guys had their spaces all laid out. They had become penitentiary-bound— this was their home now. But not me. It was not a residence for me. My attitude, like it had been on death row, was "I'm a visitor here. I'm not going to be here forever."

Around midday it would be time to head to chow. The mess hall had to feed an entire cell house. It was in a circular building, another old roundhouse, with dozens of round metal tables, each surrounded by four or five stools, and all bolted to the floor. Hundreds of guys would be in there at once, waiting in line with their trays, calling to each other in the tunnels, getting into fistfights. It was loud all the time. Everybody was trying to talk at once and the concrete and steel amplified all of the conversations. The food for lunch and dinner was no better than the stuff that came at breakfast. Everything was a mystery. There was no telling what went into the hamburger, and it was best not to guess. The Polish sausage, bratwurst, and hot dogs all looked exactly the same. The only thing that wasn't a mystery was the chicken, and even that was questionable. The fried chicken was on steroids. You'd get a thigh that was as big as your hand. That wasn't any kind of normal chicken. Soon, I stopped eating the prison-prepared food. I'd go to chow to socialize, and if someone asked I might load up a tray to give to them, but other than some special events, like Thanksgiving or Christmas, I really couldn't stomach the stuff they served. Instead, I relied mostly on what I could make out of provisions from commissary.

After chow, it was time to go to the yard.

Stateville was vast and overwhelming. But as an inmate you did not experience it the way a tourist would. You never had the luxury to take an afternoon and go see the sights. That was not your privilege. Instead you had a set way to go everywhere. You walked this way to chow hall, this way to go to church, this way to the showers. Movement was limited to just "there and back, there and back." One place where you could get a sense of the prison's outlines, however, was in the main yard. You were in the middle of everything in the yard, and you could see the movements of everyone from the other cell houses as they were transported to and from the commissary, personal property, seg, chow, everywhere. The yard held half a dozen basketball courts and a full-size running track, as well as showers and various workout equipment. We had ninety minutes of yard time. I went out and got my workout in with the weights, and then played some ball. And that was it. It was time to go in.

I was out in the yard the first time I caught sight of Marvin in Stateville. He was on the other side of the fence, heading toward the law library. I hollered at him and we embraced through the chain links. We didn't have long to talk, but there was a crucial message I needed to convey to him. I had been thinking about what had happened to me, about how Geraghty had neglected to apply to Governor Ryan for a pardon. That had seemed like a horrible mistake at the time; the regret and second thoughts I felt in the moment had almost broken my resolve to keep fighting. But now that I'd had time to consider everything, I realized that it could have been a blessing in disguise. If I had actually been released, Marvin would likely have been lost forever. A pardon for me would have made it far more difficult for him to fight his case. Our situation certainly remained about as bleak as possible, but at least we were still in the same boat. This is exactly what I told him that afternoon on the yard. "Marvin," I said, "we came into this place together, and we'll walk out together, too."

After time on the yard, there was nothing to do but play cards, or chess and checkers, and watch TV in our cells. We all had our own reading lamps clipped onto our beds. The prison didn't have a lights-out policy, no big factory whistles signaled the all clear after bed check. In the evenings, we'd just read for a bit and then one by one everyone would switch off his light, grateful to have made it safely through another godforsaken day in Stateville.

————————————

But that routine was only for normal times. When the penitentiary was on lockdown, as happened about once a week, then everything was different. We'd be stuck in our cells for twenty-two hours each day, with only the briefest interludes to go to chow or the yard. At these moments, everyone was on edge. The guards barked orders with an added growl in their voices, while the inmates moved more slowly and dragged their feet. Lockdown or not, Stateville was an extraordinarily tense place. Authorities demanded a stricter discipline there than in any other prison I'd ever seen. Many of the regulations were designed to keep large groups of men from gathering in the same area at any one time. Inmate movement was choreographed to a T. To keep down the threat of riots, or organized gang actions, prisoners were only allowed to move around the facility in small groups. Everywhere you looked you saw clusters of ten or fifteen guys in prison-issued tan or blue jumpsuits—or regulation sweatpants and white T-shirts—moving around in chains. Larger groups still congregated at chow or playing ball in the yard, but our movements were controlled to the utmost. If there were thirty cells—housing sixty people—on a single deck, then the guards would usually move the front half first and then the back half. There were never more than fifty guys transported together.

This was not just the usual paranoia of correction officers. It had only been a few years, after all, since the institution had been completely out of control.

During the 1990s, following a crackdown on crime on the outside, gangs had become all-powerful inside Illinois's prison system. Latin Kings, Disciples, Vice Lords, and others each controlled their own cell blocks, and they made huge profits by selling drugs to other prisoners. Throughout the decade, gang leaders reigned through fear. They were given preferential treatment, housed in honor dorms, and granted the right to freely circulate the yards, mess halls, and housing units. Guards who resisted their orders were beaten, attacked, and even assassinated. And administrators understood that a gang leader with influence could pick up the phone to call an associate and cause trouble all around the system.

We had heard wild stories about this situation from our isolation on death row. By the time I arrived, the guards had managed to retake control of the prisons. This process was still ongoing, though, and Stateville operated on strict alert. To cut back on theft and black market dealings, we were all limited to three plastic bins, which had to fit underneath our cots. One bin was for our legal documents, another for our personal property, and the third was for letters, magazines, and books. All of our shoes, pants, jackets, underwear, every last thing, had to fit inside these property boxes.

Even with these extra measures, everyone's nerves stayed ragged, with the authorities not yet certain they had put the wide-open days of the 1990s completely in the past. The guards were still scared, without a doubt. It was a sore subject. That's why we were constantly on lockdown and made to perform such elaborate ballets of movement. But you know what? They were right to be scared. Stateville was terrifying. I was scared. Anybody who was there who says they weren't is either a damned fool or a liar. At any moment something crazy could happen: fights in the chow hall, riots in the yard. The next knucklehead a guard let out of his cell could turn out to be the guy who had decided that this was the day to tear up his fan, make a shiv, and use it to stab the shit out of someone. And don't get me started on what the guards might do. It was a dangerous place.

The stink, noise, and rage were endless; days and nights in Stateville blended and melted together. But one moment I can never forget. I was watching the TV news on the evening of October 7, 2003. Suddenly, I realized the reporter was standing on the 5100 block of South Carpenter Street—my old hood. There had been a double homicide. My brother, Charles Edwards Sr., thirty-two, and his son, my nephew, Charles Edwards Jr., sixteen, had been murdered. Both men had been shot in the head in their home during an armed robbery. These were the last people on Earth who deserved such a fate. My little brother Charlie had been in a wheelchair since the 1980s. He was one of the kindest, and most generous, people on the block. "If anything happened, he'd be the first to help you," a neighbor said after the tragedy. "Before you'd go to a psychiatrist, you'd go to see him." His son was a sophomore in high school.

A month after the shootings, Chicago police announced they had found suspects in the crime. My feelings could not have been more conflicted. Of course, I felt rage and grief. And part of me wanted the perpetrators to be punished. But my own experience with the authorities made it impossible for me to see these issues in clear black-and-white. In any event, I knew I had to talk to my mother as soon as possible. After all her other sufferings, she had just lost her baby son and her grandson. I could only imagine the kind of pain she was feeling. At no other moment during my incarceration had I wanted so badly to rush to her side. But instead of racing out to help her—I couldn't—I had to ask her for a difficult favor. The next time I spoke to her, I insisted that she make me a promise: she had to be strong enough, even in her grief, to stick to our message about capital punishment. Prosecutors were talking about a plan to seek the death penalty for the men who had murdered our family members. But I knew it would be a political disaster if my mother suddenly came out in support of this plan. "You can't go in there and say the system didn't work for me, but it'll work for them," I told her. "If you are against the death penalty, then you are against it. You can't have your cake and eat it too."

She had the resolve to agree to these conditions. But this last heartache proved to be one too many. The next time I saw my mother after my brother's death, she looked like a different woman, a shadow of herself. She didn't mention anything, but I could tell she was sick. She tried to keep that away from me, but I saw it in her face. She couldn't hide that. As we were talking her mind kept wandering off. After the visit, I pulled my sister aside and said, "Don't let her come back." I could see in my mother's face that the pain of seeing me in prison was too much for her to bear.

This was the central tragedy of my situation in the penitentiary. There was nothing I had ever desired more in my life than to take care of my mother and my family. But as long as I remained inside I was powerless to protect the people I loved the most. Now my brother and nephew were dead. My mother was sick. All I wanted was to nurse her and provide for her. But the best I could do was just to tell her to stay away from me—because I realized how painful it was for her to come.

The guards might have reinstated some kind of order in Stateville, but they had hardly stamped out the factions. When I arrived, the heads of most of Chicago's major gang organizations remained incarcerated there. They came from all over the city: North, South, East, and West.

I got to know them on the inside, and they came to know me, too. Some were old friends and acquaintances from the street, guys I had grown up with in the 1970s and '80s. Others knew me, or my family, by reputation. Of course, I wasn't in there with my family. I was in there by myself. And that meant there was no one else to stand up for me—or defend me—from trouble. I had to handle that business on my own.

Being in general population meant the constant threat of violence. I wasn't afraid to fight, but I was afraid of being written up for an infraction, which would then damage my chance at release. Still, I had to do what was required. Guards tested you. Other guys would always try to test you. They liked to wrestle and play fight with each other. I didn't mess with that. I never would agree to wrestle with dudes. Prison was no place to play with grown men. That's how guys got punked or extorted. I was not going to let anyone size me up, or ask me what size my shoe was. I knew how that routine played out: the next thing I'd hear would be "let me get them." No, if you want my shoes, come and take them. I'm not going to let anyone size me up. If I don't wrestle or play with you, then you have to guess at what I'm about just by looking at me. I wasn't going to give you any more information than that. It's like the old saying, "You can't judge a book by its cover." That's what I was about.

On the whole, the guards were more dangerous than the inmates. Not only were they always looking for trouble, but they also had the power to punish you and thus lengthen your stay inside. Because Stateville was such a dangerous place for them to be, they had an extra chip on their shoulders. Old timers, who had once been afraid to go to work, now took the chance to push everyone around. Newcomers would swagger about just to prove how tough they were. Guards held grudges from the old days and wanted to take it out on us. They would put knives on you. They'd get in your face and say something crazy; if you responded they'd pull you out of your cell and beat the shit out of you. This was their way of getting back some self-respect.

I was never attacked by a guard. I made it known from the start that if anyone—inmate or guard—put their hands on me then I would put mine back on them. If you were thinking of putting your hands on me than you'd better put me in handcuffs, because I'd fight. Maybe it was also the fact that I'd been on death row that they took my promise seriously. There were all different kinds of guards. Some were OK. They would come by and say, "Kitchen, you have a legal call," or "Kitchen, you got a visit." And sometimes they would tell war stories about the way the prison used to be. Others were assholes; with them it was always, "Inmate, this," and "Inmate, that." These guys would want you to look at the floor when they spoke to you. I wasn't going to do that, though. I didn't have that slave mentality. I remember one time a guard looked at me, and I looked right back at him.

"Are you reckless eyeballing me?" he shouted.

"Evidently," I said. "But if you notice that then you gotta be doing the same thing to me."

That put an end to that. In general, when they saw that I was not going to let nobody walk over me, or take advantage of me, then they seemed to respect me for it. Or at least they left me alone. The flip side of this was that I had no interest in socializing with them. Some guards would stop by the cell and start opening up to me about their personal lives or their troubles at home.

"I don't give a fuck," I'd tell them. "That's your problem."

In general, I'd speak when I was spoken to. Otherwise, I made it known that I had no interest in socializing.

My priority was survival, and the less I involved myself with the guards the better off I'd be. But sometimes I just couldn't help myself. There was one corrections officer named Williams, and he walked around Stateville like he was the toughest fuck in the world. One day, he overheard another guard chatting to me about the old times. He just busted right into our conversation to brag about his exploits. He told us about a day in the 1990s when he had been on duty. He had scanned the yard and noticed a whole group of guys huddled up together. This was worrisome. Then he realized that the cluster of prisoners came from all the different gangs in the penitentiary: Vice Lords, Stones, Disciples. This was unusual and troubling. Then the huddle broke up and all of the men started running straight for him. This made Williams shit himself.

"Let me out! Let me out!" he screamed to the guards at the gate. "They're trying to kill me!"

"Wow," I said, before I could stop myself. "You was a real bitch back then, and now you're a tough dude." I got six months of "C grade" for that remark. That meant no phone, no gym, and no commissary. Like I said, the past remained a touchy subject for the guards. That was a situation I could laugh about—it wasn't a major loss for me, I was used to restrictions. But you had to be careful, because the guards didn't play. A few months after my exchange with Williams I got a taste of the serious side of prison retaliation.

By then, my original cellie in 929 had been transferred out and a new inmate had moved in with me. I had gone to chow and told this guy to watch my things and make sure no one messed with any of it. Sure enough, when I got back from the mess hall I found everything torn up. Apparently the guards had found some knives next door. Using that as an excuse, they had come in and ransacked my space.

"What you found in 928 has nothing to do with 929," I told them.

But the guards said they had discovered scuff marks on the floor of my cell, evidence—they claimed—of a potential hiding place, or even an escape attempt.

"Every cell in this place has scuff marks," I said. "I didn't do that shit."

But the guards were determined to pin something on me. Eventually they charged me with hiding hooch in a juice bottle—a ridiculous accusation, considering I hadn't tasted a sip of alcohol since I was a teenager. Once again, logic and truth had no place in the state's institutions of law and justice. They slapped me with a year in seg.

Segregated housing in Stateville was like living on permanent lockdown; almost every day was spent in isolation. Even the daily trips to the yard provided only further frustrations. In the seg yard the guards would lock you up alone in a dog kennel and leave you out there—winter or summer—for five hours at a stretch. All I had was my journal to keep me sane.

While still in solitary confinement, I was transferred back to Pontiac—and then after a few months, the department sent me downstate to Menard. Five and a half hours from Chicago, this was southern Illinois, deeply Republican and racist, real Klan country. Driving into the facility for the first time in the late summer of 2004, I remember feeling something like terror. The main entrance road was lined on either side by little red brick buildings. The prison had been constructed in the 1870s and it looked like a set for a Western film. To me it felt more like the setting for a horror flick.

Down at Menard you were surrounded by all the good ol' boys. They had a different mindset there. The guards and lieutenants were openly racist. Whereas the South Side organizations had held sway in Stateville, downstate it was the biker gangs who ran things. They were just as racist as the guards, and the two groups seemed more or less in agreement about their feelings about African American inmates. The first time one of them called me "nigger," I got right in his face and made sure he never said that word to me again. The prison assigned me a white cellie who was openly racist. He and I started bumping heads immediately. It didn't take long for things to come to a crisis. One day I was heading out to the mess hall. "When I come back from chow," I told him. "You better be out." Perhaps sensing this confrontation might not end as they'd expected, the guards transferred him to another cell.

More than a year had passed since the governor's mass clemency. I had overcome my initial shock of disappointment—especially since I realized this gave me the power to help Marvin's case. But so many other hopes had been dashed—not just for me, but for the movement itself. Ryan had put a moratorium on capital punishment and had commuted the terms of everyone then awaiting execution, but he had not actually had the power to abolish the death penalty in Illinois. New capital sentences had been issued in the previous months. Slowly but steadily, the state's death row was beginning to fill up again.

Our "victory" had proven limited in other ways as well. I watched with sadness as the Campaign—once so unified and inspiring—gradually fell apart. The movement was being torn up by in-house bickering. Activists fell off. People who had been fully dedicated to the cause now drifted away to other interests—and there was a lot going on that demanded attention in those days, especially with Bush's ongoing war in Iraq. And I understood, of course: they had "won." It was easier to celebrate that accomplishment and rally people to the cause of another egregious issue than it was to confront the messiness of the remaining work.

I could feel the sharpness of the difference. Before—on death row—I had been the center of attention. Media, activists, celebrities, had all rallied around me—around us. Now, we were all split up, in different places. And here I was, just another lifer in general population, another black inmate behind bars. Tom Geraghty and his law students at Northwestern were still fighting on my behalf, but the momentum was gone. I definitely felt the effects of that, something like withdrawal, in the aftermath of the excitement and energy of our fight. It was 2005. I had been incarcerated now—in one way or another—for seventeen years. My family was coming apart. The movement to free me had failed. I just could not believe it was taking this long to prove my case.

"I'm sitting in this cell and everything hurts," I wrote to Alice Kim one night when I couldn't sleep. "I miss me. I don't know how to be me anymore. . . . I look at these old pictures of myself and I had a smile that made people trust me, a smile I don't have now. Alice, this place is killing my soul, my heart. I know that I have to wait my turn in the wheel of life, I'm waiting. It's like the more light I see the more depressed I get." I had never experienced such a desperate depression. I was losing faith. I felt like I had no command over anything. Then my eyes fell on my precious journal. Here was something I *could* control, a wild action I *could* take.

Without thinking, I lunged for the box that contained my diaries: notebooks, loose-leaf typing paper, binders, yellow legal pads—nearly two thousand pages detailing my entire ordeal. I grabbed the documents and threw myself onto the floor. Word by word, line by line, page by painstaking page, I began to tear it all to pieces.

"Man!" My cellie yelled. "What's going on with you?"

Grimly and methodically I shoved handfuls of crumpled paper into the toilet and flushed them away. I did not want to write a story anymore about me still being in prison after nearly two full decades. Almost a whole life was stored in these handwritten leaves of paper. In one outburst of rage and frustration, I tore it all up. Sheet by sheet, I ripped out the memories.

"Are you crazy?" my cellie was shouting. "You been writing this shit for years, and now you gonna tear it up?"

I didn't answer. I erased it all. At that moment, I understood that this was the only thing I had true and total control over. It felt good to destroy the journal. I regretted it later. But I never started up another one.

9

IT'S GOOD TO BE OUT

THERE IS A type of wisdom called penitentiary knowledge, which is a combination of hard-won experience and rough-and-tumble street smarts that tends to reside in the minds of old timers in a correctional institution. I had always been around these types of men, valued their advice, and taken every opportunity to learn from their insights about what to do and what not to do. I based my movements and my thinking off what they had to offer. When they said, *Stay on top of your case*, I listened. *Don't get caught up in the folly* was one of their rules that I lived by. *Be serious, but not too serious*—meaning, respect yourself, but don't start throwing fists anytime someone says something to you—was another one I always tried to follow.

As much as I respected these elders, though, I still didn't plan to become one of them. I prized their knowledge, yet at the end of the day that's all they had. The institution was their life. It was where they were stuck, where their minds were. They were penitentiary-bound, and that was not an outcome I ever wanted for myself. But at the same time, did it really matter what I wanted? Every day that passed brought me closer to their fate. Some people say that each year in prison is longer than the one before. For me it was the opposite. It actually seemed like time started flying by. It was all slipping away from me. I turned thirty-five, and then forty years old. I was losing days faster than I could count them.

By the mid-2000s, I was sick of being depressed, tired of my mind and my memories. It felt like my brain was a tape recorder. Every night I'd press rewind, wanting to see something new, and all I'd get were the same scenes coming up over and over again: my arrest, torture, death row, prison. I felt like my lawyers were taking their time. They were about to file this motion, about to do that thing, looking into this. I knew they were busy, and yet it seemed like nothing was happening. It started to become more frustrating than anything else to me. I wanted to keep fighting. I didn't want to give up. But the longer I remained inside, the more strenuous and stressful it became to me. I didn't see any sunshine at the end of the tunnel. I didn't see no ending at all to this shit. I wanted to contribute to the world, to place my stamp on life. More than anything, I wanted to get up out of there and to come home.

And meanwhile, one by one, each day was stolen from me.

———————

It took a full four or five years of therapy, scrutiny, and dubious mistrust before the Illinois Department of Corrections finally decided that I could get a job in the prison. All that time—as a former death row inmate—I had been deemed unfit, or potentially disruptive. Finally, however, the state concluded I could be trusted with the responsibility of employment. They made me a dishwasher in the kitchen at Menard.

Working in prison-food preparation was an eye-opening, stomach-churning experience. This was cooking on a mass scale, with no oversight to speak of from the Department of Health. When it was time to scramble eggs the cooks would have to quickly break down thirty-six cases into one enormous pot. Then they had to stir the mess like maniacs to get it to scramble. I'd see them laboring over their cooking with giant paddles, sweat cascading from their brows right into the mixture. I watched them dump in whole eggs, and then stick their arms in to get out the shells. Others would spit in the eggs, or go take a shit and come back to work without washing their hands. I hadn't eaten much from the mess hall anyway, but seeing what went on in the kitchen put me off prison chow for good. Once I saw all that—come on now—I couldn't eat it no more. It only took a couple days in the kitchen before I started to just provide for myself. I immediately went on a strict diet of burritos, beans and rice, and Oodles of Noodles. It wasn't the healthiness of these foods that appealed to me—basically I would only eat things that I could prepare for myself in my cell.

Before long, a spot opened up to serve as baker. I asked for a chance to prove myself. They let me do a test run and saw that I knew what I was doing. I was fast, efficient, and quickly mastered the details. Baking had always been a part of my life. When I was a kid there was nothing I enjoyed more than sitting on the floor of my grandmother's kitchen and watching while she prepared her Sunday feasts for the family. As a young father, baking was one of my favorite activities to do with my son. In fact, I had been on the way home from the store with cookie dough when the police had arrested me in 1988. This type of cooking was nothing like that. Home cooking was more sanitized, more organized, more clean, and it tasted good. Penitentiary food ain't sanitized, ain't organized, and it sure as fuck don't taste good. The stuff was garbage.

It was my daily task to bake breakfast cakes, cornbread for lunch, and dinner brownies for the entire penitentiary—thirty-three hundred people. I worked the midnight shift. Around 10:00 PM, the guards would come down the gallery. I'd be standing by the bars, in my coat, ready and waiting to go to my assignment. For the next six hours I raced through the task; it was constant exertion every night. At home we had been dealing with one small stove. In prison, I found myself in charge of two giant industrial ovens dating back to at least the 1950s. Each one had ten shelves in it, and each shelf could hold six or seven baking pans. To feed every mouth in the prison I had to cook almost two hundred pans of food. I was constantly mixing ingredients, pouring batter, loading and unloading the ovens. As soon as I took out one pan, I'd cut it into pieces, move them out of the way, and load up the next one. Meanwhile, the ovens would be going in and out of whack; they would overheat or break down, I'd have to balance the shelves so that things didn't slide around. Finally, at like 3:30 or 4:00 in the morning, the job would be complete. The guards would escort me back to my cell, and I'd sleep throughout most of the day.

One perk of the position was that I was able to bake special treats for myself and my cellie—coffee cakes and other little things in which I could identify the ingredients and which were actually edible. In these moments, when some calm existed in the kitchen, I would often fill a cup with cake batter and eat it. Guys asked me what I was up to and I would tell them this was something I had done as a kid. Back in my grandma's kitchen, when she was baking, I had never missed a chance to lick the bowl. This was a small way to remember her, to connect with home. Even though she had been dead for more than a decade, I thought about her all the time. Working in the kitchen brought back memories of our conversations, about going over to her house while my mother was at work. Or visiting her at the office and sneaking off together to go grab lunch. Geraldine was with me all the time.

My mother was there too. It had been years now since I had seen her or spoken to her. Her visit after my brother's murder had in fact been her last. In these years, I never got much of a chance to talk to her on the phone, either. She was slipping away from the world, and the people who took care of her had little interest in making sure we got a chance to keep our connection strong. These women—the two most important in my life—were lost to me in these years. I did nothing but think about how much they meant to me, the only way to reach them was through little symbols, such as tasting that cake batter.

The outside world became like a ghost. My family wasn't trying to visit me or accept my phone calls. I never received letters from them. My youngest son, Randell, wanted little to do with me. My oldest son, Ronnie Jr., was a grown man now, with his own life and family to worry about. My family was surviving as best they could, just like I was. They had no obligation to me. I put that in my head and dealt with it and never let that go. Other people would go crazy because their family and friends weren't treating them the way they felt they deserved. It hurt me too, but I dismissed it. I tried not to blame the people who abandoned me. I had no reason to. After all, they weren't the ones who had put me here. It hurt. But, like everything else in my life that hurt, I had to deal with it. All the comments, all the things I had to hear in that place, all the bad shit people were doing to me—I called myself the bigger person and tried to let it slide off my shoulders. Of course, a lot of it stuck.

―――――――

While my family was vanishing from my side, others stepped up and kept me afloat. Alice Kim literally kept me sane, visiting and calling, sending me updates about politics, keeping me in touch with the world. Another lifesaver was my lawyer, Carolyn Frazier.

We had met a few years earlier in a makeshift attorney-client room in the Cook County Jail, where I was temporarily being held. Because I was a death row inmate at the time, the jail had chosen to house me in its most restrictive and dehumanizing space, the Abnormal Behavior Unit in Division I. I was locked up in segregated housing and shackled by the feet and at the belly. My cell was all the way in the deepest subbasement of the jail's oldest building; it was a hellhole. This was where Chicago kept the craziest of the crazy, the worst of the worst.

Carolyn was waiting in the meeting room when I arrived. Still a law student at the time, this was her first ever meeting—not just with me but with any client. Nothing about it conformed to what she'd been told in school to expect. There was no confidentiality. Instead, several attorneys were all meeting with their clients at once. It was in the immediate aftermath of 9/11 and anti-Arab posters and graffiti were plastered across the walls. The guards brought me in. I had to shuffle and stagger under the heft of my chains. Carolyn and I had talked on the phone many times, but this was our initial face-to-face moment. The setting could not have been less promising. Broken furniture and cheap plastic chairs were scattered around. Stagnant puddles of water pooled on the ground, along with countless electrical cords.

Just as we began to talk, I noticed Carolyn see something behind me and flinch.

"What? What?" I shouted, panicking. "Is it a mouse? Is it a mouse? Carolyn, please do not tell me you just saw a mouse!"

A brief moment passed and we both started laughing. Here I was, the "worst of the worst," a supposed mass murderer—and I was deathly afraid of mice. The situation was awful and ridiculous at the same time. Each of us saw both sides of it and were able to crack up.

This shared sense of humor became the basis of an amazing friendship. Carolyn was a third-year law student at Northwestern at the time, studying with Tom Geraghty, and an eager participant in his anti-death-penalty law clinic. A lot of students passed through the program, but I could tell immediately that Carolyn was different. She showed a deep concern, and everything she said was genuine. Unlike some of the others, she wasn't just trying to get extra grades or put an internship on her resume. That was not her. By the time I was moved to Menard we had built a close partnership. She immersed herself in my case and worked on it after graduating from law school, taking me with her from prestigious firm to prestigious firm as she moved from Baker & McKenzie to Jenner & Block, and then back to Northwestern as a professor. She called me her "brother from another mother." And I called her any hour, day or night, whenever I could get access to a phone. That was the relationship we had.

Carolyn made my case her life's work. It consumed her, like it did me, and she was tireless in tracking down new evidence. She worked the streets, interviewing witnesses—including Willie Williams—and trying to catch the state out in its lies. Meanwhile, I used my time inside to bring my own perspective to the evidence. Between the two of us, we were able to not only poke holes in the prosecution's arguments, but also make real progress on solving the original crime that had landed me behind bars in the first place. Just by using common sense—and a little bit of street knowledge—we made more inroads on the quintuple homicide than the Chicago police ever did with all their training, resources, and so-called expertise.

My main breakthrough concerning this horrendous crime came from reading and rereading my case records and transcripts. Back on death row, our process was to have everyone read one person's files; that way we could get multiple perspectives on a single set of facts. Four or five guys would pore over the same materials and then discuss it afterward. Our life experiences of growing up in inner cities and having firsthand knowledge with how the narcotics industry worked in Chicago gave us a certain knowledge about these topics—of which most lawyers and judges were completely ignorant. We took different routes but we all came to the identical place. The same claims struck us each as deeply improbable. We started seeing what was missing.

First off, the idea that people could sell drugs for me for three years without me knowing it was crazy. If you were selling drugs for me for three years, we were going to bump heads. You were going to see me. In addition—and anybody who knew anything about drugs knew this—Mexicans, Puerto Ricans, Asians, Cubans—they did not work for black people. That's a fact. That's just a true fact. We got our drugs from them. It also struck us as improbable that two or three black guys could visit the same house in a Mexican neighborhood as many times as the prosecution said we had without attracting some notice from the neighbors. The same was true for the clubs and lounges where Willie Williams claimed we'd met up. No way could we have gone to those places incognito. Of course, I knew that these were lies. But it was good to hear my fellow inmates come to that conclusion on their own.

Finally, after putting our heads together, we all made the only logical deduction: it was an inside job. The murderer of Deborah, Rosemarie, and their three children had to have been a family member. There was no evidence of forced entry, and the doors were locked when the firefighters arrived, so in all probability the killers possessed keys to the house. More to the point: Why would Marvin and I have killed the kids? After all, they wouldn't have been able to identify us by name. What use would it have been to detectives if three toddlers had told them that two black guys had done the crime? The person who suffocated those children and then set fire to the house knew that the victims could recognize who they were. The children were potential witnesses and had to be killed.

Meanwhile, Carolyn's gumshoeing took her all across the continent, from the South Side to the West Coast, as she tirelessly sought new leads and evidence. Everything she discovered served to back up the theory I had deduced from inside. It became clear that Deborah's husband and his brother—the children's father and uncle—were the likely killers. When the state finally was forced to release suppressed investigation reports we learned that police had actually brought in the two Sepulvedas for questioning. Both failed a polygraph test when they claimed to have been in Mexico at the time of the killings. This fact was not revealed at my original trial, in clear violation of the rules of evidence. When investigators went south of the border to pursue these leads, they found even more conclusive proof that the men's cover story had been a lie. Relatives and friends in Mexico told inquirers that the men had been around during the summer of 1988, but that they had disappeared for nearly a week in the midst of that trip, dropping from sight at precisely the time when the crime was committed.

At every court date I'd ever had, Pedro Sepulveda—Debbie's husband—had been present. From the first pretrial motion in 1988, through the entire trial, and at every appeal hearing, he had never missed a session. This apparent testament to a husband's loyalty to his murdered wife took on a different appearance when our investigators learned that DNA material from underneath one of the victims' fingernails had been preserved. New technologies that had not been widely available in the 1980s suddenly meant we could test those cells and possibly find conclusive evidence about the identity of the killer. The judge ordered that testing commence on all possible suspects.

At my next court date—for the first time ever—Pedro was absent. The conclusion was inescapable: he had not been obsessively following these proceedings out of concern for his dead wife, he was watching to see if suspicion ever focused in his direction. We never saw Pedro again. And for good reason, too. Although the testing sample had degraded in the twenty years since the murders, the lab was still able to conclude that the fragment of skin must have come from a male member of the Sepulveda family.

Among the many outrages committed by Burge and Kill in my case, one that had always shocked me was their willingness to knowingly and falsely besmirch the names of the women and children who had been killed. They knew they were peddling lies, and yet they had still been ready to defame these two hardworking women—one of them a cop's daughter, no less—with a fabricated story about their secret lives as drug dealers. As we followed more leads and uncovered new evidence a more nuanced picture emerged. The women were likely innocent of any criminal wrongdoing, but the men in their lives were clearly up to something, perhaps linked to narcotics smuggling. Not long after he stopped showing up in court, Pedro Sepulveda himself was found murdered in Mexico.

Due in large part to our own activism—as well as the work of the Campaign, and a handful of determined lawyers—public pressure had finally forced authorities to officially examine our claims of torture. Back in 2002, the Chicago Police Department had started up a formal investigation into the Burge torture scandals. After their first choice to take on this task—state's attorney Dick Devine—was ruled to have a conflict of interest, the project fell to other members of his office. My expectations were low from the start. The special prosecutors assigned the job of rooting out wrongdoing had worked hand-in-hand with police detectives for years—both as state's attorneys and judges—and they were therefore too close to the perpetrators of the crimes to actually mount a real inquiry. It was just common sense—you don't have the police investigate the police and expect any serious results.

If Chicago's leaders had truly believed in progress they would have acted already. The torture story was hardly a secret. From local newspapers, such as the *Chicago Reader*, to Geraldo Rivera on national news, revelations concerning racism and violence among the city's detectives had been in the public eye for years. It's true that Jon Burge had been dismissed from the police department, taking the fall for a culture of torture and racism that stretched far beyond his influence. But besides losing his job, he had not suffered much. The former scourge of the South Side was enjoying a quiet retirement in Florida, spending pleasant hours on his boat, and receiving a monthly pension check of more than $3,400—all at Chicago taxpayers' expense.

In the summer of 2006—after four years and another $6 million or so of public money—the prosecutors' special report was finally released. A close reading of this document revealed important facts. Although the inquiry had begun with fewer than seventy "alleged" cases of torture, by the end of the process more than twice that many victims had contacted the investigators to tell their stories. The report detailed their claims, as well as cataloguing numerous mishandled complaints, lax oversight, and administrative errors.

Yet, despite these revelations, the investigation on the whole was a sham. For instance, the report never formally charged the police with "torture." Nor did it connect the patterns of abuse to issues of racism—a word that didn't appear even once in the 292-page document. The investigators stated that irrefutable proof of abuse existed in only three cases, and cast doubt on the stories of several members of the Death Row Ten. I was furious when I read this. Again and again, they claimed that there was insufficient evidence to prove the case. And yet, to me it was apparent that evidence of torture was everywhere to see—if you were actually trying to find it. There were two hundred witnesses talking about it. And if our word wasn't enough proof, then investigators could have found the details in my medical records.

To these injuries, the city's report added one final insult. Even in the three "provable" instances of torture, the investigators concluded, it would not be possible to pursue indictments. Too much time had passed by. The statute of limitations had expired. This hypocrisy rested on the ultimate piece of faulty logic. For decades, we had been urging the city to investigate police torture. The authorities had dragged their feet all that time. Now, after finally conducting an inquiry, they were claiming that no further action could be taken—because too much time had elapsed. I was enraged but not surprised. "I had a feeling," I wrote for the Campaign newspaper, "that they were going to pull a city of Chicago method: a cover-up. They can call it whatever name they put on that report, but the fact of the matter is they are covering asses. . . . That report is a joke." That's what it was, a whitewash pure and simple. But what could we expect when the police were asked to investigate their own? Behind it all was Mayor Daley and state's attorney Dick Devine; the city would go to any length and spend limitless funds to protect them. With these two we were talking about serious gangsters—gangsters for real.

———————

The investigation report was a setback in the quest for justice, but it didn't stop me from pursuing my own case. I was working on my post-conviction appeal at the time. In this petition we'd be stating all of the fresh evidence our investigations had unearthed. After decades of effort, more and more details had gradually come to light. Each successive round of subpoenas unearthed further documents from the police—all of which had been illegally suppressed during my trial— and with each new trace we were able to discredit the detectives' lies a little bit more.

This was by far the most meaningful work Carolyn had done in her law career. Obsessed with the case, she would leave her job at the firm late at night and then go back to Northwestern, nap on a cot for a few hours, and keep at it. Whenever I could get access to the phones I'd place a collect call and we'd update each other on our progress. She'd be speaking in whispers so her colleagues at the law firm didn't realize what she was up to, and I'd be yelling over the din of the other prisoners. I was a demanding client—but in the best way. Whenever we talked I'd pepper her with questions: *What have you done? What's going on? Have you followed up with this, this, this, and this?* It was a delicate relationship. I was totally dependent on her and the other lawyers—just as I had been with Alice and the death-penalty activists. I would do everything I could from inside, but for almost all my needs I was forced to rely on others to be my eyes, ears, legs, and hands. As hard as they worked, it was never enough. As fast as they moved, it was always too slow.

It took years of effort—both inside and outside—to draft my post-conviction relief petition. I talked with Carolyn and my other lawyers about every aspect of the process. I worried about her going out and talking to Willie Williams and other people from my past. And she worried about me, balancing the need to keep me updated on progress while not wanting to give me false hopes. In the end, it took Carolyn, Tom, and a team of more than a dozen top law students to draft the motion. When I received it, I was blown away. They kept me posted on everything, so there were no specific surprises. But nevertheless when the final document was actually delivered to me—I was in segregated housing at Stateville at the time—the overall effect was stunning. I devoured it in one sitting. It was like reading a book. Everything was in there, from the evidence implicating the Sepulvedas, to Willie Williams and his lies, to Robert Edwards's innumerable failures to defend me properly at trial, to the state's sustained efforts to suppress evidence. "How are they going to answer this petition?" I asked Carolyn and Tom the next time I saw them. Every point was covered beyond dispute. To me it was apparent that prosecutors would be struck dumb by the evidence we'd laid out. There was nothing to say, nothing to talk about. Every corner got covered.

It soon became clear that the State of Illinois felt the same way. Instead of responding to our claims, or attempting any sort of rebuttal, the prosecutors just stalled for time. This process played out with excruciating slowness—six years passed. Any time my case came up for a hearing the state just asked for another continuance. They had nothing to say. They didn't know how to answer.

Then, one evening in early July 2009, I was taken in from the yard at Menard to my cell. It was late in the day, around 6:00 PM. I had been locked in for the night and was getting ready to prepare some type of dinner on my kettle when the word came down that I had an attorney call. This was unusual. The guard was mad as hell to have to take me out again and escort me across the grounds. He grumbled the whole way over to the administration building. "Fuck, Kitchen, what's going on? Why you getting a special privilege? We don't usually allow phone calls this late at night."

"I don't know what's going on," I said. "You tell me. This is your job." Inside, I was nervous. I could just tell that something terrible had happened. We got to the office and dialed Tom Geraghty's office number. It rang and rang. No one picked up.

"We are going to try this one more time, and then you're going back," the guard announced.

"No, I have the right to my legal call," I replied, "and you're going to dial that number until someone answers it." Geraghty picked up on the second attempt. My heart was beating through my chest. All kinds of scary thoughts were flooding into my brain: *Had another tragedy struck my family? Had something happened to my mom? Was I going back to death row? Had our petition been denied?*

"Ronald," he said, "I have some good news."

"What is it?" I asked nervously.

"I can't tell you," he replied. He was being vague, almost secretive.

"Well, what do it concern?" I asked, trying to get something—anything—out of him.

"I can't tell you that either."

"Then what the fuck is the phone call for?" I laughed in frustration.

"It's really good, Ronald. I can't tell you what's going on, but it's really good news."

"Tom, this is crazy," I said. "How you gonna call me, and tell me there's really good news, but you can't tell me?"

"I wish I could, but I can't," he insisted. "The guards are probably going to get you over the weekend and bring you up to Stateville. Don't worry."

"OK, that's cool," I said. "All right."

We hung up the phone. A ball of fire raced through my body. A feeling more powerful than anything I had ever experienced was telling me *You're going home.* This blast of light, hope, joy, happiness, excitement, completely overwhelmed me. After a minute or so I realized my face was hurting. I had never smiled this hard to hear some good news, or, rather—because of Tom's silence—to not hear some good news. Back in my cell I started pacing and shouting, just acting crazy—frantic, frantic.

"What's going on?" my cellie asked.

"Dude," I said, "I'm out of here."

When I went to my assignment in the kitchen later that night, I was still in the clouds. The supervisor told me I seemed especially happy. "I'm out of here," I told him. "I don't need this job no way. I ain't coming back." I was that confident. I told everybody in the kitchen, "I'm up out of here." I believed it, wholeheartedly. My work shift ended at 5:00 AM, but I was too excited to sleep. I didn't go to bed that night. I stayed up, lying in the cot, thinking about how I would tell Marvin when I saw him in the morning in the yard. But I didn't have to wait that long. Soon after the sun rose, the guards came knocking on the bars and shouting, "Kitchen! Pack your shit!"

I gave everything away. Food, clothes, gym shoes, I gave all of it away. Everything. And I didn't think twice about any of it. Just in case, though, I told the guys, "If I come back, I want my shit returned to me." The only things I left Menard with were a clean pair of drawers, socks, a T-shirt, and some shoes.

I met Marvin at receiving. No one had told him anything. He was as confused as I probably should have been. "We're up out of here," I told him.

"How do you know?" he asked.

"I just know," I said. "We out of here. We out of here. WE UP OUT OF HERE!"

They unloaded us in Stateville on a Friday and placed Marvin and me in adjoining cells in the roundhouse for the weekend. On Sunday, Carolyn called and told us to expect an attorney visit the next morning. We waited in a room in the administration building for most of Monday. No one came. Marvin was returned to his cell. Finally, that evening, after hours of delays, Carolyn appeared.

"I've got some good news and some bad news to tell you," she said.

"Oh, fuck." I thought, *Here we go again.* "I'll have the bad news first."

"Michael Jackson has passed away," she said.

"Man, I seen that shit on the news last week," I said. "What's the good news?"

She smiled. "You're going home tomorrow."

Since my sentencing nineteen years earlier, I had almost never cried—certainly never with joy. Now, all of a sudden, my eyes were flooded. Tears streamed down my cheeks. I was sobbing. Happiness. I cried and cried. Oh my god, I cried. I cried like a little baby. "Don't you be playing with me," I managed to moan between sniffs and snorts. "I'm going home for real?"

"Yes!" she said.

Back in the roundhouse I just cried without any letup. Completely deaf to everything, I didn't even hear Marvin—frantically worried—calling to me from the next-door cell. Everyone was shouting my name, but I was oblivious. After a while, the other inmates had the guards come check on me. They discovered me lying on the bunk with my feet up on the wall. I had cried myself to sleep in that position.

When they woke me for breakfast, my sheets were still soaking wet from all the tears. Hearing my voice, Marvin shouted, "I've been calling your butt all night! What's up?"

"We gone," I told him. "No more of this place."

It was Tuesday, July 7, 2009. This would be my freedom day, my Lazarus day, the day I was reborn.

I knew I didn't want to face the judge—or the world, for that matter—in a prison uniform, so I asked Carolyn to make sure I had something nice to wear. She borrowed some of her husband's suits and then popped the hem to give them a little extra roominess. She brought us two to choose from. I gave Marvin the bigger one, which hung off him, baggy as hell. Mine was a pretty sharp charcoal-gray number made by Hugo Boss, but despite Carolyn's efforts, the damn thing was ridiculously small. I had to hold my pants together at the waist, they were way too tight to fasten. If I didn't keep my hands at my belt, everything—my drawers, my belly—would have been visible. I could hardly move my legs. It was like a biker outfit, it was so tight.

"Which one of you is Kitchen?" asked the officials who rode with us from Stateville into Chicago. "You must be the man, because all anyone is talking about is 'Kitchen this,' and 'Kitchen that.' They are talking about you real heavy." We went through receiving and into the Criminal Court Building at Twenty-Sixth and California. Walking into the courtroom—that was a sight. There were a lot of people there I had not seen in more than two decades. I saw aunts, uncles, cousins, almost none of whom I had had any kind of relationship with while I was incarcerated. My younger son, Randell, whom I hadn't seen since he was an infant, was there. And he had brought his daughter—my granddaughter—to come and meet me. I guess you could say the courtroom was full of strangers rooting me on.

Geraghty and the state's lawyers did their legal mumbo jumbo in front of the chief judge. The attorney general's office, in effect, said what I knew they would say. They had no case. In a short statement

Illinois conceded that, after reviewing the evidence and our findings for six years, it could not "sustain its burden of proof." As we had said from the beginning, there was no evidence against us—because we hadn't been involved. My case and Marvin's case were both dismissed, and the judge told us we would receive certificates of innocence to clear our names. When some parole officers tried to quibble with the decision, the judge put them right in their place. "This man is not going to be on parole, or any kind of supervision," he said. "Ronald is walking out of this courtroom today. Today!" Glory.

Lo and behold, at 3:45 PM, Marvin and I stepped outside to freedom together—just like I had always promised that we would. We strode through the revolving glass doors of the courthouse into a bright sunlit afternoon. I carried my granddaughter in my arms, partly out of love—and in part because she helped me shield the fact that my pants didn't fit. Within seconds, I was surrounded by a huge crowd of friends, lawyers, and family.

Then the press closed in. Photographers snapped pictures. Microphones, TV cameras, and audio recorders were shoved in my face. Part of me was overwhelmed, but most of me was way past ready to finally speak for myself. The questions came flying in: *How do you feel now that you are free? What's the first thing you are going to do now? Why did you confess to a crime you didn't commit? What does it feel like to be released after all this time?*

I almost couldn't hear them. The clicking of the cameras, the din of the reporters faded into the background. I was taking it all in. The warm summer air. The sunlight. I was breathing, filling my lungs with freedom, sensing the lightness of my soul. I couldn't stop smiling. Was this a dream? "I haven't felt it yet. It really hasn't hit me yet. It's surreal," I told the reporters. "I guess, when I actually sit down and take a hot bath, it might hit me then. For twenty-one years, somebody's been telling me when to take a bath, when to eat, when to go outside. It's definitely good to be out."

This was an opportunity to speak directly to the public. I didn't want anyone's sympathy, or to be seen as some kind of random mistake. I hoped they would see me as proof of a broken criminal justice system. And I needed them to understand that my ordeal, Marvin's ordeal, and that of so many others, hadn't just happened by accident. There were people we could name—not to mention a larger and still-powerful culture of racism—that were directly responsible for locking us up and throwing away the key. "For someone to finally see and understand that we have been telling the truth for twenty-one years is great," I told the reporters, the cameras, the microphones, the world. "But, as long as Jon Burge is free, and his cronies, the fight has to continue. And that's that."

As soon as the crowds released me, we headed over to Northwestern for a powwow about the case. I changed clothes. While we talked, I chowed down on a slice of pecan pie with cookie-dough ice cream—a dessert I'd been dreaming of for more than twenty years. After that, we headed over to a fancy downtown steakhouse, and I ordered the biggest piece of meat on the menu. When the meal finished, Carolyn and I went shopping for some essentials, and then she dropped me off at my auntie Linda's place, on South Artesian Avenue, where I'd be staying for the immediate future. When we pulled up to the tidy brick bungalow I could see people hanging out on the porch. A whole other party was waiting for me—mostly with people I didn't want to see—but I behaved and tried to enjoy myself.

It was way past midnight when the last guests departed. Going to sleep was nowhere in my plans. I went outside and sat down on my aunt's front porch, thinking over what I'd just experienced. A whole lifetime had been crammed into this single day. That morning I had woken up in the roundhouse at Stateville, and now here I was—a free man—back in Chicago, a fifteen-minute drive from my old house. I had dreamed of this for twenty-one years, and now that it had come to pass, that's what it felt like—a dream.

The faces I had seen flashed before my eyes—and a few that had been absent. Alice Kim happened to be out of town when I got out. It had all happened so quickly that she wouldn't even find out the good news until someone told her on the phone a few days later. My mother was in Georgia, and visiting her was top on my to-do list. The most upsetting absentee, though, was my oldest son, Ronald Jr. It turned out he had missed my release because he himself had been locked up a few months earlier. No one had told me. I discovered the news only after coming home. Although he too would be coming home soon, learning he'd been locked away was yet another reminder of the long odds face by black families in Chicago facing the forces of mass incarceration.

There were other moments—small sour notes in an otherwise joyous day—that suggested some of the hurdles that lay ahead. I received my first cellphone call that morning. My hands were shaking as I pushed the buttons and tried to figure it out. I didn't know what to do. When I put it up to my ear, it turned out I was holding it upside down. Everyone was laughing at me. At that moment I sensed how steep the learning curve would be. Cars had changed, televisions had transformed. The clothing I grew up wearing was no longer in style. It was a whole different world. I'd have to learn everything there was to know about this new reality.

That first night, I sat on the porch till daybreak. In the following days, I'd be up at sunrise, marveling at the sound of the birds singing outside my window. I walked and jogged around the neighborhood. I stayed with people who would let me savor these moments. It was summertime. On many a night, I brought out a pillow and blanket and stretched out in a lawn chair in the backyard and went to sleep like that. I didn't want to miss anything. I really didn't.

10

LIFE

———————

THERE WAS SOMETHING I had to do, a youthful habit that I just couldn't quit—no matter the cost to my health, or pride. It was a big part of what had defined me as a teenager, and I had to give it one more try. I drove down through the South Side, past all the neighborhoods where someone might have recognized me, until I found a small, out-of-the way dealer carrying the specific products I was looking for. Inside, the shelves were stocked with paraphernalia from the 1980s. Memories of danger, speed, excitement, flooded back. It was as if I had never left. Adrenaline raced through me as my fingers touched the old familiar equipment. Pulling out my wallet, I purchased a pair of Gem 2 boots with black panther plates and precision wheels. It was time to go roller skating.

I laced up at the nearest rink—harder to find than when I was younger. The past—my heyday—flooded back to me as I gazed out at the glossy surface of the floor and the hypnotic pulsing of the strobe lights. I pictured my eighteen-year-old self speeding around packed skating arenas. I was a sensation, hearing the cheers from every corner. I was leaping, twisting, doing the crazy leg. In my mind, I was exactly the same guy who used to flawlessly execute all those fancy moves. Then, I glided out onto the ring and started moving. I was a little rusty, perhaps, but I felt a moment of deep relief. Much of my old smoothness was still there. Then—*wham!*—I was on the ground. *Wham! Wham!* Every time I went around the circuit I hit the deck. Whenever I tried out one of my old moves, something went wrong. One twist and turn and my knees would give out, leaving me hobbling over to grab hold of the wall. Finally, I came down with a crash that left me rolling around in pain, instantly aware that something truly bad had happened. My arm was swelling up like a balloon. It was a fractured wrist. No more crazy leg. No more of that exciting stuff. Gravity and old bones were telling me it wasn't going to happen.

Skating was the only danger I had any taste for. Otherwise, I was determined to avoid trouble. For the first few days of freedom, I kept close to my auntie's house, never straying much further than her front porch or the backyard. Before I could truly feel independent I had to get my documentation in order. I needed a driver's license, a social security card, and a birth certificate. The chance of getting questioned and harassed by the cops in Chicago, even while just walking on the sidewalk, was always high. The last thing I wanted was to go out for a stroll and find myself—without any identification—being questioned by a police officer. That would result in me sitting in a cell somewhere for a day or two until they could figure out who I was. I knew I couldn't have that. The thought of the police, let alone a jail cell, put me into a cold sweat.

Once I felt the comfortable sensation of having a driver's license in my wallet again, I settled into a steady routine. In the mornings, I took long walks and jogs around the neighborhood. Things had changed. During the 1980s, before she lived there, my auntie's street would have been considered a "no blacks allowed" part of town. It had been all Mexicans back then. As it happened, her place was only six blocks south of the address on Campbell Avenue where the murders had taken place. It was surreal to run by the house. It was still standing. A new family had moved in and was living a normal life there.

Riding through my old neighborhood for the first time gave me one of the biggest shocks of my life. In my youth, these streets had been filled with nice houses, lawns, and thriving businesses. I'd already seen some of that start to change before I went to jail, but now almost everything was abandoned. And it was hard not to take the changes personally. Sometimes it felt like the city had set out to erase my own life story. I drove around town to find old landmarks from my youth and discovered only empty spaces. The Robert Taylor homes, where I had been born, were gone. This had once been the largest public-housing development in the world, but the last tower had been pulled down in 2007. I had always had mixed feelings about the place. I was born there, and then had watched it fall into disrepair. Grateful to not have to live there, I still saw it as a place of refuge—a world where only black people lived. Other former residents clearly felt the same way. After the towers were destroyed, the families who had stayed there decided to hold an annual Robert Taylor Homes picnic. Linda brought me to one of these affairs. When she told people who I was, literally hundreds of strangers came up to me to tell me they remembered seeing me as a little kid. That said it all about the Taylor Homes. For all their issues there was a real community there.

The removal of that project was the most notable, but not the only, example of loss. Each and every one of the other houses where I'd stayed on the South Side—on Emerald, Union, Carpenter, and Aberdeen—had been bulldozed, too. They were vacant lots now, covered in dirt and scraggly grass, and blocked off by chain-link fences. No one was left to take care of them the way my grandmother had always made sure we youngsters had done in the past.

After a little while I learned not to take this too personally. It wasn't about me. The same thing had happened to almost every black district—every impoverished area—in Chicago. Where my family, and others like us, had worked to integrate housing, the neighborhoods had vanished. White residents and the leaders of the city—families like the Burges and the Daleys—had literally preferred to destroy and abandon entire neighborhoods rather than to consider breaking down barriers of racial separation. I traveled through the streets and found gaping wounds. It was perfectly normal to encounter just one or two houses still standing on a whole goddamn block. South Michigan Avenue, State Street, the old areas I'd known so well, had disappeared. When the white folks left, jobs, services and businesses had disappeared, too. And then there was the flip side of that story. With the projects gone, fancy new developments were on the rise. Mayor Daley was clearing out black people in a vain hope of attracting the 2016 summer Olympics. Projects were torn down and condos shot up. Entire areas were gentrified and prettified beyond recognition.

It was uncomfortable for me to reunite with people who had known me as a teenager. Often, they would want to talk about my youthful exploits. If one or both of my sons was around, I'd get especially nervous. I did not want them to feel like they needed to live up to some exaggerated stories that a few old-timers were telling about me. I had seen more violence than any child or teenager should. First, there had been the racist assaults on my family after we moved into a white area. Then, as a youth, I had mixed it up with others. When we were coming up, if you had a problem with somebody you would go find them and fight: win, lose, or draw. If they beat your ass, they beat your ass. If you won, you won. Things rarely got out of hand. The police never got called. No one ever pulled a gun or a knife.

My sons lived with a different reality. By the time I got out of jail, a whole new code reigned supreme. Little disagreements easily escalated. When kids got into a fight and one of them won, the other person was now likely to come back and kill them, without concern for anyone else around. These dudes didn't believe in protecting innocent people. There were no innocent people to them. Like many

Americans I watched in horror as the neighborhoods where I had grown up continued to spiral further into poverty and violence. Back in the 1980s it had been way different. We held informal block parties on summer nights, with roller skating, music, and kids running everywhere. Now in these same neighborhoods you really couldn't sit on the front porch and chill out. You couldn't sit by the window. You had to worry about people riding up and shooting you down. It was a totally different environment.

These changes were jarring and painful. The whole culture I had been raised in was largely gone. But nothing compared with the experience of seeing my mother again. It was August 2009, about a month after my release, when Alice Kim and I traveled together to visit Louva at my sister's apartment in Augusta, Georgia.

When I came in the door I saw her in her nightgown, sitting in an armchair. She was just starting to get up from her seat as I entered the room. This was the first time I had seen her in nearly six years. Her hair was damn near white. She looked gaunt and her cheeks were hollow. Her eyes had a vacant expression. She had suffered three or four strokes and was now deep into dementia. It was still Louva, and yet the disease had taken a toll on her. As I entered she was trying to go out and walk her dogs. This had been her favorite pastime, but now my sister couldn't let her leave the house anymore. If she wandered out alone she'd get lost.

We stood there and looked at each other's faces, each searching the other for some kind of response.

"Mom," I asked her, "what are you looking at?"

"I'm looking at you," she said.

"What are you looking at me like that for?" I asked.

"I'm just trying," she replied, "to figure out who you are."

My mother, the one person in this world whom I'd been close with through my entire ordeal, was so far gone that she couldn't even recognize me. That tore me up. For more than twenty years, I'd dreamed of the moment when I would run into her arms as a free man, and suddenly I realized it would never happen. I was free now, but she was locked up. She was there, but she wasn't really there. The pain was too great for me to conceal. I didn't want to cry in front of everyone. More than that, I didn't want to upset Louva. I made a beeline into the bathroom to compose myself. The whole time I was down there I remained on the verge of tears. Whenever anyone called to see how it was going, I warned them not to start crying over the phone—if they did I'd hang up on them. Hearing their pain would start me crying again, and then it would just make it even worse for my mother.

We stayed with her for about a week. The second day was a little bit better. When I came in she knew who I was and could sit there and talk to me. But then suddenly a switch would go off and she'd be gone again. One time I asked what she was thinking about and she told me that she was "waiting for Ronnie to come home." And again I had to run to the bathroom to get myself calm. Sometimes she seemed to know who I was. At other moments she could talk about "Ronnie" and remember the ordeal I'd gone through. The tragedy was that she was too far gone to put it all together. Her disease robbed her of the chance to feel the joy of me being out.

There were few people that I would have allowed to see my mother in her weakened state. But it was good to have Alice there with me. I found comfort in the thought that she had known Louva in her prime. We traded stories about my mother marching out in the streets, fighting, screaming, and hollering. She had gone everywhere and had done everything: weekly meetings, phone calls, stuffing envelopes, protesting at a Republican National Convention, participating in the Million Man March. Alice and I talked about her soft, beautiful, voice, which could work so powerfully on a crowd or connect deeply in a one-on-one conversation. Most of all, we talked about the political vision behind her advocacy against the death penalty. Whenever Louva had spoken about her work, she had always known to say, "This isn't about my son, this is every mother's son. This touches all of us."

These conversations allowed me to begin the long process of saying good-bye to my mother. But my trip south was also a series of firsts. This was the first time I had ever flown in an airplane. Takeoff was scary as fuck. I had to grab hold of something to keep myself from screaming in panic. The landing was scary as fuck. But up there in the air you wouldn't even know you were off the ground—unless you happened to look out the window. We hit a couple of potholes in the sky. A few bumps made my stomach drop. But it was all worth it to me, all part of my new adventure. I had only ever traveled through my books, or secondhand through the stories I heard from friends. Alice and Carolyn had sent me postcards in prison from their various trips. In those years I had created a long list of sights to see and places to visit, and now I had my chance to start experiencing them.

From Augusta, we traveled throughout the South. In Savannah I stood by a trading post where slaves had been auctioned. I went to Birmingham to see the church where a terrorist bombing had killed four little girls in 1963. I wanted to see the place in Mississippi where Medgar Evers was killed. I saw the National Civil Rights Museum in Memphis, at the motel where Martin Luther King Jr., was assassinated. We drove up through the Carolinas, seeing the monuments to slavery and the Civil War. I had been reading about black history and had come to understand my own story as a continuation of this legacy of racism, violence, and struggle. And now that I had my freedom these were the very first places I needed to see.

When I returned to Chicago, it was time to figure out a way to make a living. I couldn't stay with my auntie forever. I had to rebuild my life from scratch. I needed to go to school. I needed a job. I was open to anything. I just wanted to live, to be productive. Over the years, I had seen too many people get released and then struggle in the outside world to allow myself any false hopes. I had always thrived in business, but my skills were now decades out of date. This was a whole new world. It was exhilarating but also overwhelming. As much as I had longed and fought for my freedom, I also harbored deep anxieties about what it would mean.

"I'll be screwed when I get out," I once observed to a white friend, while pondering this very question. "I got the trifecta against me: I'm poor, I'm unemployed—"

"—and you're black," my friend said, interrupting me.

"No," I responded. "I was going to say 'and I'm ugly, too.'"

Although I had my certificate of innocence, I faced many of the same obstacles that anyone released from prison would confront. I fought the stigma of having been accused of murder. I had no formal education, no skills to speak of, no letters of reference, nor past job performance to report. I faced humiliation, as well as discrimination, from employers who only saw my background or who were nervous about hiring someone who had done time. I wanted to work, but I couldn't find a job. And it wasn't that I was being picky. There was nothing I wouldn't do. Hell, I had worked in the penitentiary baking cakes for pennies a day. I would be grateful to find employment for eight or nine dollars an hour. But I couldn't find a job. Nothing.

About a month or two after getting out, I heard that the Chicago Department of Streets and Sanitation had started up a second-chance hiring program for formerly incarcerated people. I gathered all my paperwork and drove downtown to apply. After a long wait I finally got face-to-face with an official from the agency.

"I just come home," I told him, "and I need a job."

"Congratulations, Brother," he said, before making a long study of my documentation. When he got to my certificate of innocence, he paused and looked up.

"I can't do nothing for you," he said. "This is for parolees only."

I stood there with my mouth wide open.

"Look," I said, "I did twenty-one years, and the state cleared me of all wrongdoing. This program is for people who deserve a second chance. Don't you feel I deserve a second chance?"

"Yeah," he said, "but this program ain't for you." And then he called the next applicant forward.

Here was yet another painful irony of my situation. Because I had my certificate, I was ineligible for the scant reentry support that existed for men and women transitioning from prison to the community. Doors were being slammed in my face. There was no winning. Months passed. I couldn't get a job because I was an ex-con; I couldn't get a job because I wasn't an ex-con. I was damned every which way.

———————

You spend a lot of time in prison thinking about women. When I was released, of course, I had hopes of finding a life partner to share my days and nights with. But it wasn't at the very top of my priorities list. I wasn't in a hurry. So, when—on my second or third night of freedom—my new cellphone started ringing at four o'clock in the morning, I was a little bit shocked to pick it up and hear heavy breathing on the other end of the line.

"*Hi.* This is Tina," said a sultry voice. "What are you doing?"

"What are *you* doing?" I answered, feeling a bit uncomfortable.

"What do you think I'm doing?" she answered. "What's your address? I'm coming over."

I was not ready for this kind of thing. Still half asleep, I hung up the phone and leapt from my bed. Running around the house, I made damned sure that all the doors and windows were closed. I even went outside to double check that the front gate was locked. This woman had me so scared.

A few days later the phone rang again with a number I didn't recognize.

"Who is this?" I asked.

"Hi, Ronald," the voice said. "It's Tina!"

My mind immediately went back to the scary scene from a few nights earlier.

"You got ten motherfucking seconds to talk," I said.

There was a long pause.

"Ronald, it's Tina Carr." I suddenly realized that this was a different person entirely. Tina, the girl from my old neighborhood—the last person, in fact, who I'd been with before being locked up.

"Tina!" I said, excitedly.

"Sorry," she hissed back, "your ten seconds are over." And she hung up the phone.

This was not my smoothest moment. Nor was it the best way to rekindle an old flame. But we got past it. Before long, Tina and I were a serious item. Many of my former friendships proved difficult to return to after my release. Too much resentment had built up on all sides to slide casually back into old patterns. But with Tina it was totally different. In all my years in the penitentiary, she was the one person I'd thought of most often. I had been with her on my last day of freedom. And we hadn't left on a bad note. I had just been taken away from her. It was easier coming from a situation that had been interrupted on a good note than it was to try to rebuild something that had ended in a nasty way. In my eyes, we had never broken up. So getting back together was the obvious choice.

Somehow she knew exactly how to be present for me. I know I'm a fucking handful. I know. I know. Tina understood that I was emotionally scarred for life, and she had a feel for when I would start slipping back into a slump. She knew when I needed comforting and when I required space. If I have any positivity left, it's largely thanks to her. Anybody that has been in the pits of hell and has come out of it will show scars. The fact that people don't immediately know this about me, that I can interact and be social and human with neighbors and friends—and not have them constantly aware that I was on death row for thirteen years—is a testament to God's gifts and Tina's love.

Another blessing was the arrival of our daughter, Madison Grace, who was born in 2011. Having another child was something I knew I had to do. Unlike with my other two babies, this pregnancy was something we had planned out. We were excited for it. But we couldn't have guessed how difficult it would be. Tina had a rough time during the pregnancy. She was in and out of the hospital and had to continue taking medicine for a year after Madison was born. It was so important for me, though. I had missed out the first time around. I knew I had a lot to give to a child. I had tried to give it to my oldest son, but then I was taken away from him. By the time my second son was born, I was already gone. I had to redeem myself. I needed to know what it felt like to watch her grow up. I wanted to hear her voice, her first words, see her first steps. I wanted to be the dad who was involved in her everyday life.

Reconnecting with Tina and thinking about starting a family made it even more important for me to get on my feet. With no help coming from social services and running up on dead end after dead end on my own, I had to turn to another source for assistance in finding a job. I would appear on national TV to tell my story.

Los Angeles was another city on my list. Just being on the West Coast for the first time was an experience in and of itself. But the most special part was being able to bring Randell along for this trip.

He and I had only ever spoken a few times in our entire lives, and we had never formed a bond. In his mind, as he explained it to me, his father was someone who was never going to come home. And the idea of having me in his life was too complicated, too painful. I understood it.

Nothing about preparing for *The Dr. Phil Show* was normal. We hung out in the green room and then came onto the set for rehearsals. The crew told us to just be our usual selves, and not to look directly at the camera. Everyone was being nice enough, but I kept waiting for things to turn ugly. I had frequently watched *The Dr. Phil Show* in prison and every episode I had ever seen had eventually involved the host confronting and humiliating his guests, acting like a vicious dog. As far as I could tell—to put it bluntly—Dr. Phil seemed like a bit of an asshole. It had taken the producer, and assistant producer, and a bunch of his staff, to reassure me that I was not going to be attacked. Still, I was anxious backstage, waiting to be called. I told Randell to be prepared. If things turned nasty, we would respond in kind. We would give as good as we got, cameras or no cameras. Once I sat down beside Dr. Phil, however, and he started asking me questions, it was clear that he was really genuine, that he cared. That touched me.

"I see you on the show," I remarked to him before the cameras came on, "and you are always an asshole to the people you interview. But now you seem OK."

"Yeah," he said, "that's because they're assholes to me first. But this is going to be a different show. I have nothing but love and respect for you and the things you went through."

Then we were in front of the live studio audience. The hot lights were on, and the producers and camera crews were frantically busy. Dr. Phil and I sat next to each other, almost close enough to touch knees. He asked me about my arrest and forced confession. My mouth was really dry and I had to concentrate on the questions.

"You were more than just beaten, you were tortured," he said. "We're talking about America here. We're talking about Chicago." I described death row, discussed my release, and some of the joys and difficulties of adjusting to the free world. Randell came on stage then, too, and shared a bit about how our relationship was developing, how we were coming to know one another.

Then we turned to the question of my immediate future.

"Well, he lives in Chicago, and I'm on in Chicago—so Chicago, I'm talking to you," Dr. Phil said, speaking into the camera. "We need to find this man a job. He's going to put me down as a reference, so don't hold that against him." The audience cheered and laughed. And a few days later I received my first job offer.

I got a call from the show telling me that Goodwill Industries had agreed to hire me in one of their drop-off centers in Portage, Indiana—about forty-five minutes from Chicago. It was not glamorous work. Basically, my job was to pick through the garbage that white folks brought into the facility and see if any of it was worth keeping for resale. I'd sort it, pick out what was good, and put a price on it. Often, the items would come in with intentional damage. For a laugh, people would fill the bags with dog shit, cat litter, or rancid meat. When I opened up the bag the stuff would be crawling with maggots. Sometimes the people would stand there and watch me, cracking up with laughter when I recoiled in disgust from their filth.

I faced more racism at Goodwill than I had in prison, or at least a more direct version of it. When I was locked up, it was rare to hear the guards come right out and use racist language. But in my job at Goodwill, the locals had no problem calling me a nigger. My coworkers were fine; I came to love them. It was the people of the town who I had to worry about. Angry customers would berate me for the slightest things. Entire families would come driving to the loading dock in their pickup trucks and their children would clamber down and start cussing and insulting me.

There was really nothing to do but bite my tongue. A few times, I stepped out and confronted them. But I never let them make me lose control. If I did that I would have gone back to jail, and that was an outcome I had to avoid. These people had no idea who I was, or what I'd been through. Maybe they had a feeling that their donations would be going to black neighborhoods, and that's why they made sure to spoil their goods. Or perhaps they didn't have a thought in their heads except racism. After about six months at Goodwill, I was asked to take on additional responsibility as a floor manager. But I had hurt my back and was sick of taking abuse. So I decided it would be best to move on and try to find another job.

While I struggled daily to get a toehold on my chance for freedom, Jon Burge—at long last—found himself facing the threat of jail time. In early May 2010 jury selection began for his criminal trial. The suit had been brought by the federal government. Chicago itself, with Daley still in control, remained steadfast in its support, even going so far as to continue paying Burge's legal fees. Although by this time it was widely known that he was guilty of torture on a mass scale, the prosecution would not be considering those crimes. Instead, due once again to the statute of limitations, Burge would only face charges of perjury—for lying under oath about past offenses. A conviction, even for this lesser crime, was far from certain. When only one black juror was chosen, my expectations sank even lower.

The trial split the city once again along racial lines. Protesters demonstrated outside of the courtroom, chanting, "Mayor Daley, you can't hide. We've got justice on our side!" Inside, police loyalists maintained their obstinate support for the ex-commander's actions. For the first time in years, Burge testified on his own behalf, denying any wrongdoing and even generating some sympathy from observers. At sixty-two years old, he appeared to be a frail old man. It was almost impossible—unless you had suffered the grave misfortune of having seen him in action—to imagine this pudgy retiree as the mastermind behind the Midnight Crew. But then the victims began to speak. Although Burge was not being charged with torture, prosecutors had to establish his actions in order to prove he'd lied about them. One after another, his victims described his tools of torture, including suffocation, Russian roulette, and electric shocks. After more than a month the verdict came in: guilty.

Many activists were jubilant. And it was certainly a major milestone. Finally, the fact of torture had been established in a court of law. But I refused to celebrate. Daley and Devine remained at large. And Burge had not really paid the price he owed. "Who wouldn't want to see him put in the same cage he put us in?" I said. Yet, as long as he avoided responsibility for his actual crimes, it would be a hollow victory. "Unless he gets up on the stand and admits what he did," I told reporters, "there's no justice in it for me."

Although a perjury conviction could, in theory, result in a decades-long prison term, the judge at his sentencing hearing called for much less. Jon Burge was given only four-and-a-half years in a minimum-security federal prison.

Determined to keep the pressure on, I called a press conference less than a week after Burge's federal conviction. With my attorneys—Locke Bowman and Flint Taylor—I went to Northwestern and announced to a crowd of reporters that I would be suing Burge, the other detectives, Daley, Devine, and Cook County for damages in my case. The previous months had been spent planning it out. We had to get all our ducks in order, figure out exactly who to sue. You couldn't just target individual cops, because they had no assets and could just be written off as bad apples. But if you took on the city itself you had to show cause as to what city officials knew about the torture at Area 3. In the end, I insisted on a sweeping civil suit, intended to force the truth out into the open. Because the civil case would be seeking financial damages, I had to put a dollar figure on what I had gone through. Literally just picking at random, I decided to ask for about $3 million for each year I had been incarcerated. But this was literally beside the point. "Let it be known that it's not about the money," I told the press. "It's about making those who were overseeing, supervising, and running the city of Chicago take notice of what happened, not just to me, but to many other people like me."

The system itself had put me on death row. It was an insult and an outrage to imagine that powerful people like the mayor and state's attorney might get off scot-free, while Burge would play the fall guy with some wrist-slap sentence. My target was Mayor Daley. I wanted him to testify under oath. Only then would Chicago answer for its sins. This was an exciting vision. I was thrilled to get started and wanted to push forward. *Let's get things moving*, I told the attorneys at every meeting. And I was just as committed to seeing it through to the end. At the press conference, reporters asked about my willingness to serve as a witness, if the case ever came to trial.

"If I have to testify, I have no gripe with that," I told them. "For me to tell my story, and just to get it out, for people to even take heed to it, that would be a satisfaction for me. . . . I'm ready to go to trial. I've been ready to go to trial since day one. So what's another year? Another two or three? Another four or five? Another ten? I'm going to be still ready."

In the lead-up to the expected trial, my attorneys took depositions from the various defendants in the case. We had discussed the possibilities in advance. Burge had testified on his own behalf at his trial, but if he was found to be lying, it could bring further perjury charges. On the other hand, he could assert his Fifth Amendment privilege against self-incrimination. This would protect him from further criminal charges, but in a civil case it would not shield him from having to pay damages.

My legal team traveled down to North Carolina to interview him at the federal prison where he was incarcerated. Ruddy and fat as ever, his white hair combed back, Burge was uncooperative. The conversation lasted about fifteen minutes. My lawyer went through a list of crimes and offenses, ranging from Burge's assault on me in the interrogation room to the longstanding enforcement of a code of silence among his detectives. Burge rarely made eye contact. He shifted in his seat. At times he seemed bored by the questions. But at the end of each question, his answer was the same: "I'll assert my Fifth Amendment right."

Other detectives followed the lead of their former commander. Only Michael Kill—combative as ever—chose to engage with the interviewers. His own words damned him more than any critic ever could.

"On how many occasions did you use the term 'nigger' . . . during interrogations?" my lawyer asked Kill.

"I would say I used it as many times as I had to."

"Would you say that was more than one hundred times?"

"In my life," Kill responded, pointing to the court stenographer. "I've probably used it more times than he's got inches of tape on his machine."

"Ok, give me an estimate . . . "

"About a million—for starters."

In other exchanges, Kill ridiculed and threatened the attorneys, mocking the entire proceedings. He sneered at the charges of torture and abuse, saying, "I didn't see anyone get beat, electrocuted, electrified, set on fire, thrown out any windows, all the accusations you're making today. None of that happened."

Now in his seventies, Kill acted with the same mad energy that had been so terrifying to his prisoners back when he was a detective. I sometimes imagined what I would do if I ever happened to meet up with Burge or Kill on the street. If I recognized them, and they recognized me—and they weren't carrying a gun—I liked to fantasize about beating the shit out of them in their old age, of putting my foot in their ass. But watching Kill's deposition reminded me why I'd probably restrain myself. Even in his frail state, he was crazy. And when you see a real fucked-up person like that, it's safest just to stay away from them.

I was the last to give my deposition. It was July 2011. Two years had passed since my release. In many ways, this was the most important moment in my case. Finally, I would have the chance to get my story in the record. Locke and Flint had prepped me. The opposing attorneys were going to do everything in their power to bait me, they would use every trick to enrage me and get me to tee off on them, just like my attorneys had succeeded in doing with Detective Kill. We were not going to do that. I was determined to keep my composure and to quiet my emotions. I wouldn't allow them to anger me, and I wasn't going to let these people see me cry.

It was a typical summer day, hot and muggy, in Chicago. I went into a downtown law firm and strolled into the interview room at my own speed. I had on a dark suit and a tie. Again, at a steady pace, I took off my jacket and draped it over my chair. I removed my tie. I made sure to be relaxed, not stuffy. I unbuttoned my shirt. I had a towel with me to wipe away any sweat. I wanted to be cool. The deposition was grueling. It lasted for more than six hours. I started by describing in explicit detail the torture I had suffered at the hands of Burge, Kill, and the others. This was painful to me. Every time I told the story, it brought me right back to that long night twenty-four years earlier. It was like I was reliving it, feeling the blows and the fear again. I could feel the tears rising up. I had to catch myself a couple times, or I would have started crying right there in the office. But I managed to keep cool.

At last, the final attorney for the city took his turn to question me. This one knew every trick in the book. He was determined to break me. Deliberately trying to be provocative, he dragged his chair into the middle of the room. He wore a bright pink shirt. When he sat down on his chair and put his feet up, he revealed to me that the soles of his shoes had gaping holes in them. It was distracting as hell. After a series of questions, he started to go in for the attack. He kept asking me about the telephone in the interrogation room, wanting to know why hadn't I used it to call for help. The answer, which I explained, was perfectly simple, "If my hands are cuffed behind my back, how can I call somebody?"

But he wasn't satisfied. Again and again he shouted at me: "Why didn't you pick up the phone? Why didn't you pick it up? Why didn't you call for help?"

He was trying to come at me, but even at gunpoint I wouldn't have broken at that moment. He wanted me to see red and start hollering, calling them all a bunch of bitches and hoes. I wasn't going to do that. I just took out my towel, patted my forehead, and kept a straight face. My attorneys finally shut down this line of questioning and the proceedings were over.

Afterward I was standing outside by myself when that same attorney came up to me and started talking. When he walked away, Locke—a little worried to see me chatting with the opposition—hurried over to ask what words had just been exchanged. I told him the man had come up to me, shook my hand, and said, "You did good. I wish I had a client like you. You're going to be all right."

This one friendly gesture aside, the city was taking the lawsuit seriously. And I knew I had to watch my back at all times. This point was made explicitly clear one night when I was driving home from the skating rink, listening to some steppers music on the radio in my pickup truck. Flashing lights spun on behind me. I pulled over and watched nervously as the officer walked up to my window.

"Are you deaf?" he demanded.

"What do you mean?" I asked. I hadn't touched the radio, and we were having a normal conversation. The volume was low enough that we didn't have to yell or anything.

"Why is your music so loud?"

"It isn't loud," I said. "If it was loud I wouldn't be able to talk to you right now."

"There's a seventy-five-foot radius," he said. "If I can hear your music beyond that distance then it's too loud."

"Ok," I said. "Well, where were you?"

"Right next to you."

"So, how do you know if it was loud outside that radius?" I asked.

"I'm not going to argue with you, sir," he said, and demanded to see my license, proof, and registration. He returned to check on the information. The whole time I was sitting there waiting, cars were flying past us with radios blaring ten times louder than mine had been. Then, after a few minutes, all hell broke loose. Suddenly, six other squad cars came racing from every direction and converged at the scene. I watched in my rearview mirror as the officers leaped onto the sidewalk, guns drawn. Officers in white shirts demanded I step out of my truck.

"I'm going to jail for my music?" I asked, in disbelief.

"No, but we are going to impound your pickup."

This was a direct message to me—that goes without saying. They rang my name up, figured out who I was, and then sent out an APB to come confront me. Why else would half a dozen black and whites roll up? Why would the officers come out with their guns drawn?

They handcuffed me, took me to the station, and allowed me to make a phone call. The next day I paid a thousand dollars and got my vehicle from the impound lot. I was seething throughout this interaction, but I stayed the course. I didn't get hysterical. I said what I had to say and that was that. Something within me told me to be cool.

Otherwise, things would have gone differently. It could have been a whole other level of bullshit.

Another time I got pulled over and the officer told me I didn't have a license plate. Once, I was riding with Tina when a cop stopped us. I gave him my current address and the police asked if I was the same Ronald Kitchen who had lived on Artesian—my auntie's place.

"You have my license," I said. "Why is that relevant?" And once again, a few moments later, I was surrounded by the white shirts.

It kept happening. Every time I got pulled over, the same symptoms would hit me: heartbeat racing, palms sweaty, mouth all dry. I would do everything I could to minimize danger. I turned on all the interior lights in the car and rolled down the windows so the officer could get a clear view inside. The main thing was to remember the situation, to keep in mind the fact that I was a black man in a nice car, and that—even though technically I had all the rights of a white driver—in point of fact, I had to control myself, and the situation, to make sure things didn't get out of control.

The police knew my name and were fixated on irritating and harassing me. I began to realize that as long as I was in Chicago I'd have problems. As my lawsuit against the city progressed I started to get the suspicion that I was being watched. People were following my movements—that's what I believed and felt—hoping I'd make a mistake. And I knew all too well that if they wanted to find some dirt on you but couldn't, then their next step would be to plant something.

Tina had grown up in the Philadelphia neighborhood of Germantown. She was living there at the time and had raised the idea of me joining her. One night, in December 2010, I packed up all my stuff and left the Chicago area for good. It was a little emotional to say goodbye to Marvin and my family, but to be honest, after what I'd been through I was just happy to leave. In fact, I was so eager to exit that I set off in the middle of a blizzard. Three snowstorms and eighteen hours later I arrived at Tina's apartment. I hadn't even told her I was coming. She was at work when I arrived. When she got home, I was stretched out on the floor asleep.

———————

Our civil case was dragging on. Months became a year, one year turned into two, then another. The city's lawyers were stalling, posturing as if they were prepared to go to trial and trying any tactic they could think of to distract us. I knew this was a bluff, that Chicago would go to any length to protect Richard Daley—who had finally left office in 2011—from the risks of having to take the witness stand. I was losing patience. When the defense threatened to subpoena Tina, I had finally had enough of the process. It was just another ruse. They knew everything about me. My past was an open book. But she was still recovering from Madison's birth and I didn't want to put her through any more stress.

Locke and my other attorneys were disappointed. They really wanted me to go through with it to the end and force Daley to testify. But I was tired and wanted to get it over with. If I would have had a little more endurance in me, I could have taken it all the way. But my race was over with. I was sick of having people watching my movements. I wanted them out of my life. I had a new family that needed my attention and I didn't want to take any more chances.

"Listen," I told the team, "I love y'all. But I've had lawyers in my life for twenty-five years now, and it's time for me to stop letting you dictate my pace. I respect you all as my friends. But I want you all out of my life as my attorneys."

I told Locke to go to the city's lawyers and get the best deal he could. Their first offer was a million dollars. They played a few more games and made some empty threats. But after a week or so, they got serious. In September 2013, we were able to announce that Chicago had awarded us a settlement of $12.3 million. Marvin and I split the sum evenly, right down the middle. He and I had been dragged into our ordeal together, we had walked out together, and now it was understood that whatever the city was going to lay down, we should get the same share. Like me, he was having health issues and had found it impossible to get a job. I had fought for this outcome for the two of us, a lot of the stuff was on my back. And no matter what, I wanted to make sure Marvin got his due.

The settlement of our lawsuit served as a major milestone in the history of police abuse in Chicago, though further revelations and lawsuits would continue for years. When the city decided it couldn't risk fighting out the case in open court, it was making an unprecedented admission of guilt. The city's new mayor, Rahm Emanuel, even took the occasion of the announcement to issue an apology for the years of torture, wrongful convictions, and cover-ups. "I do believe this is a way of saying all of us are sorry about what happened here in the city," he said, "and closing that period of time, that stain on the city's reputation, its history and now being able to embark on a new part of the city and a new way of actually doing business. And that is not who we are, and we all are one or another obviously sorry." When a reporter asked him to clarify what exactly he was apologizing for, Emmanuel added: "Here's what I mean: I am sorry this happened. Let us all now move on."

The mayor was in a hurry to put this behind him. I didn't blame him. None of this stuff had happened on his watch. He inherited Daley's and Devine's messes. And at least he tried to make things right; most other politicians never even thought to apologize. Like the new mayor, I too was looking forward to the next phase in my life. But no apology could automatically turn the page on what had been done to us. Mere words did little to help the dozens of people who had been tortured and remained locked up in prison, to soothe their babies and comfort their mothers. "The fight for justice in the torture cases will not be over," I told reporters, "until all Burge torture victims receive compensation for their suffering, the men in jail get fair hearings, and Burge's pension is taken from him." The money really wasn't a solution to anything. It wouldn't let the city escape without further reparations—we'd make sure of that. And it would not undo the experiences that Marvin and I had suffered. It wouldn't change the culture of racism and violence in the Chicago Police Department. The problems hadn't been fixed. All that happened was that two individuals were given a Band-Aid, a lifeline. Meanwhile, a hundred more people, who had suffered from Burge and the other detectives, remained in jail. As far as a resolution, this shit wasn't resolved.

Our settlement allowed us to live with fewer worries and to fulfill small dreams. While growing up, Tina had always wanted to live in a neat row house that she could see from her apartment window in Philly. Now, I was able to buy that house for her and move in there with our daughter. But we were hardly living like millionaires. The money had to last my natural life; it was there to ensure that we could live after society had taken away my earning power and made it next to impossible for me otherwise to find a decent job. After I received my settlement, many people were like, "Oh, he's all right now." No, I was not all right. Every day I lived with the thought of what I had been forced to lose to get this tiny taste of life. All of my twenties, all of my thirties. That was all snatched away from me. Now I was in my forties—an old-ass man—trying to forge some fashion of life, trying to get a grip on something I could never reach.

The emotional and mental discipline that I had used to survive in the penitentiary allowed me to get through my ordeal, but there were very real consequences and costs of those techniques. I still had a lot of bitter in me. I still had discord toward a lot of people. Just knowing that I was in a place like that for something I didn't do— the injustice and pain that I suffered has scarred me for life. I had to detach myself from pain. Looking around the prison, I saw many guys over the years who could never cope with the losses they were suffering. Whatever was going on—the death of my grandmother, my mother's sickness, my brother's murder—I couldn't let myself grieve. I was so detached from the outside world; I didn't let it affect me on the inside. I couldn't allow myself to be broken on anything. I had to put this wall up. And these walls stayed up after I got out. I still didn't let things get to me. I still reacted sometimes like I was in the penitentiary. Even though I was out, I was still in.

The Burge scandals had now cost Chicago well over $100 million, with much of that money going to defend him, Daley, and the other perpetrators against repeated prosecutions. Despite the new mayor's apology, the city continued supporting Burge, paying his legal expenses and pension. He was their golden boy. He was their case closer. And they are probably always going to defend him, because he knows all the secrets. As Chicago drifted toward bankruptcy, running up huge deficits, many taxpayers came to begrudge me the restitution I had received. Some people chose not to blame Burge or the system that created and protected him. Reading headlines in the papers about settlement awards to black victims of torture, they decided to blame us for the city's financial crises. This was a ridiculous twist of logic. People who blamed us for what happened made all sorts of claims. They said: *He shouldn't have been out in the streets selling drugs in the first place.* But what they meant was: *He shouldn't have been black.* I didn't ask to be black. Take that up with God. That one's not my fault either.

Even now that I am out of prison, with a certificate of innocence clearing my name, my truth is met with skepticism. The larger implications of my story, our story, are still lost on many. I am out of prison and have the life I have now, in spite of—not because of—our justice system. Yes, I am innocent. But it was not the truth alone that set me free. A lot of people—my mother, the lawyers, the activists, myself and the guys inside—had to work their asses off to free me. In another moment, a slight shift in the political winds, and I might still be behind bars, or dead. The truth is that everyone is in on the lie. Until we—all of us, white, black, rich, poor—can look past the stereotypes to recognize that everyone, and I mean everyone, is capable of good and bad—nothing is going to change. Until we can look past the myths of our history and see that our country was founded on the backs of people of color, that as much as white people have worked hard for what's theirs, their successes have at least in part come at the expense of others, black people, poor people, women, immigrants—until then, crime, violence, and police abuse are going to continue.

Here's another simple truth: none of this had to happen. All of these expenses and traumas could have been avoided. At any point during this decades-long ordeal, people in power could have stood up and yelled, "Stop!" But no. The individuals changed—mayors, governors, councilmen, state's attorneys, all came and went—and instead of taking an honorable stand for the truth, they each chose to smother justice beneath self-interest. It was us—the wrongfully accused and our families, activists, journalists, and lawyers—who had to take democracy into our own hands and make it work.

To call this history "the Burge scandal" is to falsely identify a social ill with a single perpetrator. What happened to me was not the act of a single bad apple but the result of an entire system. Everyone—each one of us—needs to take part in understanding our role in allowing these injustices to occur, and to ensure they cannot happen again. Our work goes on. And we will not stop until the full truth of these crimes is taken from the shadows of midnight into the light of a new morning.

EPILOGUE

IN OUR HOUSEHOLD these days, I am the first to wake up. I walk down the hallway to stir Madison Grace from sleep. We start our routine. She might feel tired, or not in the mood to go to school that day. I coax her out of bed. I brush her teeth and we wash up. "Daddy," she says, "I can't put my clothes on. Can you come dress me?" Tina fixes her hair while I make some hot chocolate, and we leave the house. Madison climbs up into the car and I buckle her seatbelt. While driving to pre-K, I ask about homework. We go over her word for the night.

"I want you to have the best day in school," I tell her as we pull up outside the building. "Remember that I love you and your mama loves you. Don't ever forget that. Whatever you do, I want you to do your best at it."

These daily rituals mean the world to me. They are ordinary and comforting. Even so, I can't help thinking about the past. In so many ways, my mornings with Madison are almost identical to the ones that I used to share with my first son—Ronnie Jr.—thirty years ago. At that time, we were preparing a big celebration for his third birthday.

But I was taken away before that could happen. They snatched me from him, and so I wasn't able to be around for my son. With Randell I was gone from before his first breath. Madison is my chance at redemption. When she turned three, we threw a big old party for her in Chicago, complete with singing cartoon characters, costumes, and a bouncy house. All of her cousins and aunties from the South Side came to make merry with us. It was a milestone for both Madison and me. At the end of that day I breathed a deep sigh of relief and said to myself, "I beat it." As a father I'd gotten past my previous record. With her, I'm around. And I'm staying around still, fully aware that every day with her and Tina is a blessing.

Nine years have passed since my release. A lot of living and dying has occurred since that day. Tina and I got married in a beautiful ceremony with friends and family. I talk with Carolyn and Alice all the time. Marvin and I speak every single day. In early October 2015, I got a call from my sister that I knew would be coming: Louva had fallen into a coma. We didn't even pack a suitcase, just jumped onto an airplane and flew to her side. For a week we sat in her hospital room, laughing and telling her our latest stories. Madison was there, playing and cuddling with her. Her eyes even opened a few times, and we felt sure she could hear us, but she never responded. We knew there was no coming back from this. After a week, I leaned down and whispered in my mother's ear, "You don't have to fight this anymore. We all here. I'm here. We all safe. You don't have to fight anymore." That night—October 9, 2015—Louva Grace Bell passed away in her sleep. I raced back to the hospital from our hotel to see her; somehow, her face was glowing again. She looked beautiful, just like in the years before her illness. We took her body back to Chicago and had her buried next to Geraldine, near her son and grandson.

It brings me a deep sense of peace to know that my mother wasn't having to fight any longer, but I have other fears to cope with. Freedom to me still feels like a dream that could be stolen away at a moment's notice. I live with the thought of the penitentiary. I feel uncomfortable on crowded buses. I keep the drapes closed and the lights dimmed. In the course of day-to-day activities, I constantly have flashbacks that make me pause and say, *Oh shit, I used to do that in the penitentiary.* A smell will hit my nose. *That's just like in the penitentiary.* A certain movie will come on TV, or a song on the radio. Something will clatter in another room, and to me it will sound like a guard is out in the corridor rattling the bars to my cell. I talk to guys who are still imprisoned, and the noises I can hear in the background of their phone calls transport me back to that place.

Peculiar habits are still with me, ones I developed to survive the pain of that life. People complain about my phone etiquette. I don't do chitchat. I just say what I have to say and then ring off—because that's what you had to do in prison. When it's time to hang up, I might say "yep," or "all right." But I never say "good-bye." On death row, the notion of "good-bye" was too emotional. The word was too final. I never said it to my mom. Instead, I'd tell her I loved her and that I'd talk to her in a week. Even in my letters, I'd pen the words "Tah, Tah, For Now" instead of using that dreaded phrase. I couldn't write it or say it—and still can't—because it sounds like I'll never speak to the person again. Good-bye sounds like forever.

Tina says I have a tell sign. On many evenings I will sit on the couch in our living room, staring at the floor and rubbing the top of my head, lost in thought. She knows, but leaves me be. I might stay like that for hours without even knowing it. When she eventually asks me what's wrong, I'll try to figure it out with her. Half the time I don't even know the answer myself. I just get lost with my face in my hands. I don't sleep well. I hope that a couple hours of dozing will be all I need. I toss and turn, or pace the house. I get panic attacks—fierce, scary episodes, where my hands will start to shake out of control.

I am glad to make it through every day with them, even though there are times when fatherhood feels more difficult than any other type of labor I've ever done. I get through by telling myself, *I just gotta do it for a couple more hours, and then two more hours after that, and then a couple after that.* Parents don't have holidays or weekends or sick days. When I'm sick, it's *so what.* When I need a nap, *so what.* I don't get days off. It's my twenty-four-hour-a-day nonpaying job. It's the hardest work imaginable, and I cherish it.

Although it would have been easy to dedicate every last bit of energy to raising a family, I made sure to stay engaged with my struggle of a lifetime—the fight against police brutality and racism, in Chicago and beyond. Death penalty politics in Illinois continued along their twisting path. Governor George Ryan, the hero who had commuted our sentences, eventually found himself convicted of corruption and ended up spending five years in prison. I never had the chance to meet him in person, but I had all the respect in the world for the man. Even if he had done some shady shit in office, when it came to doing what was right regarding the death penalty, he had gone against the grain. One night, after a political rally where people were talking about what he had done, my heart was just overflowing with love for him. I went home, sat down, and wrote Ryan a letter. "Thank you," I wrote. "I appreciate everything you did for me. You are still my governor. I think you did the greatest job you ever did when you cleared death row. If you hadn't done that, I'd be dead." Then, I addressed the letter and mailed it to inmate Ryan at the Federal Correctional Institution in Terre Haute, Indiana.

A decade after the original moratorium on capital punishment, Governor Pat Quinn finally took the long delayed step of abolishing executions in the state. These advances made it tempting to feel that progress had been made. And it's true that it would be harder today for the police to fabricate a story like they did with me and find a jury to believe it. I want to believe that the way things are going in society, we are less likely to look at someone—especially someone who looks like me—and just assume that they are guilty.

But I'm not sure of it. Every time I read in the newspaper about another person murdered by police, my hopes fade a bit more. Thankfully, another generation of activists has taken up the fight. This time the outrage was not about a secretive crew of corrupt detectives but the spectacle of naked violence in the street. Less than a year after I settled my lawsuit, I turned on the television to see reports of an uprising in Ferguson, Missouri. It did not take long before this new movement— Black Lives Matter—stormed into my old hometown. Outraged by a cop's murder of a black teenager and subsequent attempts to hide video footage of the crime, activists once again brought the nation's attention to racism and police violence in Chicago.

Nothing I heard in this case surprised me. In fact, just days before, a guy I'd grown up with had seen his son shot and murdered by police, with similar runaround and excuses. Too many of the brass still active were officers and sergeants who had come up under Burge, Kill, and the others. They all had heard the screams of suspects pleading for their lives, and they had all decided to maintain the code of silence. They had learned that they could get ahead on the backs of young black men. The department never brought out the bulldozer or gave everyone their pink slips. There had never been a real clean out, just a series of cover-ups. Those at the very top have sacrificed the least. As I write this, former mayor Richard Daley has still never had to testify to the extent of his involvement in the cover-up of the activities of the Midnight Crew. But Flint Taylor and Locke Bowman remain on the case, and the final word on that has yet to be written.

In the midst of the Black Lives Matter protests, Jon Burge himself won early release—after only four and a half years in prison—and suddenly our old struggles were back in the forefront of people's minds. By that time, the number of his known victims had risen to 120—and still counting—and dozens of them remained behind bars.

With Black Lives Matter becoming a household phrase and Chicago frightened of further protests, in June 2015 the city council passed a reparations bill—the only law of its kind in the country—ensuring further compensation for the falsely accused, the creation of a memorial to commemorate torture victims, and the education of the city's children about the history of what we had suffered, lost, and won.

It would be easy to get lost in all this history again. So for right now I just want to get back to the basics.

When I pick Madison up from school, I talk to her teachers about her progress and then get her in the car and pepper her with questions: "What was your day like? What did you learn? What did you have for lunch? What did you and your friends do?" I talk to her teachers every day, asking how she's doing and hearing the latest updates.

She has questions for me, too.

"Daddy, what did you go to jail for?" Madison frequently asks. "Daddy, why did they beat you up?" She has heard me discussing these experiences too many times not to be curious. She doesn't understand the depth of it, but she still talks about it all the time. She tells kids in school that her daddy was on death row.

"I never want to die," Madison says. "Daddy, I don't want you to die."

"You're too young to be worried about death right now," I tell her. "You should want to learn and live, get a husband and kids, become a doctor. These are the things you should be looking forward to."

I try to tell her the truth, but I don't go into details.

"When you get older we can talk about it more," I say. "But now—this stuff—as a kid, you don't need to worry." I plan out the conversation we'll share. It will be like talking to her about boys—but hopefully not quite as awkward. I'm going to have to give her the whole story, let her know all of it. But for now she's the one person I need to shield until the time is right. I have to protect her. I just want her to be daddy's baby girl. I want to do all the worrying for her, and let her live her life. I need her to be a child.

My most fervent hope is for her never to go through anything like what I had to suffer. I hope that for all my kids—for everyone's children. This is what I live for. This is the whole point of telling my story, to let my experiences be a lesson. To let my life be a stepping stone.

After dinner, I sit with Madison and we talk about her day.

I say "I love you" as I switch off the light. But I will never tell her "good-bye."